GENTRIFICATION:
A WORKING-CLASS PERSPECTIVE

For Cassie

Gentrification:
A Working-Class Perspective

KIRSTEEN PATON
University of Leeds, UK

ASHGATE

© Kirsteen Paton 2014

All rights reserved. No part of this publication may be reproduced, stored in a retrieval system or transmitted in any form or by any means, electronic, mechanical, photocopying, recording or otherwise without the prior permission of the publisher.

Kirsteen Paton has asserted her right under the Copyright, Designs and Patents Act, 1988, to be identified as the author of this work.

Published by
Ashgate Publishing Limited
Wey Court East
Union Road
Farnham
Surrey, GU9 7PT
England

Ashgate Publishing Company
110 Cherry Street
Suite 3-1
Burlington, VT 05401-3818
USA

www.ashgate.com

British Library Cataloguing in Publication Data
A catalogue record for this book is available from the British Library

The Library of Congress has cataloged the printed edition as follows:
Paton, Kirsteen.
 Gentrification : a working-class perspective / by Kirsteen Paton.
   pages cm
 Includes bibliographical references and index.
   ISBN 978-1-4724-1850-0 (hardback) -- ISBN 978-1-4724-1851-7 (ebook) -- ISBN 978-1-4724-1852-4 (epub) 1. Social classes--Great Britain. 2. Gentrification--Great Britain. 3. Working class--Great Britain. 4. Neighborhoods--Great Britain. 5. Group identity--Great Britain. I. Title.
 HN400.S6P37 2014
 305.50941--dc23

2014015821

ISBN 9781472418500 (hbk)
ISBN 9781472418517 (ebk – PDF)
ISBN 9781472418524 (ebk – ePUB)

Printed in the United Kingdom by Henry Ling Limited,
at the Dorset Press, Dorchester, DT1 1HD

Contents

List of Figures		*vii*
List of Tables		*ix*
Acknowledgements		*xi*
	Introduction	1
1	Restructuring Theory	13
2	Restructuring Class Identity	67
3	Elective Belonging and Fixity to Place	97
4	Gentrifying Working-Class Subjects: Participating in Consumer Citizenship	125
5	The Paradox of Gentrification: Displacing the Working-Class Subject	155
	Conclusions: Reinvigorating Urban Class Analysis	185
	Appendix: Cases of Gentrification	199
Bibliography		*205*
Index		*219*

List of Figures

1.1	Measures and methods of studying direct and indirect displacement (continuum)	38
1.2	Inside the penthouse suite of Glasgow Harbour, looking across to the shipyards in Govan	62
1.3	A view of Partick from the Harbour development	63
1.4	Shops on Dumbarton Road	65
3.1	Gardener Street Partick, looking towards Hyndland	117
4.1	Mansfield Park, unfinished redevelopment, 2009	139
4.2	View of Mansfield Park looking towards the upgraded, but downsized, sports court with bin with graffiti in the foreground	141
4.3	Graffiti on Glasgow Harbour promotional board	142
6.1	Abandoned promotional sign on the Glasgow Harbour site at South Street, September 2009	196

List of Tables

1.1	Production versus consumption in the orthodox explanations of gentrification	33
1.2	Theoretical divides in gentrification literature	33
1.3	Positive and negative effects of gentrification	38
2.1	Residents' NS-SeC and class identification	71
2.2	NS-SeC classifications	73
3.1	'Local' residents and tenure	98
3.2	Incomers' residential biography and tenure	99
3.3	Locals' residential biography with tenure	104
4.1	Residents' class identification and community participation	126
4.2	Increase in houses price sales at intermediate geography, city and national levels, 1997–2007	150
5.1	Components of new housing supply in Scotland	172
5.2	House sales median prices 1997–2007 by intermediate geography	173
5.3	'Notice of proceedings', court actions and housing recovery undertaken by PHA 2005–2008	181

Acknowledgements

I am a part of all that I have met.

(Alfred Lord Tennyson, *Ulysses*)

This book is based on research I undertook as part of an ESRC CASE PhD studentship and I'm indebted to all those people who have assisted on that journey, from inception to print. It would not have been possible without the collaborators who put the studentship together: Kait Laughlin (Westgap); Paul McLaughlin (Westgap); Deborah Lee (Westgap); Rowland Atkinson (University of York); Keith Kintrea (Glasgow University) and Adrian Girling (formerly at Oxfam) and ESRC. A special thank you goes to Westgap who supported this research and me on an everyday basis. They have been a registered charity operating in Partick for over 10 years. It was their vision, passion and commitment that made this research possible. I am grateful to Gesa Helms, Satnam Virdee and Mike Savage for the sage guidance they provided throughout the research process and to Katherine Champion and Elaine Webster for their wholehearted solidarity. I would also like to express my gratitude to Ashgate for seeing the merit in the message and agreeing to publish the research as a book. Thanks too to Matt Dawson and Tim Butler for patiently and diligently reading and thoughtfully commenting on the draft of the book. Kudos also to Alanna, KC, Julie, Borris, Matthew, the Dunsmores and the indefatigable Patons for getting me through the best of times and the worst of times and to Austin for championing the denouement.

The biggest thanks of all goes to all those who participated in the research, who so generously took the time to share their stories, thoughts and experiences with me. I feel deeply privileged that people chose to share those narratives with me, which were moving, funny, articulate, insightful, complex and profound often all at once.

You have been vital. Thank you.

Introduction

This book explores the working-class experience of gentrification. In general, working-class experiences are conspicuously absent from social research; they are often treated as a homogenous and undifferentiated mass with few working-class social figures in sociological analysis. Such figures are, instead, reserved to describe the middle classes; the flâneur, the gentrifier, the cosmopolitan, who are deemed to embody the ontological insecurity wrought by any given social change. Similarly the experience of gentrification is treated as a middle-class preserve of the well-heeled, hipsters and artists. This denies the working class a complex relationship with global capital processes of restructuring. In exploring the working-class experience of gentrification, this book is not a simply a witness account of displacement; the common malevolent and yet still under-researched effect of gentrification, since it is not the only experience. This misinterprets the form that gentrification takes today. Historically, orthodox accounts of gentrification are characterised by two seemingly opposed camps of explanation: economic or cultural. The former defines gentrification by a 'rent-gap', which describes the difference in the value of (devalued) inner city land and its potential value (if regenerated) (Smith, 1996). The latter defines gentrification as a back-to-the-city movement of middle-class suburban dwellers, with a focus on their lifestyle practices borne out of the post-war consumption culture (Ley, 1986, 1996). While these were powerful explanatory and impassioned positions, the debate has evolved and become more sophisticated and so too has the process of gentrification. Institutionalised as urban policy, gentrification is cast as the panacea to the decline wrought by deindustrialisation. As capital is moved out of areas, like sites of production and industry in which it was previously fixed, it leaves devastation and devaluation. Gentrification is used as the key weapon in the neoliberal arsenal of regeneration across the world: a global urban strategy (Smith, 2002) or new urban colonialism (Atkinson and Bridge, 2005). From America's HOPE VI project, mega sporting events like the Olympics, city branding, to the creation of 'socially-mixed' neighbourhoods, gentrification is pervasive. Yet we still do not know a great deal about its local use and application in policy (Lees and Ley, 2008) let alone the complexity of how it is experienced on the ground. An important point which gets overlooked is that gentrification is everyday and enduring. It is lived with as standard. Used as part of regeneration policies, state-led gentrification, as it has been labelled, targets people and places rendered surplus by economic change and defined by their 'lack' with the aim of making them more productive. While their social worlds are subject to profound change, working-class actors in these processes receive the least attention. So why this lack of analysis? Ultimately such apathy is predicated upon the notion of disconnect; a separation of processes of urban restructuring from working-class communities.

Once the bedrock of sociological analysis, the decline of the industrial working-class neighbourhood is taken as evidence for the dislocation between structural and social relations (Pakulski and Waters, 1996; Beck, 1992; Giddens, 1991). Rather, global changes in capitalism are said to incur greater levels of risk and insecurity (Beck, 1992; Giddens, 1991), which demand people to be reflexive and act individually, signifying that agency is set free from the confines of structure (Lash and Urry, 1987, 1994; Beck, 1992). Traditional meaningful place-based and class-based life patterns are undermined, signifying the demise of working-class communities' productive value and, therefore, their *raison d'être* (Pakulski and Waters, 1996). This has even been interpreted as the end of class itself (Gorz, 1980). Over the past 25 years the status of class receded from the centre of sociological analysis to become an irrelevant social signifier and a 'zombie category' (Beck, 2004). A counter trend in class research has sought to reinterpret this seeming decline by focusing on working-class people's individualistic disassociation with class, which is a concept that expresses the disjuncture between class position and (traditional) class identity (Skeggs, 1997; Savage, 2000). While this research focus has been vital, it has limitations. It does not fully interpret or recognise the material underpinnings of this process of disassociation within its analysis. Further, making disassociation the focus of class analysis disaggregates and discounts collectivity. When considering gentrification, we see that working-class people and places are the principal targets of urban restructuring and there may be a material rationale underpinning this disassociation with class which relate to the redemptive narrative of regeneration. Defined by 'lack', traditional class identity is devalued and even seen as contributing to decline and stasis in formerly industrial neighbourhoods.

Thus, here I offer a critique of responses to deindustrialisation in class analysis which reasserts this importance of place and the collective. This is not to reassert the legacy of community studies of class (Dennis et al., 1956; Jackson, 1968; Young and Wilmott, 1957; Lockwood, 1958) which, while useful, focus on collectivity at the expense of clarifying the relationship between class position and individual identity. Rather, it is done to destabilise the narratives which herald the end of class and the rise of the individual self-maker (Beck, 1992; Bauman, 1998; Giddens, 1991; Pakulski and Waters, 1996) as an unravelling of the relationship between class position and identity. While 'culturalist class theorists' (Savage et al., 2001, 2005, 2005a; Skeggs, 1997, 2004; Reay, 2005) use disassociation to express the disjuncture between class position and identity, disassociation is not merely a process of class opposition and individualisation; it reveals the material basis of a hegemonic shift towards post-industrial neoliberalism. This recognition is important in advancing an understanding of class as an economic relation of value but also a social construction and identity of Otherness which is premised upon moral value but with economic implications. In urban restructuring processes, this is evident in the devaluation which occurs as part of regeneration whereby working-class people and place are pathologised and stigmatised, verbalised through pejorative discourses of council estates, 'sink' estates, 'problem' neighbourhoods. The aim of this devaluation of working-class people and places is the realisation of potential value and profit.

Fundamentally a process of class restructuring which is spatially articulated at the local level, gentrification is defined by Hackworth (2002) as a process that creates space for the progressively more affluent user which I think captures its contemporary characteristics. Gentrification intimates that urban restructuring and working-class communities are inextricably connected yet the relationship is not always fully explicated within research, despite over 40 years of debate (Slater, 2006). The account I offer here is also, then, a critique of gentrification literature. Smith (2002: 445), in his analysis of state-led gentrification, suggests that: 'probing the symptomatic silence of who is to be invited back into the city begins to reveal the class politics involved'. In this book, I argue that probing the silences of working-class experiences of gentrification is a powerful way of elucidating contemporary urban restructuring and offers critical insight into contemporary class relations. Bringing the working class into research is not just academically edifying, the necessity for research is made more pressing by gentrification's prevalence as a global political strategy for regeneration (Atkinson and Bridge, 2005).

Gentrification from a Working-class Perspective

The story of the working-class experience of gentrification is undoubtedly complex. In 2005 I was commissioned to research the impacts of the luxury residential development Glasgow Harbour on the adjacent working-class neighbourhood, Partick. This 3,000 unit luxury housing development was built on the site once given to grain mills, shipyards and related industry on Clydeside. This land, which at one point produced a fifth of the world's ships (McInnes, 1995), was sold by Glasgow City Council to Peel Holdings group, the vanguards of dockside makeovers such as, amongst many others, MediaCityUK; the Salford locale of media industries including the BBC and ITV studios as well as the University of Salford, developed on the former Port of Manchester and Manchester Dock. Glasgow City Council proclaimed of the Harbour development:

> The £500m redevelopment of Meadowside Quay (Glasgow Harbour) will deliver a quantum leap forward in the image, infrastructure and amenity of Clydeside on a scale not seen since the industrial revolution. (GCC and Scottish Enterprise Glasgow, 2001: 42)

There was general public concern that the development would lead to the displacement and marginalisation of local working-class residents, out-priced from the change in shops, services and housing as it shifted to cater for incoming wealthier groups. As part of the research I spoke to many local residents to hear about their views and experiences and gathered 'locational narratives' (Anthias, 2005; Savage et al., 2005), through interviews, with 49 people. One of them was Sylvie.[1] She was 19, studying design at college and living with her gran in socially-rented accommodation in Partick. As part of the second generation of industrial workers, Sylvie had grown up living in social housing in the Clydeside area, moving as a young teenager from working-class neighbourhood Govan on the south side of the river to the adjacent one of Partick to live with her gran as her family felt it was a better neighbourhood. She wants to stay in the area and was registered with Partick Housing Association's allocation waiting list for her own house. Sylvie was unsure of her class position when I asked her because she felt she did not know what being working class meant but she did experience it viscerally, recalling an experience of being Othered in an encounter with middle-class University of Glasgow students who shamed her for her accent. She could also read the semiotics of class from people and from her neighbourhood's changing landscape. When I met her she was sitting in the sunshine at a table outside one of the new bars in the neighbourhood, sunglasses on, drinking a glass of wine. Sylvie had chosen the place because she liked it; I tended to arrange interviews in more traditional and established locations. She is ambivalent about the Harbour development and its local impact. Yet when I mention that I had seen inside the Harbour flats, her curiosity piques and she asks me to describe what they are like in detail which I oblige. She then asks how much a flat would cost to rent which, I tell her, is around £700 per month. Sylvie contemplates this as I do: as a flat-share with a friend it is not unreasonable or unattainable. Sylvie wants to live in the Harbour development. She pipes:

> Not all the way up, maybe halfway, with a wee balcony. Maybe the penthouse though!

Her aspiration is as lofty as the high-rise itself yet is slightly tentative, grading herself as being worthy of a place only halfway up. The key point is that she refuses to be excluded from the gentrification processes taking place despite her lack of means, and that the proliferation of this type of development is the very housing trend that sees the curtailed growth in social housing.

At this point the complexity of the issues is apparent. This encounter shows that it would be myopic for the research to focus on the effects (displacement) caused by gentrification (Glasgow Harbour) as a one way process. The Harbour development is not the only form of gentrification and gentrification is simply an intermediary of greater processes of restructuring; it is more broadly representative. It signifies the end of industry and wholesale change in land use with the demise in production and cultivation to a site of consumption. It also demonstrates neoliberal experimentation with the devolution of power to local states and their subsequent urban entrepreneurial activity (Harvey, 1989;

---

1 All respondents' names have been changed to pseudonyms.

MacLeod, 2002) brokering land sales and working in partnership with businesses. This is, in part, underpinned by the belief in the 'trickling down' of capital created through regeneration: a disingenuous idea which runs concurrent to the decline of traditional social welfare and collective consumption provisions; including social housing. It is also indicative of impact wrought by the Right to Buy policy and the growth of the private housing sector since the 1980s, precursors to the current proliferation of the private rental sector. The Harbour development then also represents a sleight of hand whereby Sylvie, second generation industrial working class, raised in social housing and facing constrained housing choices, is potentially a future Harbour resident. These beacons of modernity are the prospective high rises of the future, only this time round the landlords are private owners, not local authority. In this sense, the development also signifies a revival of the pre-1915 Rent Strike days of private landlordism. Residents of cities like Glasgow, Leeds and Manchester passionately fought against landlords profiteering from poor tenants and won, resulting in the creation of what was to become the UK council housing system which has since been, arguably, all but dismantled. The development is also indicative of changing industry and the degradation of employment with the promotion of construction over traditional engineering and shipbuilding activities which is conditional and deregulated with fewer opportunities for skills training and career progression, with high levels of self-employment and relatively low levels of unionisation (Helms, 2005). Most of all, from Sylvie's interface with Glasgow Harbour, we can see that these processes are not a totality: they are negotiated by the post-industrial working class in new ways. Sylvie, like many others, did not oppose this development, they were not displaced by it, and they even enjoyed the trappings that it brought, such as these new 'gentrified' bars. Working-class residents are invited to participate in gentrification processes and, at times, wish to be part of them. They can be colonisers, displacers and, at times, become gentrifiers. This experience is often heavily circumscribed and stratified: not on the same par as the middle class. Such positions are also frequently borne out of the restriction of choice (meanwhile maintaining the seeming illusion of greater choice). This creates what Young (2007) would call a bulimic situation where respondents are simultaneously included and excluded in gentrification processes; invited to participate but not given means to do so. This point is critical.

In this sense, the changes heralded by the Harbour development could be described as 'quantum leap' forward but this is not simply a shift from one point to the next. The effects and experiences of this are multiple and complex; they are received, negotiated and resisted by working-class residents. This point has been overlooked within the long history of gentrification debates. In this book I offer a broader examination of how urban restructuring affects, and is affected by, working-class communities, through the intermediary of gentrification. I do so to offer a new sociological perspective on gentrification. This involves not only exploring the relationship between urban processes and working-class communities, but also recognising amongst processes that are thought to be determined, mundane or irrelevant: the '"hidden rewards" as well as the "hidden injuries of class"' (Strangleman, 2008: 17). The perspective offered in this book is new in the sense that it combines cultural and material understandings of gentrification, conceiving how it is used to rule as part of a political strategy, whilst making working-class communities and their everyday lives the centre point of analysis. Hitherto, these have been the foremost shortcomings of research on gentrification (Slater, 2006; Lees and Ley, 2008). This comprises two aspects: first, restating the connection between working-class communities and urban restructuring, which I seek to do in relation to gentrification; and second, by representing working-class lives through ethnographic case study of gentrification. To do this, I explore gentrification using a framework of hegemony.

Restructuring Theory: A Framework of Hegemony in Urban Class Analysis

Hegemony is both a tool for social analysis and a concept that expresses cohesion of the social structure and political strategies that helps achieve this, and it is applied as such in this book. It is a term which has recently come back into vogue consolidated by Thomas's (2009) interrogation of what he calls a 'Gramscian moment'. While much of this writing traverses and interrogates Gramsci's legacy in relation to philosophy of praxis, here it is used specifically as a theoretical basis for understanding how changes in productive social relations are managed in the urban context. The framework of hegemony is sociological as it makes an intrinsic, reciprocal connection between structure and agency which can elucidate the relation between urban restructuring and working-class groups. In order to appreciate how useful hegemony is as a framework for understanding urban restructuring, it is essential to consider how it operates empirically, exploring the actual mechanisms for achieving hegemony, the role of the state and civil society, the degree of consensus and coercion involved, the formation of the historic bloc, new coalitions and compromises made and the emergent culture under new economic conditions.

The conditions which drive modern society must be secured socially and, indeed, spatially and it is in this juncture that the concept of hegemony becomes meaningful (Joseph, 2002). Hegemony is understood as comprising two aspects relating to, first, structures, and second, political projects that express the dominance of the ruling class over other social groups. Capitalist dynamics and political projects help shape social and cultural relations during times of economic change, in a consensual rather than determined manner, and which can be, in turn, shaped by these social and cultural relations. The range of governmental forms of restructuring and regeneration are more broadly evident today as seen in workfare policies and social inclusion initiatives which operate at varying scales. Gentrification has a distinct role as a hegemonic project as it supports flexible forms of accumulation by switching capital to the built environment (Harvey, 2003) and promotes neoliberalism via entrepreneurial individualism and consumer citizenship. This helps shape new social relations and culture in industrial neighbourhoods. Using this framework, I reconceptualise the leading orthodox definitions of gentrification as the creation of space for the progressively more affluent user (Hackworth, 2002), to suggest that gentrification policies fulfil financial and social imperatives by seeking to cultivate aspiration and realign traditional working-class identities to be more congruent with post-industrial neoliberalism. Restructuring, in the broadest sense, has much salience. To borrow from Williams (1986), it operates as a keyword, demonstrated in the following three ways.

First, restructuring refers to the empirical processes under investigation in this book. I examine how a formerly industrial neighbourhood has undergone urban restructuring. Glasgow is an illuminating case. While having its own specificities and idiosyncrasies, it is an ideal type: as an industrial working-class city par excellence in terms of industry, consciousness, politics and culture, expressed through the imagery of Red Clydeside; and as a pioneer of neoliberal experimentation and restructuring to become a 'post-industrial' city. Faced with grave economic and social problems wrought by deindustrialisation and the need to attract capital investment, the industrial working-class community is effectively problematised by these processes, deemed surplus to the post-industrial economy and in need of regeneration and modernisation. I explore the effects of this restructuring process on everyday lives and identities of residents, considering the complex impacts of these processes as it transitions to a twenty-first-century post-industrial neighbourhood. I use the term restructuring to denote that working-class neighbourhoods and identities are being reconstituted rather than disappearing. I explore this complex dialectical process whereby class is reshaped by capitalist processes and where capitalist processes are resisted and are also restructured by working-class residents. I look at how people adapt to these changes, capturing the hidden injuries and rewards of restructuring.

Secondly, hegemony is used here as a theory of restructuring which allows us to attend to these epochal prognostications of the end of historically prescribed forms, as it denotes that no such dislocation has taken place. In this context hegemony conveys how deindustrialisation and the shift to post-industrialism are managed. Rather than signifying a break in forms, historical accounts remind us that shifts in productive relations, principally, the relationship between capital, labour and the state, are recurrent and endemic to capitalism (Berman, 1982). Hegemony is a transformative political strategy relevant to transitional stages of capitalism, in which productive relations, the state and social reproduction are recomposed without upsetting the overall capitalist system (Morton, 2006). Hegemony relates to both the unity and social cohesion of the social system and how the reproduction of basic structural processes and relations is achieved through political strategies. Forces of the base and superstructure come together to form a neoliberal hegemonic bloc to ensure the new dominant conditions of post-industrialism are realised in a consensual rather than coercive way. The political economy and social relations are mutually constituting, expressing a dialectical interplay between forces of structure and agency. Thus the relationship between structure and agency continues to exist; it is just set within new parameters which emphasise individualisation and the seeming end of class.

Finally, restructuring is also a salient theme on a theoretical level. There is no one set of literature that captures these changes. Contemporary literature on regulation (Aglietta, 1987; Harvey, 1989, 1990; Jessop, 1990), gentrification (Smith, 1996; Ley, 1996; Slater, 2006) and class (Beck, 1992, Giddens, 1991; Bourdieu, 1999; Savage, 2001; Savage et al., 2005) are all inextricably linked but offer disparate accounts. Orthodox theories of regulation, gentrification and class can be relationally repositioned by viewing them as interconnected within a framework of hegemony, which expresses the dialectical interplay between structure and agency. The processes involved in urban restructuring are inherently place-based and promote individualism. Not only does the new character of productive relations require flexible, spatial forms of capital, the 'rolling out' of the market requires regulative measures which undermine the tenets of industrial working-class relations, like collectivity and state welfarism. This reinforces the idea that class is no longer a salient identifier in industrial working-class neighbourhoods and, by extension, I will argue, contributes to people's disassociation with class. While many sociologists have acknowledged that class can be socio-spatial identity, this is not always applied to the working class or seen in relation to material processes. It is essential to reconnect local political economy with analysis of culture and agency to explore how working-class people adapt to fit the demands of the new 'post-industrial' economy. People refashion their identity in ways that are classed, but not in the traditional image. Restructuring is not simply oppressive since people can take pleasure from their refashioned class identity (Nayak, 2006). In the face of lack of universal economic support the locally articulated responses to securing meaning and value and social reproduction crystallise. Understanding this as a dialectical process helps rearticulate the connection between the restructuring of capital and class identity and everyday life. This is a nod to a trajectory in class research known as New Working Class Studies (NWCS) (Russo and Linkon, 2005). This interdisciplinary research group was initially developed in reaction to deindustrialisation in Youngstown in the USA which aimed to put working-class lives back on the research agenda. NWCS explores class as both an analytical tool and a basis for lived experience, which requires representations that provide access to working-class voices and perspectives (Weis, 2004). This book is in the spirit of NWCS in that it recognises the structural interpretations of class analysis but emphasises that representation is a way of achieving legitimacy for working-class lived experiences.

Outline of the Book

Exploring these issues of urban restructuring is no mean feat given the separation of agency and structure, and culture and economy. Chapter 1, *Restructuring*

Theory, navigates the discrete sets of literature on restructuring, gentrification and class in greater detail. A framework of hegemony is invoked to better specify the contemporary relationship between capitalist dynamics and the social conditions of modernity. This chapter outlines the new hegemonic project of neoliberalism and flexible accumulation, yet the literature falls short of explaining how this is achieved and managed. Gentrification is a key policy strategy used to realise this by reshaping the relationship between state and citizens via participation. Gentrification is used as part of regeneration, not to displace, but to manage working-class populations (Uitermark et al., 2007). This new theory of gentrification aims to respond to the shortcomings of class analysis, where understandings of class identity and culture have been disembedded from structural forms. I reassert the importance of place-based studies of class for analysing the complexities of structure and agency, revealing that processes of individualisation and disassociation have a material basis, which is linked to restructuring.

Taking this unsettled notion of coherent working-class identities forward, Chapter 2, *Restructuring Class Identity*, explores how restructuring affects class position and identity. I explore residents' disassociation with their class position in order to challenge the idea that class is no longer phenomenologically or materially relevant. Residents recognise that their economic class position endures through the transition to a post-industrial economy but they do not directly identify with a collective working-class identity. I show that processes of disassociation crosscut the axes of gender, age, ethnicity and 'race'. In different ways, residents reject class identity in favour of constructing a neoliberal identity, where they are individualised and entrepreneurial. This seemingly individual act is actually collectively resonant. This is demonstrated by the way in which respondents actively restructure their identities as a strategy of coping and of exercising some control during turbulent times.

Chapter 3, *Elective Belonging and Elective Fixity to Place*, explores how working-class identity and position is articulated through place-based attachment. I examine how the relationship between one's chosen residential location and social identity is expressed through the term 'elective belonging' (Savage et al., 2005). This chapter challenges current thinking that elective belonging is the preserve of the middle-class who consume places to construct their sense of self. Given the experience of insecurity, depicted in Chapter 2, retaining a sense of residual working-class local culture is important to people's everyday life and identity. This serves both material and social ends. I demonstrate how working-class place-based attachment expresses social identity and is underpinned by material necessity. Working-class residents' place attachment is broadly, although not exclusively, characterised by strong elective belonging and poor elective fixity; that is, their choice and control over their ability to stay fixed within their neighbourhood.

With the tenuous nature of working-class identity and poor ability to control their neighbourhood position in mind, Chapter 4, *Gentrifying Working-Class Subjects: Participating in Consumer Citizenship*, explores actual existing gentrification processes. Policy-led gentrification invites working-class participation, which contributes to the restructuring of working-class identities as consumer citizens. I explore how gentrification processes attempt to gentrify the working-class subject. This reveals the class politics involved in gentrification, whereby it invites wider participation but reproduces class inequality. The promotion of consumer citizenship is advantageous for affluent gentrifier residents, who appropriate local political power. However, I show that residents are active subjects in this process, and can negotiate gentrification as consumer citizens for their own gains rather than merely being victims.

Chapter 5, *The Paradox of Gentrification: Displacing the Working-Class Subject*, extends the investigation of the contradiction of gentrification further, to explore how this process displaces working-class residents in cultural and physical ways. To realise their neoliberal identity and avoid being Othered, residents were encouraged to be consumer citizens. However, they are denied the material means to realise this. Gentrification simultaneously excludes and includes working-class residents, demonstrating what Young (2007) calls a 'bulimic society'. Increased financial and cultural inequalities put working-class residents at greater risk of displacement through gentrification. This creates new typologies of displacement where renters who are not socially and materially productive are most at risk of being unfixed to place.

In the concluding chapter I return to relationship between urban restructuring, via gentrification, and working-class identities and assess the analytical, conceptual and theoretical gains of using hegemony as a framework. Residents negotiate with processes of urban restructuring levelled at the neighbourhood in individual ways, yet these individualised practices are partly borne of their dis-identification with class, which is an inherently class based process relating to urban restructuring. Their rejection of working-class identity has a material basis, which supports neoliberalism. While industrial working-class culture is residualised by the implementation of this process in the neighbourhood, what emerges testifies to the power of working-class agency. Working-class residents participate in gentrification by negotiating and consuming the process on their own terms, for their own gains. This negotiation also reveals the fallacy of theorisations which position agency outside of structure. Thus, what transpires is a negotiated and emergent culture rather than one that is dominant and totalising (Williams, 1977). This, I suggest, demonstrates that there is a third analytical aspect of hegemony that we must differentiate – the emergent way of life. However, this emergent culture brings with it emergent inequalities. This is revealed through the concept of control. Indeed, what distinguishes working-class from middle-class residents is the degree of control they possess. This is expressed nowhere more clearly than in residents' capacity to control their ability to stay in their neighbourhood vis-à-vis elective fixity. Control becomes a crucial class indicator, revealing both class position and identity and the relationship between the two. Thus, through this concept of control, we can differentiate between classed experiences of the relationship between personal troubles and public issues in a contemporary working-class post-industrial neighbourhood.

Chapter 1
Restructuring Theory

What is required is a better specification of the relationship between capitalist dynamics and the social conditions of modernity. A principal connection is through the analysis of inequalities constantly generated by the mechanisms of accumulation which are reproduced, modulated or transformed in the discourse of mundane practices of daily life captured by analysis of the experience of modernity.

(Savage et al., 2003: 69)

To begin to explore how urban restructuring impacts upon local places, everyday lives and identities requires discrete but interrelated literatures on deindustrialisation, gentrification and class, as there is no comprehensive theoretical account of this process at large (Bagguley et al., 1990; Savage et al., 2003). They instead contain unresolved issues around the relationship between economic and cultural processes. The opening quote from Savage et al. suggests this is indicative of the wider failings of urban sociological analysis which lacks a succinct articulation of the relationship between structure and agency and cultural and economic forces in relation to their spatial setting. The focus of this chapter is to demonstrate how a framework of hegemony is useful for understanding contemporary processes of urban restructuring, particularly the specific way in which gentrification is used to manage deindustrialisation: its effects on working-class people's everyday lives and identities and forms of negotiation and resistance. To do this, I frame the discussion in four main parts. The first details the use of hegemony as a framework of restructuring; in the following three sections I apply this framework to literature on restructuring, gentrification, and class before reasserting the importance of ethnographic, place-based studies of class for understanding these complex hegemonic processes of restructuring.

I begin by outlining how hegemony works and how it can operate as a theoretical framework adept at understanding urban restructuring and the relationship between economic and cultural forces and structure and agency. Hegemony refers to a form of rule relevant to how transformations in productive and social relations are managed whilst the capitalist system is maintained overall. It involves a mix of consent and coercion which combines structural and agential processes, highlighting the reciprocal relationship between the material and the phenomenological. However, its application is not unproblematic and interpretations tend to focus on opposing aspects of structure and agency which undermines its dialectical meaning. I develop the concept from the work of Gramsci (1971) and consider how it has been usefully applied to understand Fordism. I outline cultural and structural interpretations in Western Marxism (Williams, 1977;

Anderson, 1976; Poulantzas, 1967; Hall and Jacques, 1989) which undermine the strength of the concept by focusing on opposing features. I suggest that this schism can be avoided by making an analytical distinction between two aspects of hegemony – between the structure and the surface level projects (Joseph, 2002). This can be taken forward to explore urban restructuring and strategies involved in managing the shift from Fordism and how this is experienced in everyday life.

Thus, the second part of this chapter explores how hegemony can be used to theorise the crisis of Fordist capitalism and subsequent deindustrialisation. Prevailing theories of restructuring known as the regulation school draw from a hegemonic framework (Aglietta, 1987; Lipietz, 1986; Jessop, 1990; Harvey, 1982, 1990). While they capture the economic processes involved and attempt to incorporate agency and social relations, they fall back into structural and masculinist understandings. Deindustrialisation and the rise of neoliberalism not only involve the restructuring of the economy, they result in the restructuring of urban policy and the relationship between the state and civil society, as well as, citizenship and class. Regeneration has become the leading government strategy for restructuring places and local populations, extending power to both local agencies and businesses through urban entrepreneurialism and to citizens through participation. These forms of regeneration help manage social relations of neoliberalism whilst effectively blurring the relationship between civil society and the state. This is expressed through the concept of consumer citizenship (Christopherson, 1994). Regeneration is revealed to be, in essence, a class project that decontextualises and reproduces class inequality.

In the third part of this chapter I consider gentrification as a class based process of neighbourhood transformation and as a key regeneration strategy. Contemporary definitions fail to adequately theorise how and why contemporary processes of gentrification are used as part of regeneration strategies (Lees and Ley, 2008) and the implications this has for working-class communities. This section demonstrates how gentrification is *both* an economic and cultural process which has been effectively harnessed by the state to manage deindustrialisation for material and socially productive ends. Gentrification has evolved from a means of urban renewal to a strategy for regulating working-class behaviours and practices (Uitermark et al., 2007). Thus, I put forward a new theoretical understanding of gentrification. It is defined here as part of a hegemonic project which supports neoliberal and flexible forms of accumulation. It does so by seeking to create the more affluent citizen, in a moral and material sense, recalibrating both space and subjectivities. This involves the transformation of class and productive relations through negotiations, realised at the local and individual level.

The fourth part outlines how class analysis has responded to deindustrialisation and urban restructuring. The legacy of community studies of class (Dennis et al., 1956; Jackson, 1968; Young and Wilmot, 1957; Lockwood, 1958) includes too tight a focus on collectivity and a failure to clarify the relationship between class position and individual identity, paving the way for sociological narrative on deindustrialisation which heralds the end of class and the rise of the individual self-maker (Beck, 1992; Bauman, 1998; Giddens, 1991; Pakulski and Waters, 1996). The relationship between class position and identity are said to have unravelled. Consequently, we know little of how class identities are being restructured. Exploring class and place and their complex interrelationship offers a means of countering the supposed identity-position disconnect. Contemporary class analysis has made great inroads, incorporating culture, identity and, crucially, its intersection with other axes of oppression: 'race'; gender; and sexuality (Taylor, 2010). Significantly 'culturalist class theorists' (Savage et al., 2001, 2005, 2005a; Skeggs, 1997, 2004; Reay, 2005) deploy the concept of disassociation to express the disjuncture between class position and identity. Class is, then, revealed to not only to be an economic inequality but a devalued social location subject to stigma. While this exploration has been vital, this turn to culture and identity and, by extension, a turn to Bourdieu (Reay, 2011) runs the danger of leaving the material and the economic behind. I suggest that making disassociation the focus of class analysis can disaggregate and discount collectivity and underplay the significance of place. Disassociation is not merely a process of class opposition and individualisation; it reveals the material basis of a hegemonic shift towards post-industrial neoliberalism which is a profoundly urban process. Social and physical locations are both the site of inequality, stigma and pathologisation yet the working of this intersection of place and restructuring processes in this sense is missing from class analysis. A hegemonic framework can connect issues of class identity with the material recomposition of society. This is evident in how place and homeownership express social identities (Savage et al., 2005). The neighbourhood is a crucial site for observing the interrelationship between social and physical space. People's locational narratives (Anthias, 2005; Savage et al., 2005) provide a powerful account for understanding class in relation to a process of hegemonic change. Residential biographical stories of how and where people live reveal the making of the social locations, hierarchies, boundaries and categories, and people's actual physical location in relation to their material reality. This reveals the coding of people and places – or spaces and subjectivities – as historically and materially meaningful, expressing the material and cultural aspects of class that are being reworked by the neoliberal hegemony. Thus a place-based case study usefully enables us to combine these elements.

I conclude this discussion by reassessing the application of hegemony within the context of deindustrialisation and urban restructuring. Hegemony allows us to see the connection between production and social relations vis-à-vis gentrification. This framework brings together the disparate research fields and offers a progressive understanding that transcends orthodox explanations. Understanding urban restructuring as a hegemonic project helps explain how class positions and identities, as well as neighbourhoods, are restructured. Gentrification acts as an intermediary between capitalist processes of deindustrialisation and contemporary working-class lives. Gentrification expresses the two aspects of hegemony. It captures the structural aspects through productive relations of flexible accumulation and spatial fixes, as well as, the political strategy of neoliberalisation involved in creating this hegemony. Working-class people adapt to processes of restructuring. Individualised behaviours and consumption in neighbourhoods, like homeownership, are linked to the economic base and political strategies of hegemony. This process is distinctly class based as it bolsters the powers of the ruling class and denigrates the working class, although this can be negotiated. Thus, urban restructuring is inextricably linked to working-class communities and identities. I suggest that there is a third analytical aspect to hegemony: the emergent lived experience that is the result of reciprocal negotiations between structure and agency. This is best viewed in the locale, connecting micro and macro processes, achieved through a case study. I end by demonstrating how to take this forward into an empirical application in relation to a neighbourhood in Glasgow, Scotland.

Hegemony as a Framework for Urban Change

Frameworks used to theorise urban restructuring tend to focus on economic processes and are, therefore, often deterministic. Other frameworks have been used to theorise the relationship between structure and agency in urban restructuring: Bourdieu's habitus (Bridge, 2001); Giddens's structuration (Cattell, 2004; Healy, 2003) and Foucault's governmentality (Raco, 2000; Flint, 2006) but they fail to capture this interplay in relation to both social class and economic change. Hegemony can provide a framework that is particularly adept in this respect. Fundamentally, as a concept, hegemony is a form of rule that is realised consensually, as well as, coercively. It operates as an intermediary between capitalist accumulation and social relations, denoting the reciprocal interplay between material and ontological levels and therein lies its use value as a framework for understanding urban restructuring. Hegemony is a political strategy that is responsive to transitional stages of capitalism, through which productive relations and social reproductions are recomposed without upsetting the overall form of capitalism. Unlike aforementioned frameworks, hegemony transcends economic or cultural reductionism through a dialectic perspective of the base-superstructure model (Gramsci, 1971) and puts class relations at the centre of this process. In some respects, using hegemony as a framework to understand urban restructuring is not novel (Harvey, 1989; Jessop, 1990; Aglietta, 1987) however the application of hegemony used in these studies involves a theoretical understanding of agency and class rather than one that is practical or empirically validated. Indeed, different applications of hegemony emphasise either structural or agential aspects which undermine its dialectical meaning. It is essential to maintain this balance to make the concept meaningful. In the first part, I outline the origins of the concept via Gramsci, how it operates and how it has been applied to understand Fordism as productive relations and as a way of life. I then consider some ways it has been interpreted in Western Marxist debates (Williams, 1977; Anderson, 1976; Poulantzas, 1967; Hall and Jacques, 1989) which foreground the strengths and weaknesses of hegemony. This is because the framework of hegemony is sociological as it makes an intrinsic, reciprocal connection between structure and agency which can illuminate the relation between urban restructuring and working-class groups. Appreciating its power as a framework for understanding urban restructuring requires considering how hegemony operates empirically, exploring the actual mechanisms for achieving hegemony, the role of the state and civil society, the degree of consensus and coercion involved, the formation of the historic bloc, new coalitions and compromises made and the emergent culture under new economic conditions. I suggest that seeing hegemony as comprising two aspects – structural hegemony and surface hegemony of actual projects (Joseph, 2002) provides analytical clarity which can avoid this schism and can be used to attend to the shortcomings in urban sociological analysis.

Origins, Features and Application

To understand hegemony in more depth, I will consider its origins, the key features of how it operates and how it has been applied to understand the project of Fordism. There has been a recent revival and reappraisal of Gramsci's canon of work. Thomas (2009) mines recent contributions to articulate and recapitulate what he calls a 'Gramscian moment' in social and political theory, although this trend has not developed in the same way within sociology. Thus my use of it here is less the thorough expedition such as Thomas's tour de force (see too Ekers et al., 2012) but rather to ascertain and assert its contemporary explanatory value and its empirical salience in applied sociological research. Hegemony is normally understood as a form of rule that emphasises consent rather than coercion. It is associated with the writings of Gramsci (1971), who developed it from Lenin's interpretation of the rule of the proletariat, to describe political rule more generally, reflecting on the historical context of capitalist crisis and restructuring and the relationship between the state and civil society. The capitalist conditions which drive modern society must be secured socially and it is in this space that the concept of hegemony becomes meaningful (Joseph, 2002). For Gramsci, it expresses the political strategy of bourgeois rule over the working class in a stabilised capitalist society. His interpretation is novel because it refers to the interplay between structure and agency in periods of transformative politics, whereby the state rules through force while civil society does so by consensus. This is because hegemony is exercised through society's superstructure, as opposed to its base, comprising the state *and* civil society. He based his formulation of this political strategy on the differences between Eastern and Western European states, as a shift from primordial rule to a more gelatinous yet stable rule. The Western state exemplified hegemonic power via a more developed civil society which helps rule in a more complex and balanced way than through more simplistic state-based dominance, ideology or force. This is because civil society helps rule by harnessing support and consent through different methods, such as rewards, universalising values and practices and socialisation to a create a whole mode of living, all of which convince people to support the hegemonic order. Combined in this way, the state and civil society provide persuasive moral and ethical initiatives:

> [...] every state is ethical in as much as one of its most important functions is to raise the great mass of the population to a particular cultural and moral level, a level (or type) which corresponds to the needs of productive forces for development, and hence the interests of the ruling class. (Gramsci, 1971: 258)

The point being that by emphasising the significance of consensus, a hegemonic framework of interpretation tries to explain why, despite exploitation, capitalism continues to reign rather than viewing consciousness in a reductive or deterministic sense. Nevertheless, Gramsci (1971) notes that consent is armoured by coercion as the threat of the state is pervasive, even if implicit. It is the cultivation of the balance between consent and coercion which is critical and is managed by the state and civil society and makes this a powerful conception and warrants more thorough consideration of the mechanisms through which hegemony operates.

The sociological strength lies in the fact that hegemony offers a way of exploring the relationship between structure and agency in relation to social class and economic change. This is because Gramsci's elaboration of hegemony refers not only to a form of rule but to a deeper level of organisation. Hegemony can describe the way in which dominant social groups achieve their leadership on the basis of attaining social cohesion and consensus which maintain structural relations (Joseph, 2002). Class is central to the functioning of hegemony because objective social divisions must be present in order for hegemony to occur. For a social group to maintain its hegemonic position it must have the economic, political and cultural conditions behind it which enable that group to present itself as ruling. The ruling group fights for its position and secures consent to its leadership through political projects, social alliances, coalitions and compromise, forming what Gramsci calls a hegemonic bloc. In this way, hegemony involves the agency of actors seen in the relational and intersubjective aspects of political projects which are compelling and shape social reproduction. Yet the hegemonic bloc is not only defined on the basis of relations between groups but on the basis of the relations between groups and structure (base-superstructure) so that hegemony involves the process whereby structures and superstructures co-determine and relate to one another. Thus, the organisation of hegemony at the level of social groups relates to the organisation of society at the political level and to the level of production. Thus for Gramsci, hegemony is not just a reference to the domination of the ruling class. Since the ruling social group are born out the particular stage of capitalist development, it has liberatory potential for the working class. Social classes can form their own consensus to challenge the prevailing hegemony and build a counter hegemony. Hegemony offers the possibility for change but this is set within structural confines rather than borne of social agents.

Therefore, hegemony relates to both the unity and social cohesion of the social system and the reproduction of basic structural processes and relations (Joseph,

2002). It is both structural and strategic, ensuring that social relations speak to productive relations and securing this support through consensus and compromise. Hegemony is, therefore, essential during times of economic change and crisis:

> [...] what is involved is the reorganisation of the structure and the real relations between men and women on the one hand and the world of the economy or production on the other. (Gramsci, 1971: 263)

This function is best understood empirically. Gramsci applied his definition of hegemony to Fordism as a project of productive and social relations that support capitalist societies. He deemed Fordism the ultimate stage in the process of progressive attempts by industry to overcome the tendency of the rate of profit to fall (Gramsci, 1971), encapsulating the new form of production and consumption throughout the early twentieth century which partly solved the inherent accumulation crisis. It offered a means of empirical reflection on the defeats of the working-class movement in various countries. As a mode of economic regulation, Fordism introduced new methods of production vis-à-vis scientific management through an adroit combination of force and consent whereby trade unions were attacked but compensated with high wages and benefits (Hunt, 1997), thus, Gramsci's assertion that 'hegemony here is born in the factory' (Gramsci, 1971: 285). Fordism requires workers to possess certain attributes compatible with repetitive work which by extension requires compatibility with life outside the factory, like self-control and emotional stability. Fordism also represents a lived experience; Gramsci conceives it as a whole way of life, generating coherent patterns of social reproduction which form the dominant culture (Williams, 1977). It involves '[...] the biggest collective effort to create with unprecedented speed, and with a consciousness of purpose unmatched in history, a new type of worker and a new type of man' (Gramsci, 1971: 302). Moral regulation and leadership help realign social practices towards the Fordist model, largely shaping the patterns of daily life and relations in the early twentieth century:

> [...] adapting the civilisation and the morality of the broadest popular masses to the necessities of the continuous development of the economic apparatus of production; hence of evolving even physically new types of humanity. (Gramsci, 1971: 242)

Although Gramsci did not apply his Fordist hegemony to a study of Britain, it is commonly used in reference to the post-war period when working-class men's lives were largely defined by school to work, with circumscribed but steady job opportunities in local industries. Meanwhile, working-class women were traditionally located in the home, with circumscribed involvement in the labour market, undertaking unpaid labour and related responsibilities of social reproduction. People were supported by the safety net of state welfare and public provisions, notably municipally provided housing.

However, this was not a deterministic relationship or a social totality. British production was never fully underpinned by a classically Fordist system. Instead, the form that existed is referred to as 'flawed Fordism' (Jessop, 1989). The cyclical changes and expansion of capitalism are spatially uneven, resulting in regional patterning of industry. In particular, shipbuilding areas, like Clydeside, were distinctly un-Fordist in their operations and more paternalistic, hence the Conservative government's targeting of such 'inefficient' industry in the 1970s. Further, social relations were divided, particularly along the lines of ethnicity, in relation to sectarianism in Scotland, and gender. However, in general terms, the post-war settlement was one of relative political and cultural consensus, built on the basis of growing affluence, the welfare state and state regulation in the economy. Thus, it is described as a whole historical period, with the development of regulation and a new hegemonic bloc. Industrial regions were broadly characterised by the employment of wage labour characterised by relatively secure, unionised, assembly line jobs in the manufacturing sector, traditionally based on a tripartite consensus between the state, employers and organised labour (Harvey, 1990). The notion of industrial citizenship expressed the idea that basic civil, political and social rights for the workers can be gained through collective bargaining in the workplace. In Britain, in the 1970s, Labour entered a 'social contract' with the trade union movement where the unions agreed to regulate the wage demand of members in exchange for increased participation and representation in the shaping of government policies (Crompton, 1993). Fordism was based on this compromise – involving the welfare state, higher wages based on collective bargaining and full employment – thus it gained consent but excluded the working class from having any real political power (Joseph, 2002). However, the arrangements empowered the working class in ways that enabled them to build their own hegemonic bloc. Fordism demonstrates the complex and stratified ways that hegemony achieves a critical balance between consent and coercion, where the superstructure shapes social relations to match the form of capitalist organisation, while constituting a lived experience and sense of reality for people, and yet one that is not total and can be challenged. It is a social totality but not totalising or determined. Hegemony, then, helps us to understand the relationship between phenomenological and material worlds in relation to social class and economic change. However, the incorporation of the concept of hegemony into Western, particularly British, Marxist thought has exacerbated debate from humanist/culturalist (Thompson, 1963; Williams, 1977) and structural readings (Althusser, 1971; Poulantzas, 1967; Anderson, 1976).

Interpretations: Cultural and Structural Schisms

Humanist readings of hegemony emphasise the agential and intersubjective elements. Raymond Williams (1977) is credited with articulating the cultural interpretation of the concept. Williams opposed the schematic application of the dominant base-superstructure model in Marxist orthodox theory. He critiques determination and the primacy of the economic base in a novel way by broadening the narrow conception of the base as purely economic to include a whole range of human relationships and processes. In doing so, he helps bring the base and superstructure into alignment through the notion of praxis. It follows that base determines superstructure; social beings determine consciousness (Williams, 1977). Hegemony becomes meaningful (for it is not a totality) as something that is lived in depth. Williams's considers hegemony as a whole lived process, like a tradition and way of life which is enveloping:

> A lived hegemony is always a process. It is not, except analytically, a system or a structure. It is a realised complex of experiences, relationships and activities, with specific and changing pressures and limits. In practice, that is, hegemony can never be singular. Its internal structures are highly complex, as can readily be seen in any concrete analysis. (Williams, 1977: 112)

Hegemony is then theorised as a struggle between the dominant, residual and emergent cultures. In any society, in any particular period, there is a central, effective, and dominant system of meanings and values, which are not merely abstract but are organised and lived (Williams, 1977). New emergent culture can gradually come to be dominant culture, rendering the prevailing one residual. This interpretation provides space for working-class agency and resistance. The working class negotiate with dominant hegemonic projects resulting in new emergent cultural forms. Humanist readings of hegemony not only recognise political agency in actors during organic crises, they consider what compels people's actions in phenomenological and intersubjective ways:

> It can be argued that Gramsci's theory suggests that subordinated groups accept the ideas, values and leadership of the dominant group not because they are physically or mentally induced to do so, nor because they are ideologically indoctrinated, but because they have reason of their own. (Strinati, 1995: 166)

Individuals or social groups may be subordinated but they are not rendered victims; the basis of hegemony is the acceptance of a relationship which is rooted in material forms. The explanatory potential of hegemony has been observed by a number of researchers in relation to issues of cultural identity (Hall, 1986), masculinity (Connell, 2005) and moral regulation (Hunt, 1997) (see also Green's 2011 edited collection *Rethinking Gramsci*). Indeed the humanist neo-Gramscian critique of economic determinism resulted in it branching off within British Marxism. It led to the establishment of the Birmingham Centre for Contemporary Cultural Studies, headed by Stuart Hall who utilised hegemony in his *New Times* critique on Thatcherism (Hall and Jacques, 1989). However, Williams's and other humanist and culturalist readings tend to reduce the base to meanings and values so that hegemony becomes associated with their cultural dominance. This reading gives prominence to culture in a way that replaces the social structure as the primary focus, instead of incorporating it into the social structure.

Structuralist critiques rightly challenge aspects of the humanist reading (while not discussed here, Althusser's famous critique of Gramsci in his contribution to *Reading 'Capital'* is worth mentioning). Poulantzas (1967) has argued that hegemony is central to the organisation of the dominant historic bloc more than securing the consent of social groups. He insists structure over agency is necessary. Hegemony is not reducible to class consciousness or values, rather, it is rooted in the objective social structures which relates to the relation of production.

> The domination of these classes [...] relates to relatively macrochronic structures – to "phases" of the relations of production as a whole (not, therefore, to tactical "compromises" or "alliances"). (Poulantzas, 1967: 70)

In saying this, Poulantzas reduces political hegemony to structural determination. Similarly, Anderson's (1976) critique of hegemony attests that the relationship between state and civil society is not properly differentiated. Such inarticulacy fails to characterise the relationship between capitalist society and the ideological generation of consent (Martin, 1997). Anderson (1976) asserts that this is not an accidental slippage but is instead indicative of the wider and more fundamental problems of Marxist articulations of the state. Anderson (1976) argues that culture cannot determine the normal structure of power in bourgeois democratic states. It is ultimately too fragile and coercion must be the dominant power in supreme crisis. Dominant consensual bourgeois rule is determined by the threat of force via the state; this is the law of capitalism. Yet this forecloses an open-ended explanation and exploration of the role of culture and consent and the possibility of shifting relationship between the state and civil society. Thus structuralist criticisms greatly undermine the explanatory power of the hegemony.

Both structuralist and humanist readings tend towards opposite weaknesses. Instead of connecting base and superstructure these readings undermine the dialectic by focusing on the opposing sides. Humanist readings vis-à-vis Williams emphasise the social expression of hegemony but do not elaborate the structural role of hegemony – how it ensures the cohesion and unity of social formation, while structural readings vis-à-vis Poulantzas emphasis the structural and functional operation of hegemony which does not account for the emergence of historical interactions and agency of agents (Joseph, 2002). The efficacy hegemony offers is undone and the structural–agential relationship is reduced to an impenetrable conundrum. Joseph (2002) attempts to offer some mitigation via his critical realist approach which acknowledges that while hegemony expresses the reciprocal relationship between material and phenomenological levels, we should analytically conceive hegemony as comprising two aspects – a structural hegemony and a surface hegemony of actual projects. This refers to the relationship between the state and the relations of production and the social relations that buttress this, although he notes that this distinction is difficult to make as these are interpreted rather than discrete social objects; it is an analytical abstraction but a dialectical one:

> [...] hegemony is fundamental to the unity of all human societies and is a basic material necessity concerned with the interrelation of the different parts of the social whole [...] of particular importance is the relation between the state and the economic system, although strong social hegemony will be backed up by the fortresses and earthworks of a developed civil society and cultural domain.
> (Joseph, 2002: 128)

Structural hegemony and surface hegemony presuppose one another. This analytical rendering has sociological salience. Structural hegemony operates functionally to ensure the production of social structures and this functional requirement allows for the manifestation of various hegemonic projects which try to correspond to this underlying structure. In this reading, the surface hegemony of projects and strategies involve some form of understanding of the agential/phenomenological processes in relation to class. Hegemonic projects are emergent from the structural hegemony – determined by the basic social structure but not reducible to it (Joseph, 2002). These projects develop their own specific dynamic which have irreducible elements and warrant investigation as the forms and manifestation change in relation to time and place. The concept of emergent is important as it acknowledges that the underlining necessity for social cohesion depends on a structural hegemony and that this allows for hegemonic projects which have their specific dynamic and are not reducible to their structural function (Joseph, 2002). There must be underlying social divisions in order for these projects to occur, so social groups can become dominant, if they have the economic political and social conditions behind them.

This structural/surface distinction provides constructive analytical clarity. Acknowledging the structural aspects when exploring hegemony helps differentiate the structural and agential practices and the role of social classes during economic change. This emphasis on different layers acknowledges that the working class are the product of complex social relations rather than determined or constituting a universal class subject. The framework of hegemony is sociological in this respect as it makes an intrinsic, reciprocal connection between structure and agency which can elucidate the relation between urban restructuring and working-class groups. In order to appreciate how useful hegemony is as a framework for understanding urban restructuring, it is essential to consider how it operates empirically, exploring the actual mechanisms for achieving hegemony, the role of the state and civil society, the degree of consensus and coercion involved, the formation of the historic bloc, new coalitions and compromises made and the emergent culture under new economic conditions.

Deindustrialisation and Restructuring

Here I consider how a hegemonic framework can be used to understand contemporary processes of restructuring precipitated by deindustrialisation. To do this I begin with some caveats and justifications of the terms I employ. The language of both Fordism and post-Fordism has had an important impact on the conceptualisation of restructuring (McDowell, 1991). Fordism is a largely contested concept (Kumar, 1995) and is employed here in reference to Gramsci's theorisation of hegemony. I am interested in how the restructuring of Fordism has been managed. To be clear, I am less concerned with defining features of post-Fordism as a theory of deindustrialisation. Doing so would subscribe to a set of arguments that are too limited to be useful in this context. Indeed, the shortcomings of post-Fordist theories are that they do not theorise social relations in connection to capitalist dynamics. If post-Fordism was explicated in the same way as Fordism has been (Gramsci, 1971), the task for urban sociological analysis would be less problematic. Here I explore restructuring as a shift towards flexible forms of accumulation and neoliberalism. These have significant ramifications for urban development, politics and forms of governing as capitalism affects different places, neighbourhoods and ways of life in combined and uneven ways (Harvey, 1982). In this section, firstly, I consider a branch of literature on restructuring, the regulation school, which resonates with the hegemonic project (Jessop, 1990; Harvey, 1989; Aglietta, 1987; Liptiez, 1986). It provides an account of deindustrialisation which recognises the need for recomposition and regulation of social relations to be congruent with the economy. However, this approach ultimately deviates from the Gramscian application, collapsing back into structuralist models, reducing restructuring to the logic of process of capitalist accumulation. Secondly, I explore strategies for achieving restructuring. Regeneration has emerged as a key urban policy strategy of restructuring in the UK. Regeneration denotes a break from previous Fordist–Keynesian relations, in that it is inherently spatial and localised in scale and alters state–civil society relations and forms of citizenship and class practices. Current Marxist explanations theorise regeneration as a new form of urban entrepreneurial politics (Harvey, 1989; Hall and Hubbard, 1998) which extends political power to business. In post-Foucauldian analysis it is a technology of government exercised through the extension of participation (Rose, 1999; Flint, 2006). There is no comprehensive theory of regeneration and these fissures in explanations reflect the separation of productive and social practices in theories of urban restructuring in general. Yet regeneration, as I demonstrate, is vital to the hegemonic project of neoliberalism. Regeneration is a class project which both decontextualises and reproduces class inequality through its promotion of consumer citizenship (Christopherson, 1994). This leads into the following section which identifies gentrification as a leading government regeneration strategy.

Explaining Restructuring Theory

Writing within the regulation school carries varied theoretical assumptions which are beyond the scope of my analysis here. They are considered in relation to their main thesis that the inevitable crisis in the Fordist regime of accumulation has hastened a hegemonic shift towards a flexible system of accumulation and neoliberalism, with social and political consequences. The attributes of flexible accumulation and neoliberalism stand in conflict with the rigid features of Fordist–Keynesianism:

> It is predicated upon instead a flexible labour process, labour markets and products and consumption. Including new sectors of production, new provision of financial services and intensified rates of innovation in commercial technological and organisational spheres. (Harvey, 1990: 134)

Harvey (1982) outlines the geographic dynamics of capital accumulation which he calls uneven geographical development and spatial fixes of accumulation. Capital seeks to resolve crises through geographical expansion and it is redirected into the built environment and uneven economic development. Capital fixed in place is deemed a drag upon the capacity to realise a spatial fix elsewhere. If capital is not moved, it becomes devalued in the impending recession. These processes were catastrophic for the industrial heartlands in the UK that were reliant on coalmines, manufacturing and shipbuilding, like Clydeside. Yet the processes by which flexible accumulation is implemented are the same as those in Fordism. Regulation theorists work from the premise that the system of accumulation is only effective if it has a corresponding schema of production. This transition requires a corresponding mode of regulation to ensure that it operates effectively and, by extension, has supporting social practices. Hegemony relates to the complex processes that achieve this (Gramsci, 1971). To create a hegemonic bloc, the task is then to bring all the actors' practices, capitalists, workers, the state, employers, financiers and so on, into a complementary configuration. This involves a reconfiguration of the relations between capital and labour. In Britain, the social contract with the trade unions had to be dismantled. The Conservatives spearheaded the return to market forces in the regulation of economic affairs which saw the privatisation of state industry and welfare (Crompton, 1993). This altered the relationship between the state and the market. This relates to a broader shift in political economic practices. Neoliberalism has emerged as the new mode of political economy, development and regulation. The genealogy of neoliberalism is grounded in flexible accumulation, privatisation and the financialisation of markets, and the dismantling of the social contract and previous notions of citizenship which upheld Fordism:

> Neoliberalism is a theory of political economic practices that proposes that human well-being can best be advanced by liberating individual entrepreneurial

freedom characterized by strong private property rights, free markets, and free trade. The role of the state is to create and preserve an institutional framework appropriate to such practices. (Harvey, 2005: 2)

In the neoliberal formulation, the market is the regulative principle of the state: state actions and policies are submitted to the considerations of profitability. The economic process is also distinctly re-humanised and re-socialised (Gledhill, 2004) as dimensions of human life are cast in terms of rationality. Citizens are encouraged to act responsibly by making decisions that support entrepreneurialism which is a both morally correct and a rational choice.

On the surface, this has been achieved in a coercive way, with the defeat of the trade unions, and by and large, the industrial working-class. Other methods used to achieve this are mostly based in the workplace, where consent for this mode of production is manufactured (Burawoy, 1979). However, much occurs backstage and a new hegemony is achieved through a combination of consent and coercion:

> Some mix of repression habituation, co-optation, cooperation, all of which have to be organised not only within the workplace but also throughout society at large. The socialisation of the worker to conditions of capitalist production entails the social control of physical and mental powers on a very broad basis. Education, training, pension [...] all play a role and are plainly mixed in with the formation of dominant ideologies cultivated by the mass media, religious and educational institutions and the various forms of state apparatus, and asserted by simple articulation of their experience on the part of those who do the work. (Harvey, 1990: 123–4)

Thus, the shift to flexible forms of accumulation and neoliberalism is achieved through intellectual and moral leadership where people are persuaded to accept new values, norms and practices. This part of the hegemonic project was consolidated by the Third Way alternative heralded by New Labour, as will be discussed.

While the regulation school offers a framework for critically interpreting a range of contemporary political-economic features (Peck and Tickell, 1995), its proponents fall back into structural and statist interpretations. These are expressed in three major shortcomings. First, this approach does not integrate the contemporary transformation of capitalism with the framework of uneven development. Urban processes are the 'missing link' within the regulation approach (Savage et al., 2003). Regulation theorists overlook the agency of labour, firms and individual actors (Massey, 1984) in shaping firm location, production patterns and practices. For example, shipbuilding was dominated by craftwork which allowed labour to leverage some control over this industry. Employers were reluctant to invest in technology given the fluctuating market. This afforded processes of protectionism that were divisive in reproducing jobs within certain groups – that of 'white', protestant males (Knox, 1999). Second, the local variations and impacts are such that intervention and management need to be tailored at a corresponding level which is inherently spatial. Peck and Tickell (1995) argue that the nation state is not the main arena of regulation. Deindustrialisation has led to the restructuring of the local state apparatus in the interests of the central state (Hall and Hubbard, 1996; Peck and Tickell, 1995). Power is devolved to local states, who then utilise local agencies, who become the state apparatus for governance. The whole time the state appears to be remote. Peck and Tickell's (1995) insistence on a revised regulation approach that focuses on the localised mode of social regulation seems more fitting. Third and finally, the masculinist and structuralist model of the regulation approach forecloses an exploration of how social relations and reproduction are managed. They miss the elements of gender, civil society, political mobilisation and the restructuring of services, including social welfare provisions (Bagguley et al., 1990). While regulation approaches usefully define the nature of deindustrialisation, they lose all sense of social practice and the mechanisms required to make hegemony effective. The political strategy of hegemony is understood in terms of the monetary system, wage determination and corporate structures as ways of establishing behavioural routines, rather than the personal, ontological, localised methods. These three shortcomings allude to the same issue: a structuralist interpretation of hegemony. While Harvey (1989) and Jessop (1990) are notable in their attempt to integrate agency into their analysis, this is limited to a theoretical application rather than a practical empirical one where class has little analytical currency.

These criticisms could be seen to undermine the logic of upholding the regulation approach. However, I suggest that in spite of these shortcomings the basic premise holds: that the economic regime shift towards neoliberalism requires corresponding changes within social relations. It is possible to attend to these shortcomings by offering a humanist critique. This involves conceding the gendered and racialised character of the welfare state (Bakshi, 1995). We ought to conceptualise the state, not as disembodied or detached from everyday lives, but as a relationship that is enacted through the practice of social agents at work and at home (Mitchell et al., 2004). Under neoliberalism social reproduction is shaped and constrained by the state in contemporary capitalist society, perhaps more than ever before. The regulation approach can also be supplemented by refining the analytical focus to include the spatial scale and the ontological level, as well as, class relations, where the processes of restructuring are effective. The form of flexible accumulation has a distinctly spatial element and so too do the political strategies of intervention. This is evident in the government strategy of regeneration.

Restructuring of the political economy has altered the form of politics. Urban policy, a term first used in the 1960s (Cochrane, 2007), attempts to respond to the crisis of the post-war settlement and deindustrialisation. The uneven urban problems borne of deindustrialisation generate specific new practices in urban government with an increase in the engagement of the local authority in economic development and a simultaneous restructuring and subordination of social consumption (Mayer, 1994). The pressure of economic restructuring and mass unemployment, coupled with diminished subsidies from central government and a prioritisation of economic development have meant that the local state takes less responsibility for social consumption and welfare services. In the 1980s, urban policy turned to property-led renewal, whereby problems in cities were diagnosed as poor physical infrastructure that repelled capital. 'Roll back' neoliberalism uses unbridled market forces and attacks both Fordist–Keynesian welfare principles and the social contract. Economically, neoliberalism involves the 'rolling back' of traditional forms of state intervention and politically, it 'rolls forward' a new type of government more suited to the market driven global economy. From the 1990s, urban policy under New Labour has been characterised by regeneration which is said to tackle environmental, economic and social problems in cities (Lees, 2003; Imrie and Raco, 2003; Roberts and Sykes, 2000). This so-called softer form of 'roll out' neoliberalism purposefully constructs and consolidates neoliberal state forms, modes of government and regulatory relations (Peck and Tickell, 2002). Regeneration is a specifically spatial intervention aimed at combating the area-based negative effects of uneven capitalist development. It is heralded as a panacea, defined as a:

> [...] comprehensive integrated vision and action which leads to the resolution of urban problems which seeks to bring about lasting improvement in the economic, physical, social and environmental condition of an area that has been subject to change. (Roberts and Sykes, 2000: 17)

Regeneration is implemented at various spatial levels: nationally;[1] locally, through regional governments, neighbourhood initiatives, voluntary and community groups; and at the level of the individual. In contrast to tripartite political arrangements of Fordist–Keynesianism, the 'rolling out' of regeneration as a strategy of neoliberalisation involves two key components of governance: the growth focused strategy of the state (Logan and Molotch, 1987) via urban entrepreneurialism (Harvey, 1989), and the expansion of community and individual participation and citizenship in local policy (Imrie and Raco, 2003).

To consider urban entrepreneurialism first, this is commonly interpreted using a Marxist or structuralist framework. Cox and Mair (1989) describe this paradigm shift as 'new urban politics', where the public and private sectors in city governance are blurred. Peck and Tickell (2002) suggest that the new urban politics are concurrent with the 'rolling back' of national state regulation, cutting localities free from centralised fiscal funding and controls, and the success of a neoliberal growth ideology. This paradigm shift was presented somewhat coercively under the auspices of TINA (There is No Alternative) during Thatcherism. It represents a shift in how cities operate whereby the public sector assumes characteristics indicative of the private sector: risk-taking, inventiveness, competition and profit motivation. Local government and various local interests and coalitions

---

1 Nationally for Scotland means both Westminster and the Scottish Parliament.

work together to enhance the economic value of urban space and attract mobile capital. This development is generally associated with the emergence of entrepreneurialism and competitive styles of urban governance hence the description of the 'entrepreneurial city' (Harvey, 1989; Hall and Hubbard, 1998). It is based on the belief that cities must be made attractive for people and capital to go there. Cities are re-branded into innovative, attractive sites through place-marketing campaigns, including cultural or sports events like Olympic and Commonwealth Games, physical transformation and development, and the creation of symbols of modernity such as conference and cultural sites, transport systems, consumption and leisure spaces and so on. Unsurprisingly, restructuring has been more pronounced in industrial cities like Glasgow (MacInnes, 1995). The renowned 'Glasgow model' denotes successful regeneration (Turok, 2004; Boyle and Hughes, 1994; Boyle et al., 2008; MacLeod, 2002) involving aggressive place-based marketing which utilises the cultural spectacle as a means of re-imagining the city through campaigns that celebrate it in a positive way. However, such Marxist and Marxian accounts are often deterministic and have impoverished conceptions of the social and the subject (Clarke, 2005). Regeneration involves a unique fusion of economic *and* social restructuring initiatives, targeted at local places and populations (Cochrane, 2001; Haylett, 2003). Therefore, the second crucial aspect of regeneration strategies is participation. This involves including citizens in local policymaking processes which renders regeneration a more consensual approach to regeneration than forms of urban entrepreneurialism. Participation is interpreted as a crucial mechanism for dealing with legitimation crises. Social unrest from the 1960s has seen a shift towards the ideal of participatory democracy in Western democratic countries (Pateman, 1970) with near universal appeal (Cruikshank, 1999): '[…] citizen participation is a categorical term for citizen power. It is the redistribution of power that enables the have-not citizens, presently excluded from the political and economic processes, to be deliberately included in the future' (Arnstein, 1969: 236).

Cockburn (1977) asserts that these offers of 'participation' in local level democracy in the 1960 and 1970s were made to render the actions of the state more acceptable, thus meeting and managing any spontaneous expressions of popular conflict. We have seen the community development programmes of the early 1970s give way to explicit neoliberalism in the 1980s with urban development corporations before going back to partnership based politics in the 1990s, exemplified by social inclusion partnerships (Raco, 2000). Regeneration places great emphasis on community members to practice a particular form of citizenship. Participation bestows citizens with an active role, transferring responsibility to help them to solve their own problems, with special emphasis on stakeholder roles and community empowerment (Hastings, 2003). Communities are imbued with rights and responsibilities to equip citizens to respond to restructuring by being self-supporting, flexible, employable and investors in their own pensions, of which homeownership becomes a primary form. Citizenship under New Labour was 'investment in human capital wherever possible, rather than direct provision of economic maintenance' (Giddens, 1998: 117). The 'Big Society' politics of the subsequent Conservative–Liberal Democrat Coalition are in some ways an extension of the Blairite project yet with a sharper, coercive rather than consensual edge. Under this new punitivism, underwritten by the 2012 welfare reforms, moral and economic responsibility is manifestly that of the individual, not the state. This unabashed shift emphasises the explanatory relevance and actual workings of hegemony as surface level projects; workfare and the 'Bedroom Tax' do not speak to the consensual, participatory politics of New Labour governance during the more economically buoyant times but neoliberal austerity politics where the social securing of capitalist conditions happens in a coercive way. We are alerted to how consent and coercion are simply different sides of the same coin.

Micro-level urban entrepreneurialism seeks to make the community and individual more enterprising through participation. Yet the expansion of participation is often, although not exclusively (Cockburn, 1977), interpreted using Foucauldian and post-Foucauldian rather than Marxist frameworks (Dean, 1999; Cruikshank, 1999; Rose, 1999; Flint, 2006; McKee, 2008). Foucault's (1980, 2003) concept of governmentality is used to discuss the argument that the move towards a 'rights and responsibilities' agenda is part of broader changes in the rationalities and techniques of government which alter the relationship between the state and civil society. Emergent policies that form neoliberal strategies use 'citizens, individually and collectively, as ideally and potentially "active" in their own government' (Rose, 1996: 352). These strategies seek to govern by instrumentalising and harnessing the self-governing properties of the subject in a variety of locales (Rose, 1999). Post-Foucauldian critiques of urban policy see neoliberalism as a new anatomy of power that revolves around the demise of social collectivities and the propagation of self-management, or what Foucault refers to as government through the governed (Raco, 2000). The population becomes a field of regulation or a resource to be cultivated and capitalised principally through the use of disciplinary measures or techniques in the administration of individuals' lives (Dean, 1999). Moral decisions are economically rational decisions. This reflects Giddens's (1998) Third Way motto – no rights without responsibilities. Post-Foucauldian analysis of participation is not dissimilar to the way hegemony operates. However, post-Foucauldian analysis fails to fully integrate the economic aspect of neoliberalism, particularly the privatisation of governance via urban entrepreneurialism. This is inextricably linked to the promotion of the entrepreneurial actor. Class is decontextualised in these accounts. The new emphasis on community and individual participation and citizenship development is linked to the wider neoliberal objective of creating active citizens to reduce 'dependence' on the welfare state (Raco, 2000). It is a crucial device for realigning the social contract – recasting the rights and responsibilities expected to be upheld by citizens. Reliance upon selected forms of community participation may act as a 'means of adjusting to new demands without directly challenging existing political and social structures' (Cochrane, 1986: 53), which are essentially class-based.

Thus, as a strategy of restructuring, urban regeneration is said to be undertheorised (Lovering, 2007). Regeneration represents a paradigm shift in thinking about urban problems over the twentieth century which is both an economic and moral project and alters the state–civil society relationship (Imrie and Raco, 2003; Cochrane, 2007). It is ultimately a class project but class is decontextualised from both discourses and theorisations of regeneration. The individual and community are cast as entrepreneurial actors responsible for morally correct and rational decisions. As Haylett (2003) attests, issues of poverty, unemployment and decay are considered almost exclusively in relation to the social and physical fabric of cities which pathologises those who reside there; target problems become targeted places and targeted lives. Urban problems are constructed in ways that obscure class inequality and pathologise populations in areas that have declined: 'The evasion of class and the illusion of meritocracy encourage moralising policies such as government workfare programmes which effectively pathologies individuals by holding them responsible for class disadvantages […]' (Sayer, 2005: 226).

The representation of working-class communities in policy discourse is either negative or non-existent. Either they fall under the statically delineated category of deprived or excluded groups or they have been subsumed into the middle-class. They are deemed surplus to service economies, the living antithesis to 'modernisation' and require regeneration as redemption. Regeneration is a cultural and moral intervention used to partly redefine class identities, so much so that the urban policy field acts like a 'symbolic regime partly constructed through representations of what "poor people and places" are and should be like through a modernising political imperative' (Haylett, 2003: 57). This is encapsulated in many ways by the notion of consumer citizenship (Christopherson, 1994), '[t]he rights conferred by citizenship are increasingly predicated on being a consumer-citizen of private and government services' (Atkinson, 2003: 1834). Consumer citizenship is a class based project in that it consolidates the power of urban entrepreneurs and residualises practices associated with Fordism, particularly state welfarism and trade unions which had consolidated the power of the industrial working class. I believe that processes of neoliberal hegemonic restructuring are best understood through the processes of gentrification. Housing has become the major vehicle of capital accumulation (Harvey, 1973). Analysis of the processes of gentrification reveals more about the class-based, political impetus of regeneration strategies. As the following section shows, gentrification is not merely commodification and privatisation of housing, it expresses the alteration of the social contract between the state and citizens, which realigns behaviours and practices deemed incongruous or residual to neoliberalism and flexible forms of accumulation.

The Gentrification Problematic

Gentrification was first identified by Glass (1964) in London in the 1960s and has since been an embattled concept. While the ensuing debates have been dynamic they have, historically, been defined by their cultural or an economic impasse: orthodox arguments which most researchers of gentrification would agree are outmoded. Yet a revised theoretical framework has not been advanced. Recent research highlights the challenges that current waves of gentrification pose towards its conceptualisation (Lees and Ley, 2008). Slater (2006) suggests there are three main problems that hinder research on gentrification. First, it is still haunted by the theoretical schism between economic and cultural positions, even though the debates have subsided; second, research is said to lack critical perspectives and therefore fails to include working-class experiences in the research and the effect of displacement; and third, there is only limited understanding of the use of gentrification as an urban social policy. Rather than seeking to fundamentally redefine gentrification, my concession here is that the answer to these problems lies in the reconciliation of the orthodox arguments by connecting cultural and economic accounts using a framework of hegemony which helps explain both state-sponsored gentrification and the experience of and effects upon working-class people. Cultural and economic drivers are harnessed by the state to successfully restructure places, labour markets and economies and communities. In doing this we can ascertain what urban policy is trying to communicate and achieve when implementing gentrification and therefore clarify its potential effects. This may not be physical displacement but rather the management and civilisation of populations (Uitermark et al., 2007) in a way that corresponds to the mode of accumulation. The following section considers the contributions and limitations of orthodox theories of gentrification. I then consider the prevailing understandings of how gentrification is used as part of urban regeneration policy and the effects this is perceived to have. Then I posit a new theory of gentrification. This relates to both the structural form and political strategy of hegemony, promoting homeownership and consumer citizenship. In doing so, gentrification realigns the practices of working-class communities which are deemed incongruent with post-industrial culture.

The Gentrification Orthodoxy

Exploring the historical meaning of gentrification can help elucidate the contemporary form. This necessitates a return to original discussions of the process, in an attempt to reconnect the 'inherently problematic nexus of culture and economy in the gentrification debate' (Bondi, 1999: 195). In its original conception (Glass, 1964) gentrification is deemed a process of class transformation at the neighbourhood level. In this model, gentrification is initiated by a few 'pioneers', who move into urban areas that have suffered decline, seeking out alternative lifestyles, subsequently followed by wealthier middle classes, and finally property developers. For the most part, consensus ends here with literature fractured between culture versus economic explanations of the process, expressing the paradigm wars between structure and agency.

Table 1.1   Production versus consumption in the orthodox explanations of gentrification

	Main issues	Theoretical influences
Production	Supply of 'gentrifiable' property; the workings of housing and land markets; spatial flows of capital and the 'rent-gap'; role of public and private finance; 'uneven development'.	Structural Marxism; radical social theory; geographies of class relations and class struggles.
Consumption	The characteristics of the 'pool of gentrifiers'; 'new middle-class' ideology; consumer demand and consumption practices; (counter) cultural politics; the roles of 'race', gender and sexuality; education, occupational change and household composition.	Liberal humanism; post-industrial urbanism; importance of human agency over economic structure; human geography's 'cultural turn'.

Source: Adapted from Slater (2009).

This has been expressed in a series of divided themes within gentrification literature at large:

Table 1.2   Theoretical divides in gentrification literature

Consumption	Production
Agency	Structure
Emancipatory	Revanchist
Misunderstood saviour	Vengeful wrecker

As Atkinson (2004: 125) suggests, 'a move away from the portrayal of gentrification as a simple good or evil will inevitably be an analytical improvement'.

As a capital-led process, gentrification is conceived to be part of wider processes of the uneven development of urban space under the capitalist mode of production (Smith, 1996). This has its roots in Harvey's theorisation (1975,

1982), related to the decline of geographical sites and the built environment and circuits of capitalism. Smith (1979, 1996, 2002) conceives gentrification to be the residential manifestation of the circuits of capitalist investment. He explicates gentrification with his powerfully simplistic rendering of the 'rent-gap' theory (1979) which refers to the measure of the difference in a site's actual value and its potential value. Smith proposes that suburbanisation in cities from the end of the nineteenth century led to a devalorisation of inner city and urban land. This out-migration led to a decline in investment and subsequent physical deterioration and decline in value or 'rent'. The rent-gap is the disparity between the inner city and suburban land prices. This rent-gap in land precipitated by uneven development is capitalised upon by developers and the land is put to 'best use'. This is, for Smith, the necessary centrepiece to any theory of gentrification; a fundamentally capitalist process for accumulation and profit. Oddly, while this is a highly politicised and critical account of gentrification, it does not represent working-class lived experiences. As is common to structural accounts of deindustrialisation, it pays modest attention to social forces. Marxist theoretical contentions in these urban debates can be empirically weak and offer little account of agency, especially place-centred agency (Massey, 1988) in processes of gentrification.

Conversely, cultural accounts focus on the agency of the 'new middle class' in the post-industrial economy. This perspective, of which Ley (1986, 1996) is the main proponent, attempts to theorise the social meaning of residential settlement in gentrification processes by focusing on the life and times of middle-class gentrifiers (Bondi, 1999; Butler and Robson, 2001, 2003; Caulfield, 1994; Hamnett, 2003). This gives more explanatory importance to the role of these new consumption practices and lifestyles in gentrifying neighbourhoods. Caulfield (1994) argues that gentrifiers subvert the dominance of hegemonic culture and create new conditions for social activities. Gentrification here is conceived as an expression of liberation and emancipation, seen in gay gentrification (Castells, 1983), and gendered gentrification (Bondi, 1999; Bondi and Rose, 2003) where individuals actively choose to settle in the central city as a rejection of traditional roles. It expresses bohemian tastes or post-modern, corporate or kitsch aesthetic. But this explanation focuses on a stratified experience and on consumption practices of affluent groups in the public arena. The growth of a new middle class or a middle-class-in-the-city and their consumption practices relates to urban economic restructuring and industrial changes rather than being free-floating or inevitable. It is a dialectical process. Their practices and residential settlement are not without ramifications. Their locational choices have profound impacts on the neighbourhoods they choose to occupy. Indeed, middle-class settlement is promoted and facilitated by the state precisely because it *does* have ramifications and this is aspect of their city living warrants more consideration and critique. Cultural and agential explanations draw from an uncritical account of class which can assume embourgeoisement is the outcome of restructuring. Like the production-side explanation, this reading does not acknowledge the effects of gentrification on working-class people.

Separately, these perspectives cannot fully encapsulate the dynamics of gentrification. Lees (1994: 148) remarks: '[...] juxtaposing a Marxist analysis with a cultural analysis allows political economy, culture and society to be considered together, enabling a more sensitive illustration of the gentrification process'. The demand and consumption of potential gentrifiers cannot be separated from 'rent-gap' theory and changes in the economy cannot be excluded from the formation of the new middle-class gentrifier, or, as will be argued, working-class identity. Gentrification is both a cultural and economic process. Zukin (1988, 1995) is credited with theorising a synthesis of these perspectives by arguing that cultural production is a catalyst for changes occurring in the workings of urban economies. The strength of Zukin's synthesis of culture and capital lies in her historical materialist approach which conceptualises the 'artistic mode of production' (1988). Types of housing and location become vital cultural symbols in constructing and reinforcing gentrifiers' identities. This leads to the clustering of new cultural amenities in urban areas where decline has occurred. Creative and cultural industries are pursued and promoted by local authorities as a strategy towards successful post-industrial urban economies. Gentrification then becomes a vital cultural symbol that cities are tackling decline while the 'rent-gap' on brownfield sites can be capitalised upon by local governments. The pursuit of this in policy makes the local state an important actor in contemporary forms of gentrification. Zukin's theorising importantly illustrates the use of culture as a material force but it does not offer deeper explanation of the precise role of the local and national state, nor does it consider wider effects[2] particularly those experienced by the working class. This is a crucial absence. To take forward a unified understanding of gentrification requires a more coherent approach which understands the historical context and the contemporary forms as well as the interplay between structure and agency. A corresponding theoretical framework was never designed and applied to allow culture and economy to be considered together rather than in a crude base-superstructure relationship which means we are bereft of a coherent explanation of the use of gentrification within urban policy. It is necessary to consider what local and national governments are trying to communicate with their use of gentrification, in order to assess what effects this can have. Putting the gentrification debate into a policy perspective offers the most effective way of understanding it and its effects (van Wessep, 1994).

Gentrification as a Strategy of Regeneration

The use of gentrification within regeneration strategies is evident in most towns and cities in the UK and beyond (Atkinson and Bridge, 2005). Yet, despite the range of research, Lees and Ley (2008) suggest we know little about how gentrification

---

2   Although, in later work Zukin concedes the increasing role of the state in implementing and supporting gentrification, and suggests this development adds to the chaotic nature of the concept of gentrification (Zukin, 1987).

is used within urban policy: 'Gentrification is now thoroughly institutionalised by local and national governments as part of renewal strategies. Yet conventional explanations of gentrification do not fully explain the scope, scale, and form of the processes involved' (Uitermark et al., 2007: 125).

Policy-led or state-led gentrification involves the economic development of derelict, disused, devalued land into areas of high consumption, including luxury new-build housing developments. The state recognises the fiscal benefits of attracting people and capital to areas and uses gentrification processes to help deliver economic imperatives and entrepreneurialism. Gentrification involves the creation of space for the progressively more affluent user (Hackworth, 2002). The enactment of this is multi-scalar and is evident in UK urban policies, such as the Urban Task Force report, *Towards an Urban Renaissance* (1999) and the Scottish Executive's *People and Place* (Scottish Executive, 2006) policy statement which encourage those who left the city, predominantly the middle class, to move back. Gentrification is also implicit in the policy goal of socially mixing communities (SEU, 1998) and in Scotland's community regeneration statement (Scottish Executive, 2002). Gentrification not only brings a pertinent labour group into the city to fulfil roles as key workers in financial and service related jobs, middle-class settlement also helps valorise devalued neighbourhoods. Rather than making the debate more cohesive, interpretations of gentrification now coalesce around opposing perspectives: rational policy accounts, some of which are pro-gentrification, uphold the benefits of social mix and its use in urban renewal strategies (Lambert and Boddy, 2002; Freeman, 2006); and more polemic critiques of neoliberal governance and anti-gentrification sentiments, which uphold the significance of displacement (Slater, 2006; Watt, 2008).

Lambert and Boddy (2002) conclude that using gentrification to describe regeneration is 'stretching the term and what it set out to describe too far' (ibid.: 23). They outline the benefits of this type of development, claiming it counters population decline, changes the local demographic and has a dramatic visual and housing market impact (Lambert and Boddy, 2002). In addition to these benefits, they note that the form of new-build developments means that there are no indigenous working-class communities to displace. Critically, they argue that processes cannot be called gentrification if they do not induce displacement. However, this explanation of a form of gentrification which is policy-led fails to fully account for the way that it is used. It neglects to acknowledge that gentrification has broader impacts and is related to wider changes within social policy. Policy and academic literature (Wilson, 1987) support the creation of socially mixed communities to combat 'area-effects' – the additional negative effects of being poor in a poor area such as lack of services, stigma, role models, in essence, a lack of cultural, social and economic capital. The underpinning philosophy of social mix is that social and economic capital are thought to trickle-down to the rest of the city (Kearns, 2003). Policy thinking holds that socially mixed areas can attract and support a higher level of local services, leisure activities and higher than average levels of disposable income which may create additional employment opportunities for local residents (Bailey et al., 2007). This foregrounds the cultural–material imperative of this policy. The underpinning belief is that the middle classes are not just financially 'better off', they also have high stocks of cultural, social and economic capital that can be transmitted throughout neighbourhoods, having a positive, relational and redemptive effect. Thus, their settlement is socially constructed as creating 'virtuous circles' and 'opportunity effects' to provide the means for the 'degenerated' to regenerate themselves rather than relying on traditional state welfare provisions. The crucial point is that socially mixing communities and promoting middle-class settlement is about more than regenerating places, it is also about regenerating the people of those neighbourhoods (Cochrane, 2007). The tangible and lasting benefits that social mixing brings through physical regeneration is questioned. Upgraded facilities and affordable social housing do not coexist and new consumption sites are often the first stage of displacement (Slater, 2006). Indeed Slater's (2006) counter argument to state-led gentrification is that displacement is still a very real effect of gentrification and is only less evident due to a lack of critical perspectives rather than fewer occurrences. Slater (2006) suggests that displacement has been displaced from gentrification research and the reason for this is primarily methodological, namely the prevalence of qualitative case study approaches. Another problem is that defining displacement is almost as difficult as defining gentrification, with similarly dichotomous, oppositional understandings. It is notoriously difficult to quantify and track displacement. In the UK, Leckie (1995) estimates that 144,000 people are forcefully evicted each year though only a certain proportion of this relates to gentrification-induced displacement.

Displacement will always be a part of gentrification, not only because of the necessity of spatial fixes in displacing crises in capital (Harvey, 1989; Smith, 1996), but because it exacerbates the marketisation of housing which will impact negatively on working-class residents with less material power to stay fixed in their neighbourhood. Orthodox understandings of displacement correspond, in part, to orthodox theories of gentrification. Displacement is sometimes downgraded to a process of replacement and more natural, voluntary geographical movements, characteristic of the ecological models of urban theory, or seen as emancipatory, whereby it liberates certain social groups (Bondi, 1999; Lees, 2004). This is useful in the sense that it foregrounds the consensus and agency involved in out-migration. However, Smith (1996) sees gentrification as a process of revanchism – a revengeful attack on working classes by middle classes and city elites. Here, gentrification expresses the process through which the inner city is reclaimed back from the working classes and returned to the middle classes (Smith, 1996). This coercive displacement helps make devalued inner city land more valuable and productive.

It appears to involve a mix of both coercive and consensual methods (see Figure 1.1 overleaf). The effects of gentrification and displacement are multi-dimensional: indirect and direct, positive and negative. Atkinson's systematic review of all English language gentrification literature from 1964 to 2001 reveals the varied fortunes of gentrification processes in neighbourhoods (see Table 1.3 overleaf).

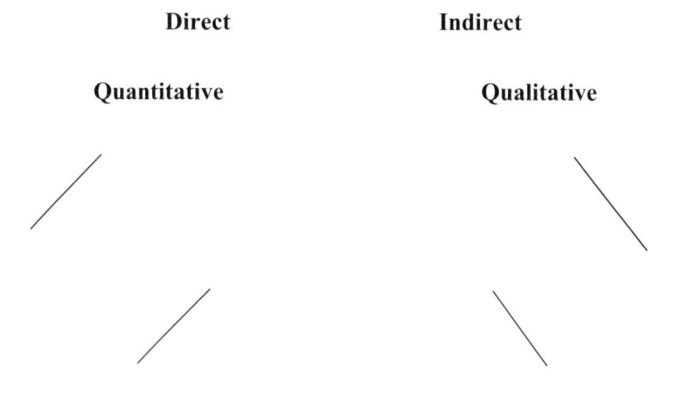

Direct	Indirect
Quantitative	**Qualitative**
Measurements: Eviction, out-pricing, replacement, changes in services and retail	Occupational changes/embourgeoisement social psychological impacts (norms/behaviours) consumption practices
Methods: census data, proxy variables, land use information, house price increase, migration tracking	ethnography, life histories, narratives qualitative interviews, photography

Figure 1.1   Measures and methods of studying direct and indirect displacement (continuum)

Table 1.3   Positive and negative effects of gentrification

Positive	Negative
Stabilisation of declining areas	Community resentment and conflict
Increased property values	Loss of affordable housing
Reduced vacancy rates	Unsustainable speculative property price increases
Increased local fiscal revenues	
Encouragement and increased viability of further development	Homelessness
	Greater draw on local spending through lobbying by middle-class groups
Reduction of suburban sprawl	
Increased social mix	Commercial/industrial displacement
Decreased crime	Increased cost and changes to local services
Rehabilitation of property both with and without state sponsorship	
	Loss of social diversity
	Increased crime
	Under-occupancy and population loss
	Displacement through rent/price increases
	Displacement and housing demand pressures on surrounding poor areas
	Secondary psychological costs of displacement

Source: Adapted from Atkinson (2004).

The effects can often be contradictory, highlighting the incoherence of the use of policy. As such, and which will be elaborated more fully at the end of this chapter, this emphasises the value of a case study approach in capturing these complexities.

State-led gentrification involves coercive and consensual measures. It is not implemented to be a zero sum game for working-class, poorer and excluded residents. On the contrary, it is implemented to have 'positive' effects, otherwise the strategy would not be pursued. The two major issues are that, first, the agency and participation of working-class people are not considered in studies of gentrification and displacement. In reality, the process is complex and people may perceive that they have chosen to move rather than been forced. This reflects the cultural meaning of homeownership and the notion of a 'housing career' associated with urban living. Second, a study of displacement has to be sensitive to specific housing policies and issues. For example, social housing in the UK has provided secure tenancies that protect against eviction but this is subject to change in relation to the privatisation of the social housing model, seen in the contentious policies around Right to Buy, the Housing Stock Transfer and, more recently, the so called 'Bedroom Tax' which reduces housing benefit based on new introduced size criteria in social housing. This erosion of social housing security suggests that new forms of displacement may come to the fore in which the state, along with social housing providers, are conduits rather than adversaries. This issue raise challenges for how we should research and understand gentrification and its effects.

Uitermark et al. (2007) assert that our understanding of state-led gentrification and its effects must become more sophisticated since it is used to both restructure people and places. In their analysis of gentrification created through socially-mixed housing, Uitermark et al. (2007) demonstrate that since there was no immediate profit from this, the value added lay in using gentrification to govern the behaviours of 'problem' populations:

> Serving the middle classes, we suggest, is not their ultimate goal. Instead, gentrification is a means through which governmental organisations and their partners lure the middle classes into disadvantaged areas with the purpose of civilising and controlling these neighbourhoods. (Uitermark et al., 2007: 127)

Social mix policy is subtly coercive. Used in this way, gentrification becomes a hegemonic process in that it seeks to realign the behaviours of the working class. Middle-class behaviours, typically supportive of the post-industrial neoliberal economy are a useful vehicle for disseminating new values. The implementation of gentrification can gradually alter dispositions and social norms over time so that they become widely embodied. It has profound phenomenological impacts, affecting people's sense of being in the world. Culture is deployed as an economic resource, but culture is more than superstructure, it is a whole way of life, including practices, values, and patterns of consumption. I wish to further advance the definition of gentrification based on a hegemonic framework. Gentrification is incorporated into policy to intervene in managing the 'decline' of people and place.

The New Theory of Gentrification

I contend that gentrification is an important political strategy in achieving neoliberalism and flexible forms of accumulation. Rather than signifying the rule of market forces and the retreat of the state, gentrification constitutes an attempt by the state to reassert its grip on social life (Uitermark et al., 2007). Gentrification is used as part of urban policy to 'gentrify' people, that is, to make their subjectivities and behaviours more congruent with the neoliberal principles of the economy. Class culture is the point of intervention. State-led gentrification demonstrates an attempt to devalue existing social practices related to industrial production, that is, municipal housing, mono-tenure neighbourhoods and local public provisions by promoting homeownership, socially-mixed communities and private and public–private neighbourhood provisions. It attempts to imbue consumerist and traditionally middle-class characteristics of homeownership onto working-class people. Gentrification foregrounds the relationship between property and propriety – aesthetics is the space that mediates between these two (Skeggs, 2005). This is not new, but a culmination of processes since Thatcher's dismantling of the welfare state and the introduction of the Right to Buy policy in the 1980s:

> Hegemony is then a kind of reach-out-and-touch mechanism of power, it involves deconstructing some previously fixed positions (for example working class support of social housing) then attaching the same social group to a new and unexpected set of ideas (for example homeownership and the property-owning democracy). This requires effort at every level of political society […]. (McRobbie, 2005: 23)

This crystallises in the way the local state 'rolls out' gentrification, hyper-legitimates owner-occupier and de-legitimates other tenures. This is compounded by the wholesale transfer of social housing stock to private non-profit organisations, which occurred in Glasgow in 2003, which effectively transforms the identity of social housing tenants into customers (Flint, 2003). Housing consumption increasingly expresses an identity and status – of good taste and responsible and moral conduct (Flint and Rowlands, 2004). As Blomely (2004: 89) argues:

> Programs of renewal often seek to encourage homeownership, given its supposed effects on economic self-reliance, entrepreneurship, and community pride. Gentrification, on this account, is to be encouraged, because it will mean the replacement of a marginal anticommunity (nonproperty owning, transitory,

and problematized) by an active, responsible, and improving population of homeowners.

The image of the working-class as degenerate and immoral is used to help reconstruct the boundaries of regulation and legitimate state control. Brought in as role models, middle-class residents' behaviour is deemed to be worthy and virtuous, as opposed to the problematic working-class. Regeneration is a means of redemptively recalibrating stigmatised spaces and subjectivities.

This understanding updates the current contemporary definitions of gentrification as the creation of space for the progressively more affluent user (Hackworth, 2002). I suggest that gentrification, as part of urban policy, seeks to create the more affluent user, within a financial and moral economy. Conceiving gentrification in relation to hegemony conceptually strengthens its heuristic in a number of crucial ways. It offers a more complex explanation of how gentrification is used within urban policy than existing production versus consumption accounts do. Gentrification corresponds to consumption and production. It becomes a wider ethic of consumption and a way of life that supports the relations of accumulation. Under the logic of capitalism, gentrification has social and material uses and functions. It is an expression of neoliberalism and flexible accumulation which have distinct spatial manifestations relating to the built environment (Harvey, 1973, 1982) and, thus, expresses the two aspects of hegemony – as a structural hegemony and a surface hegemony of a political project. Housing becomes crucial vehicle for accumulation, (Harvey, 1982) demonstrated through Smith's 'rent-gap' thesis (1979). Gentrification is used to encourage homeownership and consumption of private neighbourhood services over Fordist tenets of state welfarism. It is not implemented to displace per se, rather local residents are encouraged to support and participate in gentrification, based on the range of benefits that it will bring. However, the threat of displacement may act as a powerful coercive element to ensure its support. Despite acknowledgements that gentrification is a class-based transformation of the landscape, there have been few direct confrontations with how it affects working-class residents. Worse still, it has been suggested that gentrification should uncouple itself from its association with deindustrialisation (Butler, 2007), despite there still being no full exposition of this in relation to social life and relations. Further, class analysis has been embattled by its engagement with deindustrialisation, in implicit and explicit ways. Gentrification is seen as a process 'where the nonmanual middle classes and service employment are now the dominant mode of living' (Butler, 2007: 163). What is required is a research trajectory that combines recent trends in both gentrification literature and class analysis. This is a crucial and prescient, but surprisingly neglected, intersection in current research.

Restructuring Class

The field of class analysis has always involved contentious theoretical and epistemological arguments, transfigured into debates over whether culture and economy constitute unitary or dual systems (Compton and Scott, 2005) and how class is best measured and analysed. These challenges are as old as the study of class itself (Bottero, 2005). However, deindustrialisation and restructuring challenged prevailing analytical categories and conceptual resources of class even more so. The relative decline of industry is interpreted as undermining class as a meaningful category and identity almost altogether (Beck, 1992; Pakulski and Waters, 1996; Giddens, 1991). The industrial working class represented in the 'golden years' of stratification research are deemed an irrelevant marker in deindustrialised times. Yet, the localised processes of decline and restructuring have material and phenomenological consequences for working-class groups. Hitherto, we know little about how restructuring affects working-class identities and how this is negotiated and resisted by actors. This entails updating our conceptual resources and restructuring our analysis of class accordingly. As has been central to this chapter, I advocate an approach that acknowledges the interplay of culture and economic processes (Gramsci, 1971). The sociological task is to explicate how a changing sense of identity might be linked with the consequences of economic, social, and spatial restructuring.

To do this, first, I examine how writers have explored class within a place-based context to connect the relationship between class position and identity. 'Golden years' of industrial working-class community studies (Dennis et al., 1956; Jackson, 1968; Young and Wilmott, 1957; Lockwood, 1958) were characterised by the 'structure, consciousness, agency' approach, or S-C-A (Pahl, 1989). Even in the time of apparent class cohesion, the conceptual link between position and identity was flawed. This approach does not afford a consideration of other forms of social divisions and factors such as gender, ethnicity and individuality and fails to adequately express material relations of class alongside an understanding of how this may relate to identity. Second, I look at how deindustrialisation has been interpreted by some as heralding the rise of the individual and the 'death of class'. Restructuring is thought to have disembedded individuals from structural confines. 'Culturalist class theorists' (Reay, 1998, 2005; Savage, 2000, 2001; Skeggs, 1997, 2004) kept class firmly on the agenda in the face of this challenge, principally through the use of the concept of disassociation which expresses the disjuncture between class position and (traditional) class identities. Lack of identity is a crucial starting point for their analysis, purporting that people's rejection of class is an essentially classed process. Drawing from the work of Bourdieu (1984, 1986, 1987), they deploy a relational model of class. While their turn to culture and identity in advancing theories and conceptualisations of class has been vital, ultimately, it forsakes the material relations of class. I suggest that making disassociation the centre point of class analysis disaggregates collectivity and overlooks the coherence in seemingly individualised acts.

Therefore, in spite of the gains of these expositions, we still know very little about the correspondence between restructuring and working-class identities. Returning to place-based studies while taking questions raised by culturalist class theorists forward, synthesises cultural concerns with material analysis and connects local experiences to changes in capitalism. Some writers take such an approach to explore the middle-classes experience of their neighbourhood (Savage et al., 2005; Butler and Robson, 2003). I propose that it would be advantageous to put working-class and former industrial neighbourhoods at the heart of class analysis once again, reaffirming the relationship between class and place in the neoliberal, post-industrial landscape and exploring the articulation of localised resources and identities in the face of a lack of universal and economic ones.

Working-class Community Studies: From Boom to Slump

The crisis in class analysis has been interpreted as an inability to adequately theorise changes initiated by deindustrialisation (Roberts, 2007) and the 'cultural turn'. Crompton and Scott (2005) suggest that a return to community studies in a post-industrial context may hold the key to reviving class analysis. That is not to say these classic studies do not have their own shortcomings. Post-war community studies capture the wider problem inherent within class analysis, seen in the statement of the relationship between the economic and the cultural. Class was interpreted using a base-superstructure model of S-C-A (Pahl, 1989). In this model consciousness of your class position is an intermediary between structure and action which develops a 'class in itself' to a 'class for itself'. It follows then, that position in the structure generates consciousness. The 'golden years' of stratification research lasted from the 1940s through to the 1970s (Dennis et al., 1956; Jackson, 1968; Young and Wilmot, 1957; Lockwood, 1958). They represented the lived experiences of the boom period of industrial production through their focus on towns centred on coalmines, shipyards and factories and the articulation between this work and community, solidarity and patterns of life. Class is presented as salient within bounded communities based on a few industries where patterns of exploitation and domination are clearly evident and values can easily become recognised and shared. These communities were deemed collectivities where people coordinate their actions because they believe themselves to have a common identity with a strong sense of consciousness. This is expressed through well-developed and articulated views about membership and collective class groupings and a clear sense of their place in the class system (Savage, 2000). Lockwood (1966) is credited with theoretically elaborating the S-C-A approach to class analysis. He asserts that different forms of class consciousness were the central mediating factor in accounting for how social positions gave rise to class action. Phenomenological understandings of class related to distinctive social positions, for example, new towns or shipbuilding communities. Despite noting the differentiation in images of society, values were still reduced to social structures in these studies.

The S-C-A model is also unsuccessful in the fact that class action was not fully realised. This challenges the idea that consciousness was the necessary reflex of class position thus undermining the basic premise of the S-C-A model. It fails to avoid, on the one hand, normative functionalist claims about class based on shared social values about the status of particular occupations and, on the other hand, economic reductionism where values are simply the reflex of social location. It lacks recognition that collectivities can also be divided. The reading of working-class relations under Fordism proffered in post-war community studies elevates the status of the traditional male proletariat and forecloses the significance of gender (McDowell, 1991; Adkins, 1995), ethnicity (Virdee, 2006), sexuality (Taylor, 2007), and individuality (Savage, 2000). Savage (2000) asserts that the idea of the working class served as a moral identifier for much of the twentieth century that helped consolidate a particular notion of the working class which had a resonance for British society. In part, deindustrialisation renders the industrial male working-class figure redundant which contributes to the arguments that class is no longer relevant in post-industrial society. However, it would be folly to dismiss the resonance of working-class culture as a way of life and consciousness expressed in political action within a tripartite system. While traditional working-class identity is said to be highly problematic and empirically weak (Savage, 2000), equally it can be empirically demonstrated that patterns of social relations existed in industrial areas which corresponded to the form of productive relations. A hegemonic model is useful in this respect. Williams's (1977) reading of working-class culture can be used to examine the nature of experience, identity and beliefs in relation to space, place and time (Joseph, 2002) through the concepts of residual, dominant and emergent culture. These acknowledge that processes of economic change are secured within social relations but are also negotiated and not determined. Williams conceives the economic base as a process rather than a stage, underlying the need to reassess culture in relation to economic restructuring. Thus, hegemony can express the processes through which class cultural change occurs, namely how industrial working-class culture and identity becomes residualised with the passing of Fordism and the emergence of a new historic bloc and how a new emergent culture is negotiated from a combination of the residual form and the new dominant form. However, Williams saw working-class culture as embodying collectivism, as opposed to the individualism of middle-class culture, which raises the problematic question of how to incorporate individualism into an analysis of emergent working-class culture. This is, hitherto, unresolved within class analysis and is particularly prescient given the promotion of individualisation under neoliberalism. Nonetheless, there is much to be gained from recharging the focus of these studies in a contemporary setting, focusing on social reproduction and the broader patterns of life and culture. The neighbourhood remains an important site because it captures a cross-section of people, inclusive of the intersections of gender, ethnicity and sexuality with class. This begins with moving away from notions of a determined or archetypal class (Savage, 2000) and incorporation of thinking on individualism and agency.

The Rise of the Individual

Strangleman (2008) asserts that class analysis in the late 1990s was irrelevant or esoteric or both. Deindustrialisation and the subsequent expansion of the service sector is said to signify the end of the traditional working class. The theoretical thrust towards cultural endeavours was partly a reaction to the claims that the decline of class was part of a progressive process of individualisation (Beck, 1992). Place-based class studies were rendered tangential by a growing interest in individualisation. Pakulski and Waters (1996) claim industrial communities, neighbourhoods and cultures are eroded and fragmented. One of the main contentions is that deindustrialisation undermines the raison d'être of these communities, indeed, they have progressively disappeared (Pakulski and Waters, 1990). This so called 'death of class' thesis is compounded by the work of Giddens (1991), Beck (1992) and Bauman (1998) who hold that class no longer shapes our lives as it once did, being neither materially nor ontologically germane in a society of cultural fragmentation borne of individualisation (Savage, 2000). The relationship between class position and identity is said to have unravelled in relation to the changes that have occurred over the last 30 years. This is evident in Beck's (1992: 88) famous refrain, that restructuring has created 'capitalism without classes, and rather, individualised social inequality'.

Clear-cut class identities, distinct communities and cultures have been outmoded:

> As a result in the shifts in the standards of living, subcultural class identities have dissipated, class distinctions based on status have lost their traditional support, and processes for this 'diversification' and individualisation of lifestyles and ways of life have been set in motion. As a result the hierarchical model of social classes and stratification has increasingly been subverted. (Beck, 1992: 92–3)

For Beck (1992), individualisation is a process of disembedding which separates people from historically prescribed forms and traditional security, seen in norms and knowledge, and the subsequent re-embedding of a new type of social commitment – as reflexive authors. Beck argues that individuals can reflect on the implications of structural processes that surround them and choose how to react in relation to them. This acknowledges that structural forces are inescapable but choice is available. Set free from structural forces, people refashion their identity and self in response to these dislocations but in a highly individualised way. They are able to reflexively construct their own biographies and life-course and have the control to do so on the basis of individual choice. Similarly, Giddens (1991) invokes the notion of ontological security to furnish his theory of individualisation. This expresses the confidence of people in the continuity of their self-identity and the constancy of their social and material environment. Ontological insecurity results from restructuring which unsettles traditional class identities, values and certainties which held strong and provided self-affirmation.

To be clear, these arguments do not challenge the continued salience of material inequalities. Rather, they challenge the relationship between material inequalities and collective social identities and ultimately political action, as outlined by Marxist base-superstructure models and the S-C-A model. They assert that class does not give rise to coherent identities, rather, this relationship has unravelled. The flaw in this argument is similar to that of post-war community studies; it presupposes that a coherent class identity existed. This, by extension, undermines the role of gender, ethnicity, sexuality, and individuality and the general agency of the working-class actor. Whilst we now recognise the importance of these factors, they are not always retrospectively applied to readings of industrial working-class communities. These writers assume that these communities have disappeared rather than acknowledging that they are being restructured or displaced and such restructuring, particularly within the context of neoliberalism, actively seeks to reshape the self, undermining collectivity in favour of individualism. This raises questions of how then to understand a lack of traditional class identity within a class based analysis of urban restructuring. I suggest that a powerful way of countering these claims is by showing that the salience of class identity can be reasserted whilst demonstrating that position does not determine identity. One way of doing this is by showing the continued salience of class within neighbourhoods, as it offers conceptual and analytical reinvigoration. Insights by 'death of class' theorists are based on an exaggerated understanding of class in these bounded communities which draws upon the image of industrial male proletarian model. They deny the existence of agency historically, by assuming that only now are people able to reflect on structural processes and choose how to react. The challenge is to not overstate how the changes wrought by restructuring affect class; equally we cannot overstate the cohesion of class formation in the past. Theorists of individualisation miss the crucial point that divisions always existed and that these, along with process of individualisation, have a material context which correlates to the form of productive relations.

The emergence of a new sociology of social class (Bourdieu, 1984, 1986, 1987, 1999; Charlesworth, 2000; Lawler, 2000; Reay, 1998, 2005; Savage, 2000, 2003; Skeggs, 1997, 2004) was partially a response to theories of individualisation. Writers sought to demonstrate the relationship between class analysis and individualisation rather than perceiving them as mutually exclusive. To do so, class theorists draw from the work of Bourdieu to incorporate issues of identity, culture and lifestyle. Although too diverse to be called a school, they are known loosely as the 'culturalist class theorists' (Bottero, 2004). They work from the premise that class is still a central issue and that inequality is a result of wider social structures reflecting inequalities in the distribution of power and resources. Secondly, they display a desire to understand the subjective meaning of class and identity without collapsing this interest into a discussion of simple individualism. Thirdly, their work recognises that class analysis has to take 'culture' seriously and explore the intersection of gender and ethnicity and the fragmented and problematised notion of traditional class identity (Bottero, 2004):

[...] we need an understanding which goes beyond the economic, production and occupation which can take into account the consequences of culture, and how this is central to the making of class difference, generating new ways of attributing value, producing new forms of appropriation and exploitation. (Skeggs, 2004: 63)

In doing so, the studies move away from place-situated, collective accounts to look at more individualised experiences of class as a way of reconciling the growing disassociation with traditional class identities.

While traditional class theories maintain that the relationship between the cultural and the economic is that economic-cause leads to social-effects, Bourdieu (1984, 1986, 1987), focuses on the relational aspect of class, particularly how cultural tastes are enduringly related to class position. He holds that culture is not an effect of class whereby your class position determines your cultural practices, like the S-C-A model, rather culture is a central mechanism through which class is constituted. Tastes and culture can become a resource and have value which is deployed by groups in the stratification system in order to establish and enhance their position in the social order. Rather than using labour as the key analytic, class is understood as a space of relations by placing groups with similar tastes close to each other in space. Cultural tastes are related to class position, where groups have similar tastes are positioned together and those with different tastes are positioned at a distance. This, in part, relates to their economic position but there are also horizontal distinctions where people are positioned as having higher cultural tastes but lower economic position. Hence Bourdieu's multi-dimensional approach where class position is based on relationship between four different types of capital: economic; cultural; social and symbolic. People actively invest cultural capital to realise economic capital and vice versa and it is the complex interplay between the two types of capital that gives rise to a number of different social groups. The working class are defined as having a relative lack of either kinds of capital compared to the groups above them. Differences are then marked out by a process of distinction which contains social meanings and values.

This approach attended to some of the shortcomings of industrial class theorists' statement of the relationship between class position and identity by looking at differences within class culture rather than assuming homogeneity. Further, unlike theories of individualisation which proclaim the end of class, it recognises individual expressions of class in cultural practices that still relate to structural positions. Culturalist class theorists powerfully deploy this relational approach to class to directly confront class dis-identification (Savage, 2000; Skeggs, 1997). The concepts of dis-identification and disassociation express the disjuncture between people's class position and their identification with class culture or expression of consciousness. Dis-identification is a key concept and starting point for these researchers. Absence of class identities is taken as evidence for class because dis-identification is seen as the result of a class process. Dis-identification foregrounds the paradox of class whereby the power and effects of structural forces are not actually recognised by those people most affected by it:

> One outstanding anomaly in relation to class is that, while over 80 per cent of the UK population agree that we live in a class society where class divisions have grown, few of them are prepared to admit that class has any impact on their own lives and relationships. (Reay, 2005: 923)

Savage et al. (2001) found that their respondents often sought to establish their own 'ordinariness' using terms like 'normal' or 'people like us' rather than recognising class. This class dis-identification reveals how people have a sense of their place and the social and cultural distanciation that exists between different groups that, in turn, affects life chances. In doing this, these writers have sought to broaden and deepen Bourdieu's thin account of the working class in the very different social conditions pertaining to post-industrial economies (Watt, 2006). This begins to uncover some of the complexities involved in delegitimating forms of cultural capital, whereby prevalent practices like socially renting your home become residualised and devalued and associated with being working class, in a negative way. The relational nature of class cultures where middle-class constructions of 'respectability' are partly organised around not being 'working-class', devalues and stigmatizes the working class. This cultural hierarchy reflects the pathologisation of working-class culture by middle-class groups whereby middle class is the standard and working class is point zero (Skeggs, 1997). The middle class differentiate themselves from working-class groups through a process of Othering which is particularly important in times of economic change. Culturalist class theorists' incorporation of the private realm is inclusive of a broad range of experiences, moving class analysis beyond the traditional 'white' working-class masculinist bias. Reay (2005) suggests that this vitally restates the importance of class by elucidating the subjective realities, feelings of ambivalence, inferiority and superiority, visceral aversions and the markings of taste which have been downplayed in UK analysis. This relational Bourdieusian approach has been crystallised by Savage and colleagues' (Savage et al., 2013) spatial codification of habitus vis-à-vis the Great British Class Survey which attempts to create a new model of social class that incorporates social, cultural and economic capital.

However, there is danger of moving *beyond* economic production, occupation and inequality. While they recognise the relational aspect of class, culturalist class theorists tend not specify the nature of this relationship, namely the intricate and dynamic ways in which structural position relates to cultural identity. These studies of disassociation assume an oppositional account of class that emphasises difference rather than exploitation and the realities of the hierarchical nature of class inequalities:

> In casting such activities as class conflict or exclusion, theorists of class disidentification have allowed their concern about the inequities of class

outcomes to obscure a vital point about the processes which generate them. If hierarchy is so decisive in shaping our opportunities, our lifestyles, and our sense of ourselves and others, why is there not a more a reflexive awareness of it? (Bottero, 2004: 1994)

The problems of this cultural approach are also indicative of the shortcomings of Bourdieusian analysis in general. They do not *clearly* detail the material basis of culture which would account for how processes of class habitus can be devalued over time and space. The fixed character of metaphoric capital stock makes them resistant to change, be contradictory or incongruous. Shifts in the value of cultural stock take place over a lifetime, like working-class support for social housing. Bourdieu has never undertaken any protracted discussion of transformation in the social, cultural or political spheres (Fowler, 1997). There is a fixed quality to habitus unlike Williams's (1977) account of how culture that was once dominant can become residualised through hegemonic shifts. Whereas Bourdieu would employ the term 'symbolic violence' to express the domination of middle class and elites over the working class, the notion of hegemonic bloc helps explain the material basis for this. In the end, culturalist class theorists are undermined by the same issues as individualisation theorists; they do not articulate the material basis for these processes of individualisation. Hierarchical accounts of cultural distinction can inadvertently legitimise the values of the dominant culture. Class distinction is based not only on dissimulation but on unequal terms.

However, like Bottero (2004), Byrne (2005: 808) notes, this turn was an essential endeavour:

> The cultural turn in class, which is often also a turn toward individual experience and personal response to that experience, has been legitimate and necessary. The antithesis to economism and attention primarily to the experience of waged work was very much required, but the collective matters, the relational matters, the contextual matters, work matters.

Dis-identification has a material basis that relates to productive forces not just borne out of people's sense of place. This is evident when looking at deindustrialisation, the changing regime of capitalist accumulation and how populations are managed to be more congruent with the neoliberal, post-industrial economy (Harvey, 1990). As outlined in the previous section, this is a class project which promotes individualisation and delegitimates working-class identities. Neighbourhoods, particularly in formerly industrial areas, are the key site of intervention for state-led gentrification. Traditional industrial working-class culture is vilified, particularly through state-led gentrification which explicitly supports middle-class consumption. This compounds people's reluctance to associate with a class identity that has such negative connotations. Returning to neighbourhood based studies allows us to see the materiality of class as we can observe hierarchies in action, as well as, relational processes of inequality. The term community is important here because, first, it is used instrumentally by policy, second, it appropriately describes a neighbourhood-bound social group, and, finally, using community means that its use value can be assessed, exploring the existence of collectivities and shared and individual identities. Studying class at the neighbourhood level offers important conceptual resources.

Return to Community Studies

A recent place-based revival offers nuanced accounts of urban change at the local level (Blokland, 2003, 2005; Butler and Robson, 2001, 2003; Savage et al., 2005, 2005a). Again, taking their lead from Bourdieu, these writers explore class as a socio-spatial relationship, looking at differences in lifestyles and culture in relation to their distribution in a socially ranked geographical space (Bourdieu, 1984). To understand class processes, it is not simply enough to study who lives where, rather, it is better to study people's claims to place. This revival is partly an attempt to express local and global interconnections (Savage et al., 2005; Butler and Robson, 2001, 2003). Acknowledging this interconnection, Savage et al. (2005) hold that residential space is a key arena in which people define their social position:

> If only because it remains rare to have multiple residencies, residence plays an increasingly important role vis-à-vis other fields in defining one's own sense of social location. In addition, residential space is crucial also in allowing people to access other fields, such as that of education, employment and various cultural fields. One's residence is a crucial, possibly *the* crucial identifier of who you are. (Savage et al., 2005: 207, emphasis in original)

This provides an alternative and complementary insight to social identities than that offered by the field of employment alone.

> As occupation has receded as the primary determinant of cultural preference, where you live has become an increasingly important source of identity construction for individuals [...] The process is, if anything, more extreme, as a greater spread of people feel obliged to express who they are by where they live and with whom they share their neighbourhood. I argue that these behaviours are essentially those of "class clustering" [...] on the basis of choice rather than force of circumstance. (Butler, 2007: 163)

Choice is a key conceptual motif. Social identities are expressed through chosen residential location. Savage et al. (2005) critique common and limited analytical binaries invoked in community studies and suggest a new orientation to place. Contra to the locals who are trapped in the past and the transients who are 'here today, gone tomorrow', 'elective belonging' defines the unique place-based attachment of incoming groups whose chosen place of residence is congruent with their life story (Savage et al., 2005). Places are seen as sites where identities are performed:

> Individuals attach their own biography to their "chosen" residential location, so that they tell stories that indicate how their arrival and subsequent settlement is important to their sense of selves. People who come to live in an area with no prior ties to it but can link their residence to their biographical life history, are able to see themselves as belonging to the area. (Savage et al., 2005: 29)

This exploration of place attachment reasserts the existence of shared identity, social collectivity and belonging, expressed by the post-war community studies, but in a way that recognises agency and individuality. It shows how people consciously seek out places that reflect their identity, situating themselves with 'people like us'. This resonates with Saunders's (1984) assertion that the home offers people a sense of control over their environment. The notion of home represents a response to the problem of ontological security (Giddens, 1984, 1991). It is strongly linked to the material environment. Dupuis and Thorns (1998) go on to suggest that in times of ontological insecurity the home can act as a site of constancy.

Places, in this context, are not historical residues. Rather, people choose their identities and choose where they live in a free way borne out of a conscious choice – this is deemed elective belonging (Savage et al., 2005). Such people have economic and social resources to make such choices which afford the creation of an intimate relationship between residential location, social identity, and forms of social action. Savage et al. (2005) argue that the term elective belonging is preferred to 'outsider belonging' because this would, by extension, infer that 'insider belonging' existed, which they say was largely absent. Given the spread of gentrification throughout the UK, the category of 'insider belonging' is most representative of working-class residents. The notion that working-class groups do not share in the same place-attachment as middle classes is compounded by Allen's (2008) study of working-class housing consumption. He reports that working-class respondents saw their houses as 'bricks and mortar' and 'places to live' rather than as expressions of their identity. They have a basic functional attachment to where they live. This differentiation in attachment to place resonates with the categories of cosmopolitans and locals. Literature on cosmopolitanism seeks to understand globalisation from the individualisation/subjective perspective as a form of spatialisation and distinction (Hannerz, 1990, 1992; Binnie and Skeggs, 2004; Beck, 2006). Cosmopolitans are at the privileged end of the power geometry of time–space compression, as identified by Massey (1993). Cosmopolitanism is an embodied subjectivity that requires accumulating cultural resources to generate appropriate dispositions (Binnie and Skeggs, 2004), of which residential location is a significant aspect. Hannerz (1990) defines cosmopolitans as willing to engage with the Other. Cosmopolitanism is an attribute that regeneration policies seek to harness (GCC, 2003a). It is a desirable trait to have in residents as it supports gentrification and the use of social mix policy. Whereas locals are seen as 'representatives of more circumscribed territorial cultures' (Hannerz, 1992: 252), Blokand's (2005) study compounds this by demonstrating how working-class identity is constructed in opposition to incoming ethnic groups, which suggests that locals are unwilling to engage with Others.

While the revival of place-based studies heralds a welcomed reinvigoration of class analysis that generates useful conceptual insights into place attachment, this is presented as being more meaningful for middle-class groups. There is the implicit suggestion that neighbourhood mobility is a middle-class proclivity. Gentrification is part of elective belonging through which the contemporary middle classes define their right to claim territory and express their social identity. I agree with Savage et al. (2005) that residential space is an important arena in which people define their social position and identity. However, the way in which this is recognised is disconnected from urban restructuring and deindustrialisation and the material realities needed to choose residential location. People's sense of community is more than just an ideology cultivated by capital (Jonas, 1996). Instead, community and, more pertinently, its different factions become not only an agent in, but also a critical part of, urban restructuring (Helms and Cumbers, 2006). While Charlesworth's (2000) research in Rotherham acknowledges such material realities he does so at the expense of working-class residents' choice and agency, conceding only injuries and not rewards. Similarly, the concept of elective belonging is not based on the dynamics of choice in a way that relates to material resources and power. It expresses the perceived freedom of choice and not its stratification. The latter may be a more insightful indicator of class in neighbourhoods. The notion of elective belonging also denies choice and agency to people who live in the neighbourhood they are born into and choose to reside in, which has particular resonance with working-class communities. This suggests that those who are 'born and bred' in a neighbourhood are not making a choice to live there nor could they express their identity by living there. This is because historical attachment to place is interpreted as nostalgic. This denies (working-class) people a historical attachment to place or that their attachment is a valid social identity which is both socially and materially meaningful. It also belittles the historically embedded social relations in neighbourhoods that provide meaning, a sense of collective membership and place in the world (Williams, 1977).

Charlesworth's (2000), Allen's (2008) and Savage et al.'s (2005) interpretations reinforce the binary distinctions between working and middle-class groups. This can actually proliferate the idea that differences can be assuaged through housing consumption which, in turn, supports gentrification and the neoliberal hegemony. The extent of these differences can be explored through an enquiry into working-class place attachment. This would begin by viewing past working-class culture within context, and through a perspective of hegemonic change, with reference to dominant, residual and emergent culture. In doing so, Young (2007) suggests we may find that those inside and those outside the 'contented minority' are far from dissimilar, sharing comparable desires, passions and frustrations. Young (2007) suggests that the more marginal groups are *simultaneously* excluded and included.

He calls this a 'bulimic society'. Barriers, divisions and separateness exist but their solidity is exaggerated – hard lines are imposed on a demarcation which is blurred in reality (Young, 2007). This resonates with Mooney and Danson's (1997) critique of the 'dual city thesis'. They argue that the representation of Glasgow as a city of two distinct social worlds of poverty and affluence is misrepresentative. The poor and working-class are not as culturally, physically or economically corralled as is often depicted. Identities are highly overlapping and fragmented. The danger of evoking the idea of middle-class attachment to place is that it fetishises and subsequently reifies it, thus reproducing precisely what urban policy is trying to achieve. These binaries can be deconstructed through empirical research which would challenge the notion that the working class have deficient cultural and social capital.

This research agenda is supported by Byrne (2005: 809):

> [...] we know little about how they think, how they feel about work, about their identities in these places, about their schools and about their hopes for the future.

This challenge is taken up by NWCS whose primary aim is to reassert class as a crucial category of experience:

> Discussions of class should consider class as a category of identity, a socio-economic category, an aspect of social structures of power and privilege, and as an aspect of discourse. We must also consider the complex relationships among class, race, ethnicity, gender, sexuality, place, and other social and political groupings [...] how class works in the lives of individuals, communities, and societies. (CWCS, 2009)

NWCS are not so much concerned with agreeing what class is, but rather how it operates, both as an analytical tool and as a basis for lived experience which requires representations that provide access to working-class voices and perspectives (Weis, 2004). Importantly, it focuses on both hidden injuries and rewards of working-class experiences (Strangleman, 2008).

Researching working-class lives offers a useful method of critiquing theories of individualism as well as acknowledging the multiple intersections of inequalities and identities. Instead of beginning with the assumption that working-class culture has dissolved or degenerated, it is useful to acknowledge the material basis of nostalgia by viewing it as form of culture that has been residualised through processes of change. A good example of this is Weis's (2004) longitudinal study of working-class high school students in a formerly industrial town in America who grew up 'in the shadow of the mill'. She saw that they were encouraged to cultivate 'freedom dreams' of individual achievement, independence and opportunities but these were circumscribed by economic conditions in adulthood. Another example is Nayak's research (2006) which explores the impact of global change in the industrial economy on local class identities of 'white' masculinities in Newcastle.

Connecting local political economy with cultural analysis, he examines how young men with generational labour histories adapt their identities to fit the demands of the new post-industrial economy. They refashion their identity in crucial ways which are classed but not in the traditional image of working-class masculinity. Restructuring is not simply oppressive since people can take pleasure from their class identity. NWCS does not seek to place one approach over another but rather provide a channel through which they can come together. It is not opposed to the structuralism of class analysis but does suggest that the formation and experiences of the working-class remains important (Roberts, 2007). Through representation, they hope to achieve legitimacy for working-class lived experiences. This is a crucial research agenda since policy increasingly delegitimates working-class experiences and hyper-legitimates middle-class practices. What is required is to salvage what we can of class, as structurally determined, including new forms of inequality, employment and unemployment created by restructuring and assess the relationship between these contemporary forms of consciousness and identity and socially constructed Otherness.

The Value of Ethnography of Working-class Lives

To this end, an ethnography of class is a powerful resource for exploring class, uncovering what class means to people, how it is experienced, how it is embodied, and the interplay between material, social and cultural aspects. Reay (1998: 272) makes this case:

> Class is a complicated mixture of the material, the discursive, the psychological predispositions and the sociological dispositions that quantitative work on class location and identity cannot hope to capture [...] Now what is required are British based ethnographic examinations of how class is "lived" in the gendered and raced ways to complement the macro versions that have monopolized our ways of envisaging social class.

My approach to class analysis is informed by the same dialectic, grappling with existing flawed class categories and crisis in stratification theory (Anthias, 2005; Crompton and Scott, 2005). Thus I define class objectively, as whether or not one is forced to sell their labour, therefore, including the majority of the population within modern society, but I also acknowledge the intersections with ethnicity, gender and sexuality (Virdee, 2006; Skeggs, 1997; Taylor, 2010) and have incorporated a Gramscian understanding of consciousness: I understand class as a structured relationship; materially based but not determined. Further, an orthodox Marxist reading of class has major analytical shortcomings in the context of this study principally because it does not analytically capture the struggles of cultural and material differentiation between working and middle-class groups and the material basis for these. This is crucial to the process of restructuring and to how hegemony, as rule of one social class over another, is achieved. The task is to try to understand these struggles between social groups, and the material basis of this, in the context of urban restructuring. Willis (2004) suggests that the enduring features that delimit who are working-class can be seen through the positions of agents, and in groups and their relationship to each other in systematic groups; they are separated by power and/or capital. The working class then occupy subordinate positions in the sense that they have less power and capital. The relationship with those who have power are characterised by domination, through the exercise of this power. Willis (2004) says that this can crudely be defined as being told what to do, not just in production, but, in his field of expertise, education. This has resonance with the experience of neighbourhood life and power over being able to stay in your neighbourhood or move out. The neighbourhood is a crucial site for observing the interrelationship between social and physical space. To understand this, I gathered people's locational narratives (Anthias, 2005; Savage et al., 2005). Locational narratives describe people's residential biographical stories of how and where they live – reveal the making of the *social* locations, hierarchies, boundaries and categories, and people's actual *physical* location in relation to their material reality. They provide a powerful revelatory account for understanding class in relation to a process of hegemonic change. Exploring how people understand their social and physical position, and how these relate to each other, expresses both the material and cultural aspects of class that are being reworked by the neoliberal hegemony. In practical terms, to explore class, even in an inductive way, we need to be able to identify respondents' class position. To do so, I employed the National Statistics Socio-economic Classification (NS-SeC) framework. While not Marxist, utility underpinned this choice as this measurement correlates with neighbourhood-based census information (which also employs this measurement). While acknowledging its limitations, this classification was useful within a broader context alongside qualitative, ethnographic data to explore connections between NS-SeC position, self-identification and levels of power, exploitation, domination and differentiation between residents in the neighbourhood.

Towards a New Sociological Perspective of Gentrification

As the opening quote from Savage et al. (2003) indicated, a better specification of the relationship between capitalist dynamics and social conditions of modernity is required. This is essential in order to understand how urban restructuring affects, and is affected by, working-class communities. There have been various attempts to examine the relationship between structure and agency. In post-Foucauldian interpretations of the relationship between state and subject have been popularised within urban studies (Rose, 1999; Flint, 2003). In current studies of class, the use of Bourdieu's (1999) habitus has been popularised (Savage, 2000; Butler and Robson, 2003; Reay, 1998). Hegemony has similar doxic qualities to governmentality (Foucault, 1980) and habitus (Bourdieu, 1998) yet transcends them because it involves a process whereby structures and superstructures codetermine which recognises the reciprocal interplay between the material and the phenomenological. Throughout this chapter, I have explored how this process can be understood through literature on regulation, gentrification and class but without a framework which states the relationship between material and phenomenological forms, these literatures remain disparate and unable to capture the reciprocal processes involved. Hegemony offers sociological insight into the relationship between capitalist dynamics and social conditions. It helps connect issues of structure and agency and transcends economic or cultural reductionism through a dual perspective of the base–superstructure model (Gramsci, 1971). Hegemony provides a theoretical basis for the restructuring of the existing capitalist system without upsetting that order (Morton, 2006). It is a practical conceptual tool for analysing the dynamics of change over time. To recall Gramsci (1971), hegemony pertains to the reorganisation of structure and the relations between men and women, on one hand, and the economy and production, on the other.

The regulation school provide a critical starting point, defining the changes in the political economy towards neoliberalism and what correspondence is required within social relations, but lack the finer level of analysis required to understand the social aspects of hegemony, agency and the forms of local level restructuring strategies. Readings are too structuralist and do not consider, in depth, the surface hegemony and agential aspects involved in specific political projects. Notably, despite its economic focus, regulation school readings do not connect with the way in which the tenets of neoliberalism – individualism and housing consumption, are promoted through urban policy in consensual and coercive ways. Regeneration is the main strategy of restructuring and signifies the reorganisation of state–citizen relations by extending participation via consumer citizenship. This emphasises individualised consumption practices and self-sufficiency over collective social practices and state-welfarism. It is essential to make this connection as individualisation is taken as evidence that the working class are obsolete, and that agency is set free from structure. This very idea helps reify the neoliberal hegemony. Similarly, place-attachment is taken as a middle-class proclivity that expresses their social identity. Gentrification is a pivotal strategy in urban restructuring yet the cache of existing research inadequately conceives the relationship between culture and economics. The notion of restructuring through gentrification captures the political strategy of hegemony, as an organising principle that operates as an intermediary between capitalist accumulation and social relations. Yet theories of gentrification are disconnected from class analysis, despite it being an intrinsically class based process. The absence of the working class in the research is partly related to shortcomings in class analysis. Class consciousness, identity and collective membership are deemed largely irrelevant in a post-industrial, culturally fragmented society. However, working-class people and places are the main targets of such strategies. We know little of how they may adapt their identities in response to restructuring process and how they may shape these processes themselves and the positive or negative effects or hidden injuries and rewards this may create. In this way, there is a third analytical aspect of hegemony. This is the way of life and emergent culture in post-industrial working-class neighbourhoods, negotiated through processes of restructuring.

Understanding these experiences reveals economic and political issues that help construct everyday life in a material and historical way, revealing a rejection of a traditional subjective position thought to reflect one's material position, like being working class. Capitalist restructuring unsettles social formations and can result in ontological insecurity (Giddens, 1991), which leads to struggles over new standpoints. The interplay between dominant and residual forces can result in a new emergent culture (Williams, 1977). The emergent culture reveals restructured standpoints that have been negotiated and won, for example, Nayak's (2006) account of repositioned 'white' masculine working-class identities in post-industrial Newcastle. Therefore, people experiencing the sharper end of restructuring in places like Partick are privy to a particular knowledge and experience, which can create a certain negotiated standpoint. By drawing from situated knowledge of residents' personal experiences, we can see how class identity is being remade and fought out and that it is inextricably linked to place. Understanding gentrification as part of a hegemonic shift involves exploration of how the everyday contributes to the maintenance of power. In particular, how the cultural, material, and ideological aspects of restructuring may relate to new working-class identities. It is often in the minutiae, interactions, social and cultural practices, and people's experience of their position that we can clarify how hegemony may be realised, negotiated and resisted. Hegemony helps us understand the changing fissures yet the enduring relevance of class through daily activity. It is community based, ethnographic studies that help us realise this. This can offer a unique perspective on the relation of how we analyse and study class.

From Red Clydeside to the New Black: Case Study of Restructuring

In order to explore this we need first a word on Glasgow. Researching urban restructuring as a case study emphasises the relations between systems of accumulation and the ensemble of state forms of political norms, institutional practices and social relations, which constitute the mode of regulation. The urban element is paramount. It foregrounds the local specificities of restructuring, including the uneven effects of capitalist development, the strategies of restructuring used, and local agency (Massey, 1984). That said, within the discrete paradigms of regulationist, gentrification, and class research, the case study approach has been criticised. Most notably, the predominance of case studies in gentrification research has been blamed for the continued impasse between competing economic and cultural interpretations (Slater, 2006). Indeed, Slater (2006) suggests they may have contributed to the eviction of critical perspectives in gentrification research. This is reinforced by Lees's (2003) call for a geography of gentrification. Individual approaches to class analysis have meant, until recently, that place-based studies had fallen by the wayside. In addition, case studies are subject to many general methodological criticisms. However it is central to a historical materialist reading which illuminates the hegemony processes at play. Used as part of a Marxist-feminist epistemology, an ethnographic historical materialist approach reveals the situatedness of knowledge and phenomenological experiences.

The local specificities are central to understanding class and urban restructuring in general. Contrary to the depiction of 'Red Clydeside' political radicalism, Glasgow is now positioned as cosmopolitan and 'the new black', via a city marketing campaign, revealing the evolutionary development of neoliberalism. However clichéd, Glasgow is often presented as the epitome of the British industrial working-class city (Damer, 1990); the second city of the Empire; the furnace of the world's industrialisation (MacInnes, 1995); and a proletarian city with a working-class cultural dominance which constantly refers back to itself and its own history rather than the rural hinterlands of its origin (Mitchell, 2005). The myth of Red Clydeside belies the multiplicity of lived experiences and divisions along religious and gender axes, which have a clear material basis and effect upon contemporary politics and restructuring. Working-class collectivity and formation was never coherent. In spite of the successes of collective class action, the struggles were divided. Aside from the Rent Strike action, women remain hidden from Glasgow's history (Gordon and Nair, 2003; Glasgow Women Studies, 1982). Class politics in Glasgow were also deeply divided along religious lines and sectarianism. The influx of predominantly Irish Catholics to Scotland demarcated the Catholic religion as a key indicator of an Irish Other within a predominantly Protestant Scotland. Irishness denoted by religion, was racialised and presented as a threat to Scottish nationality. As a result, anti-Irish discrimination was rife in nineteenth- and twentieth-century Scotland (Miles, 1982; Gallagher, 1987) and this was more pronounced in Glasgow, particularly on the Clydeside area, where the biggest influx occurred.

With regards to industrial capitalist production, there is no doubt of Glasgow's working-class credentials. With the River Clyde as its powerhouse, the local proverb goes: Glasgow made the Clyde and the Clyde made Glasgow, referring to how the river was dredged to facilitate industry. Being a port facing the Americas, the tobacco and cotton trade grew in the early eighteenth century. Then in the 1830s, with the advent of the industrial revolution, Glasgow developed as a key area for glass, paper, textile, cotton and chemical manufacturing and distribution (MacInnes, 1995). In the period from the 1860s through to the turn of the twentieth century, Glasgow famously became the shipbuilding centre of the world (MacInnes, 1995) while also the site of class struggle and the association with Red Clydeside action.[3] It is important to consider that the politics of social reproduction have been a critical element of struggle for working-class communities, perhaps more so than industrial action alone. Indeed, struggles over housing, health

---

3   Clyde Workers Committee. Within this era of political activism, one well-known dispute over a 47-hour working week led to 40,000 Clydesdale workers going on strike and culminated in 'Bloody Friday' and the famous deployment of tanks in the city's main civic square, George Square, in 1919.

services and the creation of social provision at the local and municipal levels in places like Glasgow and the mining valleys of South Wales (Cooke, 1982; Mark-Lawson et al., 1985; Hudson, 1989), laid the foundations for the post-1945 national welfare state (Helms and Cumber, 2006). The Glasgow Rent Strikes in 1915 were a response to landlords who had opportunistically increased rents in the hope of capitalising on the influx of munitions workers. As a result, the 1915 Rent Restrictions Act was passed which froze the rent at pre-war levels and introduced the campaign for state intervention into the regulation of the private housing rental market for the first time. This paved the way for the 1919 Housing and Town Planning Act and the advent of council housing. Whilst the conditions of many inner city tenements were inadequate, rent control and low council rent rates meant that private landlords were unable to lead housing renewal which had a lasting legacy in Scotland. Having housing regulated by the state rather than the market has protected residents against displacement, eviction and privatised landlordism – but this regulation is blamed for Glasgow's underdeveloped housing market (MacLennan and Gibb, 1988). Public intervention in the provision of housing undoubtedly shaped tenure pattern profoundly. Of the 73,630 houses authorised to be built in Glasgow between 1919 and 1939, only 9,106 were for the private market (Pacione, 1979). The amount of private housing built since 1945 is negligible, by which time housing had become a subsidised social service with the Corporation, as the local city government was then known, acquiring power, through the house-letting system, to determine the social composition of large areas (Pacione, 1979). In 1965, private landlords owned 38 per cent of houses, owner-occupiers 19 per cent, and the Corporation 43 per cent (Pacione, 1979).

Added to this, the post-war period of policy planning was dominated by Keynesian manipulation of macro-economic variables (Keating, 1988). There was a strengthening of the decentralisation of housing and industry which precipitated slum clearances in the inner city and resettlement of tenants in peripheral estates. Twenty-nine areas in the city were identified for comprehensive redevelopment (CDAs) including clearance of 97,000 dwellings (Pacione, 1995), the first and most famous being the Gorbals CDA. The overspill policy resulted in a dramatic shift in the city population, with a 15 per cent drop from 1,065,017 in 1961, to 898,848 in 1971 (Mooney, 1988). This was accompanied by a tenure shift, with a dramatic increase in council housing and a decline in opportunities for owner-occupation in CDAs, which is said to have precipitated an out-migration of 'upwardly mobile' households from the city (Pacione, 1995). By the 1970s, the Clydeside shipyards were facing severe financial difficulties and without Government assistance were liable to collapse. The unemployment rate in Glasgow was 5.7 per cent, compared with 4.8 per cent at the Scottish national level and 2.7 per cent in Great Britain as a whole (Mooney, 1988). This, combined with the overspill policy, contributed to a depleted tax base in Glasgow. It was not only the global market that changed, policy planning shifted again, away from Keynesian planning towards a more neoliberal approach to urban problems. The 1970s 'rediscovery of poverty' saw attention paid to the Clydeside's disproportionate amount of the worst 5 per cent of enumeration districts (Pacione, 1995). What followed was a neoliberal experimentation aimed at reversing decline in the 1980s through a combination of aggressive place-marketing campaigns to attract people and capital back to the city by eradicating its old industrial working-class image. This resulted in a raft of place-marketing campaigns: Glasgow's Miles Better (1984); the Glasgow Garden Festival (1988); the European City of Culture (1990); Glasgow's Alive (1997); the City of Architecture (1999); Glasgow: Scotland with Style (2003); as well as being the 2014 Commonwealth Games host city.

By the late 1980s, it looked as if these campaigns were beginning to have some success. Place-marketing was putting the city back on the investment map. The city had £800 million of inward investment which grew to £1 billion in 1989 and then to £2.5 billion in 1990, which was more than any other city outside London (Boyle et al., 2008). Much of this investment came from finance capital, especially pension funds and insurance companies based in London and abroad. Boyle et al. (2008: 324) point out the shortcomings of 'rolling out' market forces in this way:

> What jobs had been created were poorly paid, weakly unionized and flexible, to the detriment of the worker. There was little to be gained from turning welders into waiters. Regeneration had failed to reach the most needy sections of the Glasgow population.

Working-class people who have suffered most from the effects of restructuring are deemed a 'problem' and a deterrent to investment and are subsequently targeted by neoliberal policy (Law and Mooney, 2006). The shift towards regeneration in the 1990s was a turn towards conceiving urban problems in relation to people and place (Scottish Executive, 2006). Policy-led gentrification allows the council to explicitly combine industry and housing issues whilst seeking to reverse the damage of deindustrialisation and decentralisation.

By the 1990s, GCC accepted that it could not tackle its socio-spatial problems alone. The ascendancy of New Labour in 1997 heralded the birth of the regeneration approach. Rhetoric on 'partnership working' and 'capacity building' emerged along with Community Planning Partnerships (CPPs), to help minimise welfare dependency and maximise the abilities of communities to be self-sustaining (Boyle et al., 2008). This was evident in a range of New Labour initiatives (Urban Task Force Report, 1999), and in those executed by the Scottish Executive (2006) which cited both people and place as their focus:

> The long-term decline of traditional industries has left a legacy of under used assets – both land and people. Almost 100,000 people of working age in the city are currently economically inactive and dependent on incapacity and other state benefits. Glasgow City contains 12 per cent of all vacant and derelict land in Scotland. (Scottish Executive, 2006: 31)

GCC, alongside partners Glasgow City Marketing Bureau and Scottish Enterprise continued in its endeavour to rid the city of its gritty, violent reputation (Pacione, 1995; Mooney, 2004) by using marketing campaigns and strategic spatial planning to revitalise the central city and entice wealth back (GCC, 2003, 2003a). Glasgow is redefined as a metropolitan, stylish and cosmopolitan post-industrial city. The celebratory discourses on 'new' Glasgow are constructed in sharp contrast to the 'old' Glasgow (Mooney, 2004). This profitable cultural reinvention has progressed so much that Glasgow is now promoted as 'the new black' courtesy of a £1.5m campaign by the Glasgow City Marketing Bureau. Again, the Clydeside has been central to restructuring processes. The Scottish Executive deems the Clyde the national regeneration priority area. This 'rebirth' involves around £2 billion of private and public investment (Magee, 2003). It is anticipated that the Clyde project could provide up to 35,000 jobs, mostly in the finance sector, while Glasgow Harbour development proposes to get 270 unemployed people into work or further education (Clyde Waterfront, 2007). The emphasis on middle-class settlement denotes the perceived value of their social reproduction and labour in the emerging 'professionalised', post-industrial city. The reification of middle-class dispositions as vibrant and cosmopolitan and the centrepiece to regeneration legitimates their cultural practices. GCC's preoccupation with this group is also evident in their housing strategies. The regeneration approach in Glasgow combines trickle-down economics with the promotion of self-help, bolstered by the manufacturing of aspiration via promoting homeownership:

> Increased owner occupation [is seen] as an important aspect of urban regeneration and in support of the economic competitiveness of the area. (Communities Scotland, 2008)

Whether as visitors, residents or workers, urban policy consistently pitches the middle classes as the main protagonists in restructuring the city. The myth of 'new Glasgow' is based on the myth of the benefits of middle-class settlement. This is done with the intention of also regenerating neighbourhoods situated on the Clyde such as Partick.

Typical of the Clydeside, Partick is a predominately 'white' working-class area, dominated by tenement housing and home to around 5,000 people. The neighbourhood sits across the river from Govan and cheek to jowl with Glasgow's salubrious West End. This is a double-edged sword, as will be explored, giving Partick kudos and positive working-class associations but also making it ripe for gentrification. Partick's motto, *Industria ditat* translates as 'we are enriched by industry'. The Meadowside granary together with the Meadowside yards, Inglis' Pointhouse and D & W Henderson yard became the hub of industry in the area and a major source of employment during much of the twentieth century. Partick also played an important role in working-class life in Glasgow as a place where people both worked and relaxed. Residents, now in their seventies and eighties, delight in recalling the three cinemas, the skate-rinks, dancehalls and department

Figure 1.2   Inside the penthouse suite of Glasgow Harbour, looking across to the shipyards in Govan

stores. Partick was known as a 'punters place' where the 'Mile of Shopping' was a 'must-see' (*Evening Times*, 1956). Dumbarton Road was renowned for its varied and affordable shops, 'Between Church Street and Crow Road, you can buy ANYTHING – a bedroom suite, a pram, a new suit or a smart blouse, a roll of linoleum […]' (*Evening Times*, 1956). This echoes the saying many residents used 'if you cannae get it in Partick, you cannae get it anywhere'. However, these had become distant memories due to the decline of industry and investment in the neighbourhood bringing with it decline in these ways of life. Partick mirrors national trends over the past 25 years; the local economy has been severely 'streamlined' with the closure of the yards and activities at the harbour, including the granary.

Mitchell (2005: 29) comments 'Partick was always that bit different from other working class areas in Glasgow'. One reason for this is that Partick has survived as a traditional and architecturally consistent working-class neighbourhood in the city. While other neighbourhoods were razed in slum clearance actions, local community action protected Partick from demolition and the fate of other inner city working-class neighbourhoods. Local residents staved off the plans for long enough that the policy shifted from demolition to rehabilitation. The outcome of this rehabilitation strategy has been referred to as 'benign gentrification' (Bailey

Figure 1.3   A view of Partick from the Harbour development

and Robertson, 1997). This describes the process whereby local authorities encouraged homeownership and community housing associations as a strategy to rehabilitate older tenements that lacked modern amenities like an inside toilet, a bath or shower, or even running hot water. This enabled working-class people, especially situated residents and young people just starting out in the housing market, to inexpensively purchase property. This local authority-led project did not lead to gentrification because of the tight rental controls which protected people from being evicted but it can be said to mark the beginning of breach of the municipal housing tradition which has since been all but dismantled. Prior to this happening, rehabilitation helped preserve the social make-up in the working-class neighbourhood, processes which cast Partick as a strong community with historical ties to the locale adding to its perceived value and, ergo, rent-gap.

What also sets it apart is its location next to Glasgow's West End and its proximity to the University of Glasgow which not only offers prestige but a burgeoning student and academic population seeking accommodation. Partick emerges as an attractive location, with cheaper rents than the West End yet with easy access to its amenities and strong transport links to the rest of the city.

Given its history and features, the neighbourhood has become fairly socially mixed and diverse, comprising mixed tenures; owner-occupation and socially-rented housing managed by Partick Housing Association [PHA] and privately-rented accommodation. That said, intermediate geography data, which is not used for regeneration funding allocation, indicates Partick has pockets of poverty with two areas in the top 10 per cent most deprived SIMD classification. Twenty-one per cent of the Partick population and 19 per cent at Glasgow Harbour Partick South are income deprived,[4] compared with 15 per cent at the national level, and this figure has increased since 2002. Given this funding criteria and the lack of brownfield land, due to the successful prevention of demolition, Partick is not subject to interventionist regeneration initiatives. It is subject to the other approach of regeneration based on the trickle-down of social and economic capital. This worried residents. There was a lot of concern about what impact this type of regeneration initiative would have on the area. The social mix was finely balanced and the issues faced by those on very low incomes or living in poverty in the neighbourhood were being overlooked. As such this research was borne out of discussions between Westgap (West Glasgow Against Poverty), Oxfam and the University of Glasgow in 2003. All three groups came together with a shared concern with the effects that regeneration policies were having on the communities and neighbourhoods that they claimed to help. As an anti-poverty group run offering an independent advice service on money issues, welfare rights, benefits, housing and homelessness in Partick, Westgap saw first-hand the extent of such financial problems and the impacts changes in Partick were having on people's lives which the urban regeneration development of the former granary site into the Glasgow Harbour was potentially exacerbating. While imagery of 'sink' council estates on the peripheries of cities and towns are dominant in media portrayals and research studies of place-based inequality, such inequity is much more 'normal', everyday and pervasive. As Lees (2003) points out, the majority of poor people do not live in areas of concentrated poverty and 'pure' working-class neighbourhoods have become increasingly obsolete through successive waves of urban policy. This was the experience of many residents in Partick who are part of a contemporary, restructuring working class whose stories are not often heard, some of whom are working, some not, some social renters while others are homeowners. While diverse, the commonality in their experience and what emerge as a key class indicator, which I explore throughout this book, is their power and control or, indeed, lack thereof to stay fixed in the neighbourhood. What was happening in this neighbourhood was subtle and nuanced processes of state-led gentrification based on the rolling out of neoliberalism and undermining of traditional state and municipal provisions, processes which met Hackworth's (2002) definition: shaping urban space for the more affluent user. In the following sections I will explore some of the processes of gentrification occurring in Partick however detailed analysis of cases studies of the varied gentrification processes that were occurring are outlined in the appendix.

---

4 This indicator encompasses adults and children living in households in receipt of Income Support, Income Based Job Seekers Allowance, Working Families Tax Credit below a low income threshold or Disability Tax Credit and is derived from data provided by the Department for Work and Pensions and the Inland Revenue

Figure 1.4   Shops on Dumbarton Road

This telling of the city and the neighbourhood is, of course, only partial. I will now move on to explore how these changes have been received, negotiated and resisted on a personal level. The complexity of this phenomenological experience is, in part, expressed by how local resident Agnes understands the increase in homeownership in the area:

Kirsteen: Have you ever thought about or wanted to buy your house?

Agnes: No, never. That's not something I want [...] I was brought up with that council house mentality and I'm happy just paying my rent. When that Right to Buy came out it just never appealed to me, no, it just never [...] I feel like it's something that's more than it's made out to be [...] I suppose you are just brought up with it: working-class folk rent. You just paid your rent and got your repairs done. It was a working-class thing. You always paid your rent, you might not pay other things but you pay the rent.

Agnes's attitude towards homeownership explicates the previous hegemony associated with industrial production and patterns of life this generated. It also suggests that she does not accept this hegemony specifically; she resists it. The task is to understand, then, how the changes in productive relations and the effects of uneven development are managed within the current social formation, without challenging the existing order. This is explored in the remainder of this book.

Chapter 2
Restructuring Class Identity

In this chapter I examine the relationship between residents' class position and identity amidst transitions and occupational changes brought by urban restructuring. A common narrative in discourses on the decline of industry heralds the end of traditional work (Rifkin, 1996) and the rise of the individual self-maker (Beck, 1992; Bauman, 1998). Class is said to be neither materially nor ontologically relevant in a society of cultural fragmentation linked to individualisation (Pakulski and Waters, 1996; Giddens, 1991). Yet working-class culture is the main target of current neoliberal, urban-social policies (Law and Mooney, 2006), which support gentrification via regeneration. Gentrification is promoted whilst old ways of life that correspond to industrialism are residualised to raise the population to a particular cultural and moral level which corresponds to the needs of productive forces for post-industrial development. Being the subject of a political project signifies that working-class culture is being restructured rather than having dissolved. Exploring class identity not only lets us speak to such epochal prognostications (Savage, 2000), it foregrounds the process of hegemonic change. It emerges that residents recognise the nature of structural changes but do not attribute their private troubles to these public issues (Mills, 1959) in an explicit way. They acknowledge their objective class position but reject the notion of a 'traditional' working-class identity. Residents constructed narratives that emphasised their perceived control over restructuring processes. However, their class disassociation is not merely a process of differentiation and individualisation (Savage, 2000; Skeggs, 1997); it reveals the material basis of the hegemonic shift. By delegitimating working-class culture and legitimating middle-class consumption practices, neoliberal urban-social policies try to foreclose people's desire to identify with the former group, which, as I discuss in Chapter 4 is an exploitative class process. Such devaluation and stigmatisation can lead people to disassociate with class. This expresses occupationally working-class residents' ambivalence towards working-class identity. This is, in itself, a class process that expresses struggles between middle and working-class groups (Bottero, 2004; Skeggs, 1997; Savage, 2000); constructing a sense of self that invokes a narrative of individualism which correlates with the rise of neo-liberalism.

End of Work, End of Class?

Discourses on the 'end of work' are closely aligned to claims of the 'end of class' (Strangleman, 2007). They assert that there has been an irrevocable qualitative and quantitative difference in the type of employment available now when compared with the past and that this is directly linked to profound changes in capitalism (Strangleman, 2007). As outlined in the previous chapter, the labour market in Glasgow experienced a shift to post-industrial, service based economy which suggests that work had irrevocably changed. While occupations were diverse, residents (with exception of Stuart, Angus, Alison, Loretta and John) were working-class in an occupational sense in relation to the NS-SeC[1] employment aggregate approach. Almost a fifth of residents interviewed were receiving long-term disability allowance, whilst others, like Sylvie, Rachael, Gordon and Sean, moved in and out of being benefit claimants. Unlike Charlesworth's (2000) 'inescapable' conclusion that dispossessed people understand their lives least and are less able to articulate their existence, residents were keenly aware of these wider structural changes in industry or 'the end of work' and the attendant impacts on the local labour market and their neighbourhood. They did not interpret that is heralding the 'end of class'. Lisa, 48, pinpointed the moment she noticed life in the neighbourhood transform:

> Lisa: I went to Edinburgh to study and I came back and noticed a change when I came back '92. I left in '88. I noticed a difference in people. Folk were depressed. There was a real downer going on. I just found people, I mean a lot of people, my mates were out of work when I came back, guys from the pubs, a lot of them laid off at the yards. After the Thatcher years there was a bleak feeling. I came back from Edinburgh, living in a good area but working Granton and the like, and to see your own area, community, to come back to this ... I thought what is going on here? I walked into the pub, maybe they were just older but things had changed.

Lisa's moment of critique (Weis, 2004) after four years away acknowledges the effects of long-term unemployment and changes in the labour market, which relegates residents, principally men who worked in the yards, surplus. Lisa implicitly expresses that the work that one performs underpins class practices and identity. This 'end of work' thesis is evident in 45-year-old English Language teacher Mhairi's recollection 'these were places if you wanted a job you just walked in somewhere and got one. Now it's a wasteland'. Not only is this narrative of decline used to justify neoliberal policies, accepting it renders people passive, submissively accepting the 'end of work'. Gary, 37, and his peers experienced the highly circumscribed job market during the 1980s and 1990s. He was angry at

---

1 Those in categories eight to three are conceived to be working-class. While all categories are contentious, category four is obviously so and can relate to working- or middle-class positions (in my sample category four refers to a middle-class respondent), while categories one and two represent middle-class groups. Those who were retired or unemployed were classified by their previous employment.

not being given a chance to participate properly in the labour market and compete globally:

> Gary: Why not replace good paid jobs with others that are good paid? Why instead are they focusing on the service sectors with the short-term contract? Why not skill people up? It might take longer but skill them up so they can compete with other sectors like around the world, so we can [compete] rather than skilling them up for working in a call centre. Not everybody wants to work in call centres and the bubble has burst for call centres.

Similarly, Steve berates the poor quality of work available and defends people's decision not to take up poorly paid jobs. In reference to migrant workers he said:

> They are working for pennies in the jobs we wouldn't do, £3.20 an hour, 20 of them sharing one flat. We're quite relatively well off in that way. Today I'm skint, next week I'm skint, but I get by.

As I did not survey people over time, I cannot fully assess whether residents have experienced proletarianisation and precarity, downward mobility or degradation and do not foreclose the fact that that upward mobility could have occurred. I interviewed some who, in middle-class occupations, had benefited from neoliberalism and the creation of jobs under the processes of entrepreneurial urbanism. Stuart and John, who both moved to Partick to buy their first flats, claimed to be from working-class backgrounds. They both held jobs in an agency responsible for dextrous city branding and marketing to lure incoming companies to settle in Glasgow. Loretta made a living from developing property in Partick, speculatively buying new build apartments to let out.

Bemoaning the end of work is a historically recurrent theme but one that does not render it imaginary or reducible to pure nostalgia. It is recurrent because the nature of employment, the structures and practices governing it, as well as the jobs themselves, change to accommodate transformations in capitalism (Strangleman, 2007). So instead we see a qualitative change in work rather than its demise or total transformation, as Tim acknowledges:

> There's people still working in different trades; office cleaning; working as a bouncer. There's not all skilled jobs running about the place, there are ones where you're just going to make money. That's the past, there's not all those jobs out there and that's not going to change … it's a working class community 'cause people have to go out and work. It's not the type of area where people have a lot of leisure time. That's what I base it on, we have to go out and work.

Despite changes in the labour market, for Tim, the neighbourhood and people of it, remain working-class. This explicitly expresses a Marxist interpretation of class position. Complexly, residents express class consciousness in their recognition of the vagaries of capitalism, particularly the global division of labour, the loss of industrial work and workers and the poor supply and quality of jobs and felt the material impacts of this on their lives. Yet few identified with class. The end of this type of work correlates with a distinct change in patterns of life and social reproduction and even people's point of identification, as Betty recounts:

> My family were all Red Clydesiders, that kind of thing. I was brought up with Friday night was party night. There was great "work" thing; [we] worked all week. I'd say the '80s started the culture [*sic* – change]. Before that you didn't not work. You were looked down on if you didn't work. Work, work, pay your rent, go out on Friday get drunk and go back to work again. It changed, it really, really changed. Even the likes of my granny would look down on people like [...] Then it became people you knew, you couldn't be judgemental. Giros become the big thing [...] you would sign on, things like that. They are really cutting down on these things now, they are wanting everybody off the dole [...] it's the big thing to have disability benefits. And see now the job situation is crap, £5 an hour. Someone got me a book at Christmas, Hard Work, Polly Toynbee, it was London, right enough, and it was porters and stuff. It's all these agencies and sometimes an agency for an agency. In Partick it's the same. You can work in a shop or do cleaning.

Betty refers to the traditional idea of working-class jobs and related cultural and social practices. She acknowledges both the cultural and political defeat of the industrial worker as the central reference point for class. Betty's family, who she identifies as Red Clydesiders, were faced with unemployment and state benefits as a substitute for the loss of manual jobs. This led to the demise of entrenched social patterns of reproduction around the working week and the wage packet. She clearly identifies the change in the labour market as the root cause of unemployment rather than blaming benefit dependency. Her account highlights how discourses on decline have been used to intellectually justify policy responses – the introduction of the dole, disability allowance and later the growth of workfare rather than welfare.

Transformations in productive relations and subsequent consumption and reproduction changes have profoundly impacted upon notions of, and attachment to, working-class identity. There is a high level of consciousness of the impacts of structural changes of global capitalism on people's lives. While working-class residents concede that they remain in the same economic position or a worse one, they increasingly dis-identify with class identity (Skeggs, 1997, 2005; Savage, 2000). That is, they do not connect their class position with a coherent identity or collectivity. This paradox of disassociation is expressed by Steve who clearly relates his private troubles to public issues, recalling how difficult life was under Thatcherism with his dad getting paid off, struggling with YTS (Youth Training Scheme) and limited opportunities and fighting against the Poll Tax. Yet when it comes to identifying with class, he is ambivalent:

Kirsteen: See when I mentioned class is that something that you identify with?

Steve: No, not anymore. Used to say working-class but now I say socialist.

Kirsteen: Why?

Steve: Because there's no such thing as working-class anymore now is there?

Kirsteen: Why would you say that?

Steve: Too many unemployed and on benefits but they still come from the background so I would say that because most of us aren't working, not legit anyway now.

Steve suggests that the traditional industrial working-class occupation no longer exists and therefore neither does working-class identity. The relationship between class position and class identity is divorced. He notes that class position has been restructured when he expresses the idea of an underclass or classlessness of a group who are delegitimated as surplus, which does not correlate with what he understands as a subjective or phenomenological class identity. This leads him to dis-identify with the category of working-class, which he sees as obsolete. This was not limited to Steve and Betty; many respondents rejected this identity and displayed increased ontological insecurity.

Table 2.1   Residents' NS-SeC and class identification

Name	Age	Identified with being working class	NS-SeC
Betty	49	Yes	7/8
Brian	63	No	5/8
Leona	37	Unsure	7
Mary	67	No	3
Bea	62	Yes	3
Alison	32	Yes	2
Loretta	42	No	4
Gary	37	Yes	5
Robert	73	Unsure	3
Natasha	39	Yes	5
Jimmy	42	Yes	5
John	35	No	2
David	59	Yes	3/2
Stuart	34	No	2
Gordon	24	No	7

Name	Age	Identified with being working class	NS-SeC
Fi	64	Yes	7/3
Phil	37	No	5
Nick	58	No	5
Alan	41	Unsure	7
Kathleen	33	Yes	6
Louise	41	No	2/3
Bill	68	Yes	8
Danny	51	Yes	8
Tim	43	No	7/5
Sean	25	No	7
Agnes	69	Yes	7
Mhairi	48	Unsure	3
Betty	78	Yes	5
Rachael	49	Unsure	7
Molly	37	Unsure	8
Paul	41	Yes	8
Steve	38	No	8
Sylvie	19	Unsure	6
Bilal	37	No	3/7
Rhonda	66	Yes	7
Darren	25	No	6
Lou	42	Yes	8
Angus	36	Did not ask	2
Lisa	48	Yes	8
Stephen	54	Unsure	8
Sonny	67	Yes	6
Janey	44	Yes	5
Norma	38	Yes	5
Gareth	52	No	5
Maggie	53	No	8
Angie	37	Yes	8/6
Dylan	19	Yes	5
Donna	50	Yes	3
Rosa	54	Yes	5

Table 2.2   NS-SeC classifications

	The National Statistics Socio-economic Classification
1	Higher managerial and professional occupations
	1.1 Large employers and higher managerial occupations
	1.2 Higher professional occupations
2	Lower managerial and professional occupations
3	Intermediate occupations
4	Small employers and own account workers
5	Lower supervisory and technical occupations
6	Semi-routine occupations
7	Routine occupations
8	Never worked and long-term unemployed

Twenty-one out of the 49 respondents who identified with being working-class also made statements which contradicted this. However, dis-identification does not undermine class theory because dis-identifications are the result of class processes (Bottero, 2004; Skeggs, 1997; Savage, 2000). This can be explored by looking at how people make sense of the new situations they find themselves in with the 'end of work' as they knew it and the reinforcing of their class position yet the seeming end of their class identity. To do this we must move beyond work and look at how identity intersects with other factors such as gender, ethnicity and generational differences and how these are actively being constructed alongside class.

Femininity, Respectability and Dis-identification

Female respondents, arguably, experienced more changes than men. Ostensibly, deindustrialisation, the feminisation of industry through the growth in the service sector and the expansion of education has extended their labour market opportunities. They were no longer so tightly bound into traditional gender or class positions. Of those interviewed of working age, more were in employment than men. Women found themselves in much greater demand with the rise of part-time service based work, rather than surplus to requirement. The downsizing of the public sector and the expansion of the low-wage service sector creates greater opportunities for women's participation in social care work. They were especially affected by welfare reform through the 1980s and 1990s. Women's increased entry into the labour market increased the burden on them as parents, carers and workers (Lister, 2000). The new gender order under neoliberalism has deepened the subordination, trapping them in peripheral work and increasing the class divisions between women (McDowell, 1991). Deindustrialisation has arguably increased their exploitation, but rather than increasing class identification, there were stronger claims to respectability (Skeggs, 1997).

Respectability and femininity have a long historical association but the meanings of these have altered in increasingly secularised, post-industrial times. Respectability is no longer intrinsically linked to the heterosexual norm of marriage. Younger generations did not have to make bad gambles on marriage as older residents might. Mhairi, Alison, Loretta, all unmarried and earning decent incomes, held power and material and social status that their mothers did not. Loretta owned and developed properties, Lisa and Donna were in a same sex relationship and Mhairi, 45, Sylvie, 19, Norma, 38, Louise, 41, Molly, 37 were all unmarried, living independently with no children. Many of the mothers were single or in long-term relationships but had not married. However, there was still a clear relationship between respectability and femininity, which expresses class position and identity. While women were not bound in the traditional patriarchal sense, they faced economic pressure as single earners and parents, and pressures to be respectable which involved supporting the social reproduction of the neighbourhood community. This was historically rooted. Residents such as Bea and Mary had witnessed the unpaid labour efforts their mothers had to produce. Mary wistfully and bitterly remarked, 'I would kill myself if I had to live their life'. Bea felt that women were 'treated as slaves'. Femininity and traditional gender roles are a double-edged sword, epitomised by the toil of washing laundry and social reproduction undertaken at the city's municipal washhouses known locally as the 'steamie':

> Bea: Lots of marriages were sorted out in there, because it was groups of women, it got opened out and discussed and by the time they were leaving, everyone was fine. That was their way of seeing psychologists, as you would today [...] they're not going to discuss it [with people outside of the steamie] because they were *in the same boat*. Life was not easy and although they say "the good old days", it was hard, especially the hardships for woman. There was no central heating, nothing. A fire: that was it. Back breaking stuff. I watched my granny cook. She could cook; she could do anything that woman. She could paint, build, do anything. [My emphasis]

While the back-breaking labour of the 'steamie' was assuaged, women lost their 'psychologists' and support networks. That said, Bea continued the tradition of pastoral and kinship support that she saw her female family members provide. She worked relentlessly, in a voluntary unpaid position, despite arthritis and heart problems. At 62, she ran a social support club, Golden Friends, at a local church. This was a lifeline for women from around 60 years of age upwards, often widowed, some still living in the peripheral estates, who travelled to Partick for the club. Most knew each other from childhood in Partick. They met regularly at the church for tea dances, bingo and raffles. It had 60 or so members and a lengthy waiting list for membership. It was entirely grassroots and had no public funding; its main source of support was Bea. For her, class meant looking after your own and being responsible for the community and its social reproduction. Paradoxically, this was often done to help others move out of their class position, whilst keeping women anchored (Skeggs, 1997). Skeggs asserts that the production of the caring self is a means of taking responsibility for social reproduction, via traits like unselfishness and altruism. Caring is also something they are unlikely to fail at. Acting responsibly in this way signifies respectability, which counteracts the negativity of the working-class female status.

Thirty-three-year-old Kathleen's life had been a battle against adversity, growing up in care but also fighting against bullying from her peers. She no longer lived in Partick but came back often to visit. I asked whether she met many people she knew and grew up with:

> Kathleen: Most are junkies. One guy, a friend, had done well. He has a business round the corner. Some others have done well for themselves, I don't mean a business as well, I mean *they're respectable*. They fit in nicely, they're not jumping about streets, reliving their youth, think that drugs matter. Unfortunately that's what a lot of my friends from school think. And it's heartbreaking seeing them. You want to say to them you know, "Right! Enough!". It's so sad. It really is [...]. [My emphasis]

Success in life is not a measurement of material achievements; rather, the desired and worthy accolades are moral ones. Gaining respectability means you have done well, breaking the classed cycle set out from your youth, which potentially could have resulted in her 'jumping about' and taking drugs:

> Kathleen: I need to tell you something. I remember all these people saying to me when I was pregnant at 17 [...] "what a wee slapper. She'll amount to nothing good, she's a right wee cow". Well, I tell you what, not blowing my trumpet, not looking at all of them but some of them; I could be living in a cardboard box with my kids and I've still done better than them, some of them. I really have because I'm not letting my kids make the same mistakes that I have. I'm really not and they can't say that. And those same *moral principles* just don't kick in with young ones these days. I don't think so, I really don't. [My emphasis]
>
> Kirsteen: You sound exceptional though Kathleen.
>
> Kathleen: No, not exceptional. You've just got to fight for what I got. I'll always be the 17-year-old lassie who dropped out of school with no education, getting into trouble fighting. *But I changed it to suit me.* I need to look after my kids now, not myself. [My emphasis]

Kathleen's view of her life chances suggests that this cycle was compounded by being 'unrespectable'. It was not her education attainments or career which helped her transition from these difficult times, it was her commitment to being respectable. Thus she felt she had truly earned her status.

Skeggs (1997) argues that the pathologisation of working-class women as disrespectable by middle-class groups means they shrink from claiming this identity. However, slightly fewer women dis-identified with class than men; 12 out of 24 women compared to 8 out of the 25 men said they identified with being working-class. Those women who were long-term unemployed or on disability benefits did not see themselves as working class, suggesting that, similar to Steve, they felt un-entitled to do so. Contrary to Skeggs's account, many women identified with being working class as they were able to reconcile negative connotations by being 'respectable', which they achieved through cultivating the caring self. Those women cultivated a caring identity directly identified with being working class. Natasha saw herself as working class although she was confused about official measurements. She described her transition from claiming benefits to becoming a drugs worker as 'going legit'. Being a community worker, rather than single mum and benefit claimant, gave her legitimacy, which she was proud of. Janey articulated her view of class:

> Well I'm a worker, my mom is Scottish, dad is American. I developed through my mum. In America it's about working and Glasgow is the same and I like that. Well there was the dole thing. When I first came over here everyone was on the dole and it wasn't considered anything. We weren't unemployed scumbags […]. In African countries where people are allowed to go to university here, this chance to go away and they go back to help because that is who they are, that is their culture and Partick is the same, everywhere is just the same. People who have done well for themselves should do their best for others, you know?

For Janey, class was implicitly about respectability via responsibility to your community and social reproduction. Reminiscent of Kathleen, this is not about personal ambition, or wealth, it is about accumulating social capital. The topic she spoke of most was her children, their development, well-being and young people in general, how to inspire them and promote education so to advance their position. And for her, the experience of intersecting class and femininity meant doing this yourself. So these women were working-class, but counteracted the negative aspects associated with this by being self-motivated, responsible and compassionate. Having caring roles levelled up respectability.

This could be empowering for women, as they substituted this social capital for economic capital by creating employment. Natasha became a drugs worker and was training to be a social worker, Janey and Louise set up after-school and breakfast clubs, Norma set up a community group, Kathleen became a junior football coach and Rosa a community worker. All created employment by extending their caring role. They were able to make a virtue *and* venture out of this necessity. While this empowered these women, it ran concurrently with the decline in welfare spending. These women found there was demand, as previous public sector social care jobs were outsourced to the third and private sector, which created employment opportunities, but also the necessity for their unpaid labour increased as social welfare services declined overall. Women had to deal with the personal fallout resulting from these transitions and the effects of increased male unemployment. The drugs pandemic in Glasgow has been acute (McKeganey and Barnard, 1992). Mothers, wives and partners of addicts are often unacknowledged victims, burdened with this caring responsibility. Fi at one point had five cleaning jobs, and as well as taking care of her home and children, she stood by her son through great emotional and financial difficulties:

> Fi: It's only in the last 20 years I've started to be alright. We've kinda paid the place off and the kids are away. Up until 1984 my son was an addict and he cleared us out, the house out, I mean everything. Curtains, everything. It took us up to last year to pay off the debts. We had nothing, we had to start again. There are no winners in that situation. No one wins.

Local support was vital for Fi. A local community nurse helped arrange for Fi's son to be placed in a rehabilitation unit. Fi turned to Westgap for advice and advocacy with her debts. She has since become a volunteer drugs worker and is assisting at a day centre for the elderly, paying back to the community, as Janey describes it. Fi, like the other women, were particularly dependent on the networks of family and friends and local, often voluntary, services, like youth and after-school clubs, for material and social support, as well as paid employment.

It is clear that these women felt empowered through being workers and therefore financially independent but also, because their job involved the caring self it helped make them respectable. While labour saving devices may have assuaged women's unpaid labour, arguably modernisation heralded by neoliberalism intensifies gender roles of femininity and respectability. Women sought legitimacy from caring roles, yet paradoxically, these bound them further, creating more exploitation and reinforcing gender roles. This is oppressive in the first instance because it is moralising, which has ramifications for women more than men. Notwithstanding, whilst Skeggs (1997) attributes this pathologisation to middle-class groups, it is clear that there is a material basis to this moralising ideology. It is borne out of urban restructuring and neoliberal policies aimed at dismantling the welfare state and manifested in the double burden of paid and unpaid work. This is a crucial point which is often missed.

Redundant Masculinities: Class Identity and Control

Men employed in manufacturing industries often had to become as mobile as production: seeking employment to match their skills in different parts of the world, retrain, or face unemployment. Brian, 63, divorced and living alone in Partick, worked in engineering at the shipyards. As a skilled worker 'demand' took him across the world. His kids joked that he had been to more places than Alan Whicker. Yet having to frequently work abroad was extremely demanding on family life. Tim, 43, a part-time bouncer and photographer living in Partick with his girlfriend and their baby daughter, took the retraining route, a process he saw as inevitable:

> One of my mates got back from the navy in the early '80s to start working in the Govan shipyards and, at one time, that was where you went to learn a trade but the economics of things, I mean, if you want to pay the wages that they used to get, it's a lot more convenient if you get someone you don't have to pay that much for, and there's lots of places in the world where you don't have pay as much. Cheap. So I think it's economics rather than, you know, supplying a good workmanship or something – it's like if you want cheaper builders you move abroad for that.

Male residents over 35 years of age displayed strong class disassociation. Their class denial and dis-identification stemmed from a rejection of the 'mythology' of class: old labour and solidarity, trade unionism, etc. In the post-industrial period contemporary masculine transitions have to negotiate opportunity, 'risk', uncertainty and labour market insecurity (Nayak, 2006). Tim was one of many male residents who took the perspective 'adapt or die', 'modernise or be left behind'. He saw himself as independent and detached but explained:

> I definitely empathise with other folk man, you know what I mean? I'm not sitting here saying, well I've got this I've got that – I can see where that whole situation can lead to. I've got friends who are not working themselves and not finding anything really. So, as I say, I've been in that situation myself. It's only since my daughter came along that I've been in full-time employment as a bouncer. *You've got to be practical.* [My emphasis]

Being practical meant giving up on a dream of being a full time photographer. He originally trained as a printer and found himself at the mercy of restructuring and technological advances in skilled industries:

> Tim: It was because of the trade union, the papers decide they were going to get rid of the unions and that changed everything. That meant there was no jobs catering for what I wanted to do, so basically that's how I got into photography. Being a bouncer, doing wedding photography [...] it's just a sign of the times *you have to modernise or you get left behind in the past basically.* [My emphasis]

Phil, who had moved to Partick from Australia two years previously, echoed this:

I left school in 1975 [...] I realised that I would have to retrain a few times. Lifelong learning is good but that idea of settling down and being comfortable seems less and less likely.

Working-class men have 'riskier' and insecure labour market experiences with an increasing number of employment transitions and ongoing training or 'lifelong learning' (Nayak, 2006). Phil's account also foregrounds the universality of this experience throughout industrialised countries. Tim believes dealing with this insecurity requires self-reliance and practicality. This means having to face-up to this reality rather than holding on to old class allegiances. Many of his peers were 'left behind' by failing to adapt:

> Tim: Eh, I think people who couldn't move on from the businesses they grew up with and couldn't diversify a bit to different things, or be open minded to working in different things, people my age really who, when they got out of school, got a trade but they haven't adapted to the changes. I mean you look around the world and you don't get people saying "well we don't want this" or they're fully behind it. They know the value of being able to change and just work basically.

Tim believes that labour needs to be malleable and move alongside changes in the job market or be left behind as global capital *re*fixes in another location. Tim perceives that he has been in control of his career shifts from printing to bouncing and photography because he has chosen to adapt. Similar to their female peers, male residents' experience of class shows a dis-identification with their material position and instead a striving for control. Managing restructuring means taking things into their own hands and one way of doing this is by rejecting the identity associated with traditional industry and constraints and disappointments in the past.

Brian adopted the 'adapt or die' outlook and said that he would never cross the shipyard gates again even for all the money in the world. He followed capital and moving labour markets around the world looking for employment. This was part of his strategy of 'forward planning'. Brian said that he had never done any forward planning previously but after experiencing the sharp-end of restructuring in the 1980s, he used it to take control. He recalls how his wife came to get her house in Knightswood. An inclement winter in the 1970s known as the 'big freeze' in Glasgow led to burst pipes which damaged lots of properties and affected residents were temporarily housed in community centres. Brian had separated from his wife but did not want her and his kids living in a centre temporarily. He managed to secure a socially rented house for her by doing free work for the Glasgow Corporation. He realised there was a shortage of plumbers, then identified someone who was assessing the empty houses in Glasgow to see if they were fit for habitation or should be condemned. He followed him and worked for free. When he correctly identified that a water tank was frozen solid, he received a call from the worker's boss who offered him an empty house for his wife to take.

He also did unpaid work securing properties for PHA, which, he said, led to him getting a house for his mother-in-law and himself:

Kirsteen: So you did that for free?

Brian: Yes.

Kirsteen: Sounds like they [PHA] got a good deal.

Brian: Well at that time my neighbours would have been flooded so it was just neighbourly. They've been fair with me and I've been fair with them [PHA]. [...] I got *the choice* of the house I'm in because I was doing work for them free. So basically what it is *you look after your own, respect*. You think of me doing work for the Corporation? I wasn't. I was doing free work for my wife and kids. [My emphasis]

Brian adopted an individualised, entrepreneurial role as a way of responding to restructuring. This was reflected in his attempts to have prescient knowledge of the job market:

Brian: When my son was looking for a trade I had to talk him out of it because he wanted to follow in my footsteps, just like my father, but the jobs weren't there anymore and I knew that, so I steered him into the electrical side of engineering.

Brian even offered me some advice – that my boyfriend should look towards fibre optic cables for the new leading skilled manual employment. Staying in control meant not being controlled which leaves you unemployed and excluded, 'if you can see beyond the immediate, you have some sense of control'.

Tim recalled how, eventually, he was made to pay his council tax, not having done so for years. He had accumulated a debt of around £5,000:

Kirsteen: Did you sort that out yourself?

Tim: Aye, basically talking to them and telling them you know, "this is what I can pay this month and this is what I can't", you know, "if I can't pay this month then I'll tell you that I can't pay you this month". It's hard getting out that situation. It's a spiral; *you're not in control anymore*. [My emphasis]

Even in adverse situations, where Tim owed the council money, which could result in legal action, he attempts to exert his power over the situation, to claim back a sense of control. I commented that it must have been a difficult thing to sort out. He explained:

> Well I learned it's something I needed to do. If you need to pay, you need to pay or they come and take your stuff away. I don't like people with power having influence over me, you know, so if can be like "no", do you know what I mean? That's the way I'd prefer to keep it.

For Jimmy control meant refraining from buying his house and dealing with problems himself. His partner Natasha told me about the advice and advocacy they received from Westgap to manage their debts:

> Natasha: It's brilliant – well not that we need it as we got referred back to the council.
>
> Jimmy: See, I don't like that, I don't like that. I don't like folk interfering in my shit. I prefer to do it myself.
>
> Natasha: Well you can go bankrupt! [laughs]

The collapse of Christmas hamper firm Farepak[2] had just occurred. Tim was angry about this, and the vulnerable position the savers had been put in:

> Tim: See, that to me is classic, you know? These people have got nothing. [Farepak] Taking your money over the year and they've went bust and they can't help you. They should at least say here is your product. It's a slap in the face to be told you're not gonna have anything at Christmas. These people are in control and you don't know what's going to happen at the next turn or whatever.

Of course, the flipside to this is those who did not adapt (or 'died'). Men who were of the same generation of Willis's (1977) 'lads', whose cultural worlds were shaped by the journey through schooling, training schemes, modern apprenticeships, found themselves unskilled, unemployable, and surplus (Nayak, 2006). The only 'choice' available was 'shit jobs and govvy schemes' (Coffield et al., 1986: 86). Now they were more likely to be 'learning to serve' (McDowell, 2002) or 'schooling for the dole' (Bates, 1984) rather than 'learning to labour' (Willis, 1977). Thirty-seven-year-old Gary's formative training and employment years were during the 1980s. He got a place with the local council:

> Gary: I done well at school, got O Levels, stayed on at school to fifth year and it was waste of time. The best I could do was get a YTS with the regional council and I got quickly disillusioned. I was one of the lucky ones. See, my mates they

---

2 Farepak was a Christmas hamper scheme which allowed people to spread the costs of Christmas over the year by paying for hampers by instalment. The company collapsed and customers lost what they had paid in and were not compensated.

got YTS with local employment, small businesses, where after two years "ta-ta, we'll get someone else at 30 quid a month".

By pursuing public sector employment, Gary fared better than his peers, but he does not rate this, believing he got the best from a bad bunch of opportunities, or indeed lack thereof:

> Gary: A lot of my peers have got the easy route out: some taking casual employment; some selling drugs, some died with drugs, heavy drugs. The rise of unemployment runs parallel with that. It doesn't take a genius to work out that one affected the other [...] There was no jobs and we were all just trying to get by.

Steve was close in age to Gary but unlike him, took the 'easy route out'. This began with a YTS placement in cabinet making but took a downward spiral:

> Steve: Aye, for a young boy it was alright, you know, it was alright earning decent money. There was no apprenticeships, Mrs Thatcher scrubbed all that. So I just got sick of the crap wages after a while when I should have been getting higher rate, working causal, scaffolding, on roofs and that for £15 a day? Aye. [sarcastically]
>
> Kirsteen: What did your friends do? Similar things?
>
> Steve: Out of my pals, only one got an apprenticeship in the shipyards in Govan, proper training. None of us got anything, any training like that so it was just labouring jobs doing anything like that.
>
> Kirsteen: Is that what your friends still do now?
>
> Steve: Well the Parks department, it isn't skilled, it's just cutting grass.
>
> Kirsteen: Are you working at the moment?
>
> Steve: Skiving, doing scaffolding, labouring [...].

Steve's account of his life was a testimony to the ravages of deindustrialisation and neoliberalism which marginalises and disenfranchises many young men with a generational industrial working-class history (Nayak, 2006). He bore the scars of being 'left behind'. He was caught in a cycle of intermittent informal employment, benefits, drugs and alcohol abuse and semi-illegal activities. Steve took it badly when his boss, as a YTS cabinetmaker, refused to send him to college:

It was a classy job; making classy furniture. [When he did not have the opportunity to go to college] I just hit the ground and hit drugs, I said this job didn't matter but it did matter, obviously.

Reminiscent of Kathleen, Steve embodies this world of pain:

> Steve: You know one of the first drug deaths was in Partick. The first guy in Glasgow to die from drugs was in Partick. It was a friend of mine. I've lost about 20 friends through that, just young boys. The hurt is so big ... it's an easy way, you make money selling that and everybody seems to want to take it. There's nothing on the horizon for them. The only thing that saved me from that was that I was scared of needles. Seriously. I took everything else in my life. It gets to you. It affects your head, your head goes down and you chase your tail. It's a bit depressing. You take it hard at times.

Steve candidly expresses the stark effects of restructuring on men and masculinity. It is a degrading experience that forces his head down and he 'chases his tail', which reflects the spiral he feels he cannot break free from. Adapting is no longer an option but his comment about preferring to 'be skint' than working in the poorly paid jobs that migrants do suggests that Steve also feels he has some control of his situation.

Implicit in some of the male residents' life stories is a sense that class had failed them, whether they adapted or not. They had fought low pay, poor conditions, yard closures, the poll tax, and, in the end, gained nothing. Their dis-identification became a survival strategy, a means of looking after oneself or a manifestation of dispossession, alienation and fatalism, or indeed all of these things. The men adapted to the neoliberal demands of Thatcherism, which they all disparaged, and then again to New Labour, of which they were equally suspicious. Brian and Tim espoused values attuned to neo-liberalism: individualism; responsibilism; and consumer sovereignty. This 'adapt or die' attitude amongst the men offers a means of control through turbulent economic change. This reveals how masculinity, in relation to class and employment participation, is reconstructed and reinforced through control. This illustrates the significance of this particular historical experience for these men. Younger generations living in Partick experiencing labour market participation under New Labour have a qualitatively different experience again.

Youth and Class Identity: 'It's not clever', 'It's not cool'

Unlike Willis's (1977) Hammertown lads' anti-school culture and an education system that systemically failed and reproduced them as working-class, respondents in their early twenties grew up in a time without a steady stream of jobs but with wide access to both further and higher education. Subsequently, through access to education and higher levels of consumption, younger generations growing up in the 1990s were more inclined to extol the virtues of meritocracy and individualism. This creates an epistemological fallacy where life chances are extremely structured but young people respond to these in a highly individual ways (Furlong and Cartmel, 2006). The young people, those under 30, I interviewed saw themselves as their own biographical authors who created their own destiny (Beck, 1992). This was expressed through the narratives they constructed around individuality and choice.

Darren, 25, rejected class in an explicit way. I met Darren through snowball sampling, when his friend, a theatre director, recommended that I speak to him. I felt Darren was annoyed that he had been implicated as being working-class and was slightly hostile:

> Darren: I don't think I could say I was any specific class. Everyone normally says they're working-class, when there are so many different versions of what that is. I mean they thought it was defined by your attitude or job and from where you are but I mean it's something that's not very relevant in today's society because these things have changed. It's more a financial thing. So, people are people, all doing the same kind of jobs, call centres and that. There are a lot of people doing that kind of work but maybe doing that after something else. So you're maybe jumping into two different classes, which don't really make sense with a census.
>
> Kirsteen: You wouldn't identify yourself with one class?
>
> Darren: I mean I wouldn't say I'm someone who goes about thinking if they are a different class. I know I'm friends with people who are from the bottom all the way to the top and similar to people who don't earn any money at all. As I said, it's not something I go out and do, and it's not something I'd think about. I think it's illogical to use in today's society, the way that some jobs have only just appeared. Why should we be labelling ourselves all the time? It's crazy trying to categorise it. But yet you can think of it in that way. I mean in every area there are some pockets of the area that are better off or worse off than the others, the medium? *It's just not really a clever thing to go and categorise, when you know in every area there's a good bit and a bad bit. It's not cool is it?* [My emphasis]

For Darren the traditional political subjectivity related to being working-class is extraneous. He equates this as a mismatch between occupational position and social and cultural beliefs and attitudes. He resents being labelled and challenges the usefulness of classification measurements and interprets their inadequacy as signifying the end of class. For him, it no longer works as a meaningful subjectivity or form of political action, yet he recognises that class differences exist amongst his friends as well as being geographically perceivable. Darren is from a working-class background. He did well at school, got a degree and obtained a Master's qualification. In doing so, Darren felt that class was no longer a restriction, which deactivated the usefulness of such a classification or as a phenomenological experience. He spoke of the neighbourhood to me:

> Darren: Historically it's lower working-class, a lot of the people in the area I knew never really went to university and that. A lot of them in my area *would have been forced* to go to Victoria Drive as their secondary school and that closed down ... That would've been the high school I would've went to but my parents were adamant I shouldn't go there because they knew it had a bad reputation for being a bad school. They wanted me to go to Hyndland, in fact they wanted me to go to Jordanhill but the waiting list was too long and I wouldn't have been offered a place until I was in fourth year. So I decided to go to Hyndland ... Kids that have been maybe in my group, who left school at 16 and *forced into vocational* jobs and they had society kind of looking down at them. They are the ones who are actually doing better off because they have been forced into jobs and apprenticeships like plumbers and these are jobs that are in shortages. [My emphasis]

This school closure reflects the cuts in welfare spending but this goes unacknowledged. Instead Darren makes a distinction whereby he chose while his peers were forced. Forced into these jobs, they were also forced Victoria Drive School, which he deems to be less prestigious than schools Jordanhill and Hyndland, both of which are located in more affluent neighbourhoods. This then ensured that they followed a vocational rather than educational path. He identifies class as a structure which restricts and reproduces class locations. However, Darren experienced mobility, geographically, through moving to London, and social mobility through education. Class was not only a meaningful part of his life that located and positioned him, it was something that he fought to change and get control of by creating the prospect of choice:

> Kirsteen: So what university did you go to?
>
> Darren: *For my sins*, I went to Paisley to do my undergraduate degree and when I graduated from there I went down to Manchester University to do a Master's.
>
> Kirsteen: Why Manchester?
>
> Darren: Well looking on websites I looked at what universities I could go to and what was the best university for what I was interested in and Manchester was in the top five. [My emphasis]

Darren's use of this idiom 'for my sins' implies that attending Paisley University, a former polytechnic is punishment for being bad. This is a reference back to his working-class upbringing. While Darren disassociates with class, it remained palpable through how he negotiated and dealt with his own class position. He works to make sure that class does not control him, taking control of his own destiny by choosing (and paying for) a Master's at Manchester. Yet Darren is presently living back in Partick and is working in a low wage job in a social security call centre, demonstrating the circumscribed career choices of working-class graduates (Furlong and Cartmel, 2005).

Sean believes that, while he had opportunities, he fell victim to making the wrong choices but that those choices related to his environment. He was 25, living alone in a PHA flat. He had been homeless at 17 after a dispute with his dad. Social Services and a community psychiatric nurse supported him to set up his tenancy:

> Sean: I had loads of opportunities. I started an apprenticeship as an electrician but that's the first time my dad threw me out when I was 17 and I had to get to Paisley and I couldn't manage it. I've had opportunities … I just find I float through life. Here I am, 25, the time has went by so fast and all these things that have happened.

Sean initially blames himself for not taking up opportunities but contradicts himself by wishing he had the chance of being born into a different class position where he had more opportunities:

> Sean: […] if I could choose things differently I would have chosen to be born into a different environment, more opportunities and focus.

He now leads a relatively solitary life. He does not drink alcohol or go to pubs and he converted to Buddhism. I ask him if he identifies with being working-class:

> Sean: I dunno you see … the class thing bothers me … see I've stayed in what people call working-class areas but people just seem to think I am different at work. The class thing, you know, I just don't feel like I belong to a particular kind of class. People could say to me you are working-class because of "a", "b", "c" and "d". I think *I'm just me, I don't see myself.* I would say I am working-class because I am working, because the wage I get and the area that I stay in. I would say my dad and my step-mum have a lot of money and they part raised me and my girlfriend was middle-class and I lived with her for years. *But because of where I work, I am.* But people in my work, they don't read books so if I start talking about things I need to be careful, if I talk about books or use a word they don't know. They'll ask "what did you do last night?". I'll say "I was reading a book – Ernest Hemingway – have you heard of him?". You cannae say that. What would their reaction be? They would think that I'm an odd ball. [My emphasis]

Sean conceives of a traditional working-class culture: masculine, manual, and not literary. His perceived cultural dissimilitude with co-workers undermines his class identification. Sean does manual work in a fish factory – quintessentially working-class by occupational standards – but, culturally, he feels more middle-class. Yet at the same time he recognises the restrictions and immutability of class:

> Sean: I think people are restricted. People can say they are classless but class is something that we cannot escape from. You are born into a certain family and environment and that environment will only present so many opportunities to you. You can say that you are classless but there are things that restrict you, if you are born into a family with more money [it] helps you.

Again, despite consciousness of class, he attributes accountability for his life situation on the environment and himself.

Sylvie, a vivacious and fashionable 19-year-old, had an unsettled upbringing, living with her gran in Partick from the age of 10, while her mum and boyfriend live in the South Side of the city. Sylvie looked at me blankly when I asked about class. After some deliberation, she responded:

> Sylvie: I would say I'm working-class. But I asked my mum that when I was younger I asked her what are we, lower or what? And she said working-class.
>
> Kirsteen: How did she explain it to you?
>
> Sylvie: She didn't, I just accepted it and to be honest I don't know the proper definitions for class. To be honest, I mean, I don't really think there is one. People that just go through their life working in their job and trying to pay their mortgage – is that it?

Sylvie had no experience of life in Partick during its industrial heyday, encapsulated in Betty's recollection of Red Clydesiders and no identification or sense of collective membership of a class. However, later in our conversation she was vociferous about her own understanding of class. She talked of knowing class on the underground train, identifying who will get off at Partick and Kelvinhall and who at Hillhead, the West End stop for the university:

> Sylvie: It's weird. You sit on the underground and you can tell the people who are going to Hillhead. Honestly. You can say this carriage is going to clear and it does and the people left sitting you can say "Partick", "Partick", "Hillhead", and they will be sitting there give or take a couple but it seems to be more and more I get wrong and folk are going to Partick to Kelvinhall.

Sylvie is clearly consciousness of the increasing number of middle-class people moving into Partick. Her understanding of class also resonates with Walkerdine:

[...] class is not something that is simply produced economically, it is performed, marked, written on minds and bodies. We can "spot it a mile off" even in the midst of our wish for it no longer to be there. (Walkerdine, 2001: 215)

Sylvie does not experience class in a coherent collective way that but she knows that class exists and can read it off people on the underground. She reveals how she experiences this personally:

Sylvie: Sometimes we sit up the park. I don't speak really polite. I'm speaking more polite because I'm talking to you. And sometimes we go up Kelvingrove and some folk sit with guitars. And me and my cousin were up talking to people and because we were saying "aye" and "naw" I felt there was a guy who was like, he wasn't giving us the time of day as soon as we started talking. He was talking to other people and it was like we were getting a wide berth. It was like "stay away". So my cousin could see from my face that I wasn't happy and I walked away, but I felt like saying something, you know? You're not better than me because you stay on Byres Road [prominent street in the West End] in a house that your mam and dad bought for you. Bloody ... you know? And they speak with a different accent, you know? It's like higher pitched or something. They sing their sentences.

Sylvie occupies a working-class position yet does not recognise it. She may not feel a collective class membership or coherent identity but she knows her place. She reads a class distinction from university students – including me – but infers that she and the students are not necessarily dissimilar, it is just that some students are privileged enough to have their parents buy them property. This gives them a material upper hand but Sylvie the moral high ground. Having things bought for you in such a way is not necessarily an accolade. She retaliates by deriding their accents, but I am the only witness to this.

She spoke confidently and passionately about her plans, of which she had many. Yet there was a discernible undercurrent of uncertainty and self-doubt:

Kirsteen: What do you see yourself doing?

Sylvie: What, with my life? Well three or four years studying design in Falkirk, then hopefully teaching, maybe teaching but I've never tried interior design and I'm getting to try that. My friend Tracey is really into textiles and she's older, in her 40s, I think we should start our own business but she's not sure but I'm saying "don't give up, we can get a shop". Maybe not be loaded but comfortable. A wee house. And go out when I want. I'd be happy. I get nothing from the college, a loan, it's no much and £300 or £400 wages and I pay my gran digs and I have big Visa bills. It just goes dead quickly. My mum doesn't know, she says "you're the best dressed student I know!" You know what I mean? "The only student I know that's out every weekend". But just to be comfortable not to worry about money. Nice wee house, nice wee car. But how do you know you are going to like your job? No boundaries, well there will be some I guess. But being able to say I'm doing this or that at the weekend, instead of saying I can't do this or that. That's the story of my life!

Sylvie's life is bound by restricted opportunity, finances, mobility, in other words, class. She claims to go out every weekend but her closing statement claims that these boundaries and restrictions on doing what she would like is the story of her life. Her movement and choices are constrained. Sylvie resonates with Weis's (2004) Freeway female high school graduates. They voice their 'freedom dreams' in passive, class terms using phrases like 'maybe', 'I hope', 'hopefully', rather than statements of certainty. Her ambitions are modest, to be comfortable, to have a nice house and nice car, nothing excessive, not much more. Yet the future is uncertain, it is a risk. Sylvie's lack of finances may prohibit her from completing her college course. Young people's transitions to the labour market and housing are characterised by disruptions, although this is particularly acute for young people from working-class backgrounds (Furlong and Cartmel, 2005, 2006). But education is undoubtedly perceived by the respondents as the means to a better life, as Natasha relays in relation to her teenage children:

Natasha: Hyndland [Secondary School] is achieving really high so whether you come from a poor background or an affluent background you've got the education, it's there ... there's a chance then isn't it? There's a chance that people can get out of the circumstances they're in and I think that is the only way people can. That is why I say that hopefully through education that my kids would aspire to more than Tesco, fucking hopefully. I think they are going to be social workers, which is even more of a nightmare!

I was surprised by this. I thought Natasha and her family would be critical of the idea of meritocracy, because she and her partner Jimmy worked with disadvantaged young people. But it was clear they wanted better for their kids than they had themselves, and not for their chances to be limited by the local job market.

This is set within a context where working-class youths are vilified as 'yobs', 'chavs' and 'neds', as Law and Mooney (2006: 524) comment:

[...] "ned" culture [...] and antisocial cultures of violence, drugs and alcohol, fuelled in no small part by the Scottish Executive's determination to publicize its commitment to "law and order".

Respondents were keen to disassociate with this, seen in 24-year-old barman Gordon's recollection of school:

Gordon: My year was a brilliant year because it was mixed, you had your "chavvies" and the "neds" and then the "norms", like us. There was always the real intelligent ones and they moved away and actually done something because they are off studying, doing their degrees.

He positions himself as distinct from the 'chavvies' and 'neds', as a 'norm'; normal, and not above the 'intelligent ones'. This offers further insight into the reticence towards class from the young people I interviewed. They did not relate to class on a phenomenological level and there was a sense that what they understood by class was culturally outmoded. Yet class demarcated them and shaped their lives; Darren's mobility and Sean and Sylvie's lack of this, demonstrate the prevalence of class as an inequality. They not only felt that class was an anachronistic category, identifying with being working-class undermined their belief in meritocracy and doing so would circumscribe their opportunities of mobility. Being working-class reflected that you had not tried hard enough to change your position and the fear that you could be branded a 'chav' or a 'ned'. Recognising class and that their lives and opportunities were highly structured would render their individualised responses, plans and freedom dreams futile.

Class and Ethnicity and Neighbourhood Identification

In the previous chapter, I noted how class identity was racialised in relation to Catholic religion which played out at the neighbourhood level. These divisions had a material value and were upheld in labour processes. While commentators have recently debated the prevalence of 'Scotland's shame' of sectarianism (Devine, 2000) it was notable that younger respondents did not mention religion at all and it had little resonance with class identity. However, it was implicit in Darren's account. From an Irish Catholic family, he was sent by his parents to non-denominational schools which were deemed better than Catholic schools, leading him on to further education, thus gaining 'freedom' from social class. Steve and Gary, both Catholic and in their late thirties, referred to their experience of sectarianism in the neighbourhood:

> Steve: I'd like to get rid of the Orange Walk in Partick […] That brings a lot of trouble, it did on Saturday. I'm older now […] I'm not republican minded. I wouldn't go out to see that but why should they get to come round here and wind us up?

He went on to say that if he were younger he would have got involved in a fight afterwards, but if the Orange Walk had not occurred only a few days previous I doubt Steve would have mentioned it during our interview. He is not republican minded as he says, he does not identify with being Irish in this way. The same could be said for Gary:

See in Partick, it was always violent. It's not as much now but see in "Old Firm" games, you do not want to be in Partick after an "Old Firm" game. There was like, and again it goes back to religious segregation, but this Partick East is still kinda Catholic orientated pubs and Partick West [is] Protestant and it kinda keeps like that historically.

Sectarianism is perpetuated through the Rangers and Celtic football clubs' 'Old Firm' rivalry. Bilal, the only South Asian Muslim respondent, remarked that the only threat to his safety growing up in Partick were the football affiliated pubs, or 'cardigan shops', where you would go in wearing a jumper and leave with a cardigan, having been slashed. It was more dangerous to be Catholic or Protestant in the wrong place than Muslim. Notwithstanding, it would be inaccurate to say that sectarianism is relegated to 'Old Firm' matches and pubs (or that the only racism is against Irish Catholic, as will be discussed). Economically, the impact of sectarianism is still evident in statistics of neighbourhood Multiple Deprivation levels with many Catholic areas being in the top 10 worst wards (Walls and Williams, 2004). The area south of Dumbarton Road formally the Quarry area, which is the poorest in Partick, is the Catholic side and has experienced the most amount of gentrification, with housing prices rising from £36,000 in 1997 to £160,000 in 2004, whilst in wider Partick they rose from £47,850 to only £116,000 (Scottish Neighbourhood Statistics, 2009). However, sectarianism is now more residual rather than dominant so that social class and religion are as strongly correlated in the same way as they once were. A local Priest told me that he joked when parishioners asked whether homeowners in the new luxury development around his church actually attended: 'I say even the Tims[3] have money nowadays, sad to say!' Ethnicity and religion were also highly socially cohesive and a material resource for women. Bea's Golden Friends club members at the chapel were mostly Irish Catholic.

Akin to nationhood, neighbourhoods and cities can be racialised referents in people's imagination and identity construction (Virdee et al., 2006). The Scottish population are said to have proportionally higher levels of national identity (McCrone, 2001) and this can operate as a racialised referent at the neighbourhood level. Historically, Scottish identity has compounded sectarianism, seen in the racialisation of Irish Catholics as the disrespectable, recalcitrant, reactionary faction of the working-class non-Scottish Other. This decline in sectarian divisions could, arguably, be attributed to neoliberal neighbourhood based policies that construct the working-class identity in a more homogenous way as 'white' and poor (Haylett, 2001, 2003), rather than differentiating an Irish Other. While policies which operate at a national level, relating to security or immigration for example, construct racialised referents around 'extremists' and 'terrorists' as the Asian Other, neighbourhood level urban policies racialise the 'white' working-

---

3   This is a derogatory slang term for a Catholic, derived from the Irish slang for a Roman Catholic Taig or Tadhg.

class poor as the abject limit and antithesis to modernisation and regeneration (Haylett, 2001, 2003):

> [...] poor white working-class residents of council housing estates [...] have effectively been rendered "illegitimate subjects", symbolic of backwardness within a national discourse of progressive British multiculturalism. (Watt, 2006: 777)

In the US this same set of policies racialise 'black' ghettos as places responsible for perpetuating their own poverty, highlighting the material basis of this ideology, which is levelled at the most disinvested areas. This racialised Othering is used to justify the pursuit of policy which supports social mix and gentrification, particularly under the auspices of cosmopolitanism. Some residents, like Nick, expressed this ideology. Moving to Partick 25 years ago, he saw himself as a cut above other 'born and bred' residents and enjoyed the increasing social mix brought about by incoming affluent groups:

> Nick: There's a doctor upstairs, one next door, a computer programmer, an original family and others are professionals. They work in computer design. No social housing. I like it. It's better. The one family we had we had a problem with. *A typical Partick mother, balling and shouting.* She took a stroke and lost her voice so that solved that problem. She was always balling at her kids. [My emphasis]

He uses the term 'typical Partick' to describe someone 'born and bred' in the area whose behaviour he finds disrespectable or vulgar. Being 'born and bred' is an implicitly racialised referent, for 'white', racist, backwards and those who refuse the tide of modernisation. Yet contra to the image and representation of working-class estates as abject, homogeneous masses, they are, in reality, more heterogeneous and often multi-ethnic (Mooney and Danson, 1997, 1998). Partick has a higher mix of nationalities of residents than in Scotland overall. For 87 per cent of the national population Scotland is their country of origin, while this is 78 per cent in Partick, but it is predominately a 'white' population. Thus only two respondents were 'non-white' and Scottish born; Tim whose parents originate from West Africa and Bilal whose are South Asian, whilst Phil was from Australia, Natasha and Sonny from England and Molly and Janey from America.

There was some evidence of racist views amongst 'white' residents. Rhonda and Margaret complained about what they saw as privileged housing allocation to migrant groups, using the racialised referent 'bogus asylum seekers' and blaming the growth in Asian owned shops for the deterioration of the retail on Dumbarton Road. This view was not shared by other respondents. Partick actually provides a source of more positive aspects of working-class culture and identities (Haylett, 2003; Russo and Linkon, 2005; Ward et al., 2007) which is described by the residents as 'cosmopolitan'. This was akin to Hannerz's (1990, 1992) definition of cosmopolitan as a willingness to engage with the Other. David moved to Partick from across the river in Ibrox:

> David: This side is more cosmopolitan, it's a bit more integrated. You meet all sorts of walks of life in Partick.

He elaborated that this mix referred to diversity in ethnicity, sexuality and class. This was echoed by Natasha, who was English:

> Natasha: As a Londoner if I went to somewhere like Drumchapel, and I don't mean this in a bad way, I think that there is a racist problem in Glasgow, right? Not necessarily as much here because it is bordering the West End and near the university. When I first moved up here the West End would be the only place where you saw someone who was "black" or Jewish or someone who was gay. There was that cosmopolitan mix that has spread out into Partick and I'd never experienced any racism from anyone within this area, from people that I don't know, or if I go out. Maybe that's about my confidence but I don't experience it. If you were to experience any racism it would be predominantly from them [incoming gentrifying groups].

Tim identified with being working-class and he drew comparison and distinction between class and ethnic identity:

> Kirsteen: Would you say then that you identify with a class, would you say you are working-class, for example?
>
> Tim: Yeah, yeah, yeah I wouldn't hesitate on that one at all. It only matters to the people who it means something to, on a different level from other folk 'cause that's the way human beings like to define each other.
>
> Kirsteen: What, like a group, cultural thing?
>
> Tim: It's human behaviour, you know when you think about it, my parents come from a different country and coming here, you know, seeing how the Muslim community and the African community get on with certain things, they're kind of considered a different community, different citizens yet again, when I was younger. But now there's a kinda mentality, the kinda the same now. I mean if you've got lots of money, you've got lots of money but if you've not, you're working-class basically, so there's a clear divide there man, with people who are coming from a different community, outside the community from something its totally different yet again.

Tim feels that categorisations, which may have distinguished African or Muslim groups as the Other in Glasgow, have blurred. Nonetheless he reifies these, suggesting that being Muslim or African provides a distinct but similar phenomenological experience to being working-class. He believes that working-class and ethnic groups share a mentality which is different from that of powerful groups, those he describes as having lots of money. Working-class is presented as an inclusive category but being African or Muslim exists alongside being working-class. The phenomenological idea of working-classness and ethnicity are closely aligned. This suggests a commonality of experience. This was echoed by Bilal, who in contrast to Natasha, did not believe that racism was a problem in Glasgow:

> Bilal: Glasgow [City Council] had this campaign to curb racism in Glasgow and within Scotland itself. It was concurrent with migrants and illegal immigrants coming here. I was quite surprised that Scotland had to have a campaign like that especially with my memories of Glasgow and living in Partick. It was just so, you know, there was no demarcation between your colour, your ethnicity, who you are and what you did, you know? It was just a case of you just got on with it, as long as you are good to us we are good to you and certainly for me Partick was synonymous with that growing up and that attitude.

Being from Partick is a referent for being working-class which is inclusive of different ethnic and racial identification. This suggests that Scottishness articulated at the local level as a form of neighbourhood nationalism is not ethnically bound (Virdee et al., 2006). People's identification with being from Partick was not strictly a racial referent, rather neighbourhood nationalisation was an expression of cultural belonging and, specifically, of being working-class. This was a way of expressing a sense of identity and collectivity that was class based without identifying with the denigrated working-class identity. This also challenges the ideology within neoliberal neighbourhood based policy and attests to the idea of the working-class cosmopolitan (Werbner, 1999), who is Othered and willing to engage with the Other.

Conclusion: Disassociation as Calculating Control

While traditional class collectivities have weakened, we can see that class still endures as a meaningful experience. Complexly, working-class respondents were conscious of the vagaries of capitalism and neoliberal policies and acknowledged that their occupation was working-class but did not relate this to their personal situation and disassociated with class instead. However, there was coherence in this action of disassociation which must be disentangled from issues of gender, age and ethnicity and 'race'. Disassociation with class has a broader resonance across these axes. We can see male disassociation with class in relation to the displacement of industrial hegemonic masculinity. The cultural and political defeat of the masculine proletariat figure sees local men reject class identity and traditional allegiances, like trade unionism, and instead express a narrative of adaptation.

Women who, by contrast, are ostensibly 'enfranchised' by deindustrialisation in the sense that they increasingly enter the labour market via the expanding service economy. Their labour market entry extends their traditional caring role which contributed to them rejecting class and constructing a narrative of respectability (Skeggs, 1997). Young people, disconnected from the same traditional class cultural experience, position themselves as being in control of their own biography (Beck, 1992) through a narrative of individuality. Class identity is rejected across these axes, pathologised as lacking respectability, power, or individuality.

Residents sought to calculate control through individualised responses, acting in a self-motivated and responsible way. This is evident in Brian's 'forward planning', or residents who focussed on gaining and retaining some control through respectability or educational achievements. Featherstone (1991) identifies middle-class 'calculated de-control' as a shift in moral behaviour, whereby they become less restrained without losing privileges of their status. In a similar vein, the notion of the edge worker (Lyng, 2005) has been created to explain the behaviours of those in privileged positions who attempt to lose control, by operating on the periphery of risk. These are highly stratified interpretations. The experience of being working-class offers less control over ones' life and the capacity to take or manage risks. Dis-identifying with class is a tactic of control, was acted out by individuals to manage their experiences of inequality. The writers who apply the concept of disassociation have attributed it to middle class cultural differentiation from the working class. That is, they do not fully concede the material inequities and basis for this ideology. Yet it is no coincidence that the individualised values of self-determination support neoliberal politics. Seen in this way, residents' narratives of individual choice and control which efface old Labour, social welfarism and industrialism, are a class based process and a response to urban restructuring and neoliberalism. Therefore, the epochal prognostications which claim class is no longer relevant amidst cultural fragmentation and individualisation are not only overstated, they miss the point. We can see a clear material basis in the promotion of individualism and residents' desire for control, which results in this dis-identification. However, suggesting that the human subject is created via ideology and economics only (Althusser, 1971) implies a mechanical view of human beings whose actions are determined by forces outside of their control. This debilitates purposive action and promotes fatalism. Residents' disassociation with class could then be interpreted as their incorporation into the dominant ideology but the picture is highly complex and much more nuanced. Understanding this as a hegemonic process recognises that structure is not wholly determining. Residents identify and dis-identify with class simultaneously. Consciousness itself is more than a reflection of a basic or more material level of existence, but an active mode of social being (Williams, 1986).

So while the connection between class location and cultural identity appears to have unravelled (Bottero, 2004) it can be reconstituted through residents' relationship with place. Traditional working-class culture can operate as a racialised referent (Blokland, 2005). Urban policy denigration of traditional identities also racialises neighbourhood problems in relation to the poor 'white' working-class (Haylett, 2001, 2003). The material underpinning of this ideology is that it justifies the need for social mix. Non-Scottish and 'non-white' residents are not pathologised in the same way as the 'traditional' 'born and bred' working-class. Subsequently, they displayed *less* disassociation and had a more positive association with this identity, perceiving solidarity between the working-class and ethnic experience. 'Neighbourhood nationalism' expressed a covert, complex and positive class referent. This suggests that class location and identity and consciousness may be reconstituted through attachment to geographical location. Here place-based attachment acts as a proxy for class. The relationship between place and social identities can elucidate both class position and identity, via mobility and embodied subjectivity (Savage, 2000). There has been an acknowledgement of middle-class place-based attachment. Their location in residential space is seen as marker of their identity and social position. Middle-class self-making via elective belonging (Savage et al., 2005) is a response to ontological insecurity, relating to the restructuring of social positions and class relations. This is not considered in the same way for working-class residents. Belonging can express ontological security and physical attachment to place. Whether your location is secure or threatened by displacement, can become a key indicator for understanding class and socio-spatial neighbourhood relations. The following chapter inverts the notion of 'elective belonging' (Savage et al., 2005) to look at how class is experienced *coherently* in face of the processes of dis-identification via a relationship to place. It looks at the interrelationship between psychic and physical landscapes of class, exploring the impacts of restructuring on material and ontological place-based attachment.

Chapter 3
Elective Belonging and Fixity to Place

It is vital then to explore the relationship between class, place and urban restructuring through residents' narratives of location (Anthias, 2005). Class position and identities were expressed through residents' attachment to place on both phenomenological and material levels. It is commonly assumed that the traditional relationship between working-class identity and place attachment was compromised by deindustrialisation and the decline of industry-based communities so much so that the focus of contemporary sociological studies of the post-industrial neighbourhood falls on the relationship between middle-class position and identity. Savage et al. (2005) develop the concept of 'elective belonging' to express how people attach their residential biography to their 'chosen' location despite having no prior ties to it. Neighbourhood attachment is nowadays thought to be a middle-class reaction to ontological insecurity (Butler and Robson, 2003; Atkinson and Bridge, 2005). Their chosen locations articulate and stabilise their social identity by expressing their social self through where they live (Butler and Robson, 2003; Savage et al., 2005; Rofe, 2003), whereas, 'locals' have poor ties and do not choose to attach their social identity to their neighbourhood. Working-class attachment to former industrial neighbourhoods is relegated to nostalgia, where people remember the past in a selective, positive way and by contrast have a negative interpretation of the present situation (Chase and Shaw, 1989; Blokland, 2001). Alternatively, their connection is conceived as one which lacks agency, suggesting that they are trapped in a degraded locality (Bauman, 1998; Kintrea et al., 2008; Charlesworth, 2000). This forecloses a meaningful working-class relationship to place. As intimated in the last chapter, residents' neighbourhood attachment may be a proxy for expressing class amidst restructuring processes that denigrate more traditional class identities. With this in mind, here I explore the complex and reconstituted place-based identity of both 'local' and 'incomer' working-class residents, and consider how these categories are constructed in the process, to examine working-class agency and place-based attachment, particularly 'elective belonging' (Savage et al., 2005). To date, this is a term reserved to capture middle-class place-attachment: how they express their social identity in relation to their chosen location. I challenge and extend its usage by applying to working-class place-attachment, conceptualising their material and cultural place-based attachment as a response to ontological insecurity wrought by urban restructuring. This then allows us to problematise issues of choice and control over one's ability to fix oneself in the neighbourhood and, importantly, remain fixed in the neighbourhood. It is in one's control over their fixity to place that class experiences of place connectedness are elucidated.

There is much analytical usefulness of residential location in understanding class. Locational attachment can reconnect the relationship between class position and identity through the concept of elective fixity. Belonging and fixity to place seem to have more purchase if understood in relation to choice and control and related to the neoliberal hegemony.

Elective Belonging in Partick

The analytical categories 'local' and 'incomer' have traditionally been applied to describe the relationship to place in community studies. Savage et al. (2005) suggest a new orientation to place whereby local attachment is detached from historical communal roots. Contra to the 'locals', who are nostalgically trapped in the past and have weak ties to the neighbourhood and the transients who are here today, gone tomorrow, elective belonging defines the unique place-based attachment of incoming groups whose chosen place of residence is congruent with their life story (Savage et al., 2005). Overall, most of the respondents made strong claims to place but this was often complicated and contradictory and did not relate to whether they were 'locals' or 'incomers'. Residents demarcated as 'locals' or 'born and bred' are those people who were born and grew-up in the area. This only constituted about 30 per cent of those residents I interviewed.

Table 3.1   'Local' residents and tenure

Name	Age	Employment status	Currently living	Tenure
Betty	49	Not working	Partick	PHA
Leona	37	Bar worker and park ranger	Partick	PHA
Mary	67	Retired accounts worker	Partick	Private
Bea	62	Long-term disability	Partick	Homeowner
Loretta	42	Business and property owner	Partick	Homeowner
Gary	37	Local council officer, p/t student	Kelvindale	Private rent
Gordon	24	Bar worker	Partick	With parents
Kathleen	33	Catering worker	Clydebank	Social housing
Danny	51	Not working	Partick	PHA
Agnes	69	Retired cleaner, debt collector	Maryhill	PHA
Darren	25	Call centre operator	Partick	With parents – Homeowners
Dylan	19	Apprentice electrician	Partick	With parents – PHA
Rosa	54	Community worker	Partick	PHA

Name	Age	Employment status	Currently living	Tenure
Robert	73	Retired Archivist	Unsure	Unsure
Rachael	49	Full-time single mum	Partick	PHA
Bilal	37	Nurse	Partick	With parents – Homeowners
Alice	37	Retired social worker	Partick	Homeowner

'Incomers' were those residents who were not born in the area but moved there. They were not generally gentrifiers, most were working-class and social renters who negotiated the move into the neighbourhood through PHA, with the exception of Stuart, Angus, John and Alison who were homeowners. 'Incomers' originated from diverse areas: London, Chicago, Sydney and Northern Ireland.

Table 3.2   Incomers' residential biography and tenure

Name	Age	Employment status	Area of origin	Currently living	Tenure
Brian	63	Long-term disability	Glasgow West End	Partick	Homeowner
Alison	32	Lecturer	Ireland	Partick	Homeowner
Natasha	39	Drugs worker	London	Partick	PHA
Jimmy	42	Youth care home worker	Glasgow North west	Partick	PHA
John	35	Urban regeneration officer	Ayrshire	Mavisbank Riverside	Homeowner
David	59	Retired policeman	Glasgow East End	Partick	PHA
Stuart	34	Urban regeneration officer	Aberdeen	Partick	Homeowner
Fi	65	Retired	Glasgow South Side: Gorbals	Partick	Homeowner
Phil	37	P/t masseuse	Sydney	Partick	Private rent
Bill	68	Long-term disability	Institutionalised	Partick	PHA
Alan	41	Library assistant	Glasgow East End	Partick	PHA
Louise	41	Community worker	Hyndland	Partick	PHA
Nick	66	Retired engineer	Clydebank	Partick	Homeowner
Tim	43	Bouncer p/t	Glasgow West End	Partick	PHA
Sean	25	Factory worker and audio typist	Glasgow South Side	Partick	PHA

Name	Age	Employment status	Area of origin	Currently living	Tenure
Mhairi	48	TEFL teacher	Clydebank	Partick	Homeowner
Molly	37	Full-time single mum	Unsure	Partick	PHA
Paul	41	Long-term disability	Glasgow North: Possil	Partick	PHA
Steve	38	Long-term disability	Glasgow West End	Partick	PHA
Sylvie	19	P/t student, p/t PR assistant	Glasgow South Side: Ibrox	Partick	With gran – PHA
Lou	42	Long-term disability	Glasgow North	Partick	PHA
Angus	36	Lecturer	Did not ask	Partick	Homeowner
Lisa	48	Long-term disability	West End	Partick	PHA
Sonny	67	Retired builder	England	Partick	PHA
Janey	44	Masseuse instructor/ full-time mum	Chicago	Dumbarton	Homeowner
Norma	38	Community worker	Ayrshire	Partick	PHA
Gareth	52	Masseuse/community worker	Glasgow West End	Partick	PHA
Maggie	53	Not working	Glasgow West End	Partick	PHA
Angie	37	Long-term disability, former transport worker	Glasgow South Side: Ibrox	Partick	PHA
Donna	50	Special needs teacher	Dumbarton	Partick	PHA
Stephen	54	Long-term disability	Glasgow West End: Hillhead	Partick	PHA
Rhonda	66	Long-term disability	Glasgow West End: Yorkhill	Partick	PHA

Both 'born and bred' and 'incomer' residents tended to have equally strong local attachment which they expressed through the axiom 'I belong tae Partick'.[1] This was historical reference, judging by its frequent use amongst older residents.[2] Use of this axiom had strong class connotations, which related to the former industrial production and social reproduction that had dominated the area. Usage of 'I belong tae Partick' was especially common at Golden Friends. A number of the female only members had moved out to peripheral estates, like Mary, who

---

1   I received a heart-warming hand-written letter from a former local resident. She wrote seven pages on her life in Partick and why she loved the neighbourhood. She signed off 'I belong to Perdic, a Perdic girl I will always be' – 'Perdic' the old Gaelic form of Partick.

2   It is likely to be a reference to the fact that Partick used to be a burgh independent from Glasgow.

lived in Knightswood but said, 'I belong tae Partick, this is my home', and all the other women at her table agreed. The loss they express for their former way of life was palpable. Bea gave me a very incisive account of the experience of the women at the club:

> There was a big sense of promise because you knew that these women were moving out to new houses and things were going to change and oh boy they did. They loved the houses they moved to but they didn't like the areas because they were then isolated, whereas Partick was such a community of people, you could go to anyone's door. Major problems could be sorted without the police. So in that respect it was great for the big change to come along but in the other hand it lost a lot. They may have had a phone and eventually a television, and mind that, that was fantastic but moving away from Partick was something that people were not happy about, even if they had their phones and their bathrooms.

Older residents who had responded positively to the overspill strategy regretted doing so. The promise of indoor toilets and central heating did not pay off in the long term. The loss of networks and support they experienced through this helped make the club so popular. It revived locality as a social and material resource. The club ran on the miniscule submission fees from members, rather than receiving any public funding. Bea organised a weekly bingo activity where the prize was food items. They also ran a free raffle every meeting, which distributed tinned goods. The women were practical and frugal and, above all else, relied on each other. They had known each other so long they often caused confusion by using maiden names when telling stories. It was a close, small network, strikingly predicated upon spatial proximity and kinship. Having grown-up together and never leaving the wider West End, now, in their 60s, 70s and 80s, they find solace from one another at the club. Strong claims to place were not simply an identity marker, although it did serve this function, it was a means of survival. This was a strong articulation of belonging rather than nostalgia. Belonging expressed an identity and way of life they associated with Partick. Harking back to the past was a way of expressing how things had changed rather than claiming that things were once better:

> Bea: [...] Don't get me wrong, life was not easy, and although they say the good old days, it was hard [...] I don't like to dream about the poorer side of it because it was poor, it was a hardship. But there were happier times of singing and dancing.

This was particularly meaningful for women, who rejected the past industrial times which had entailed back-breaking labour. Their expression of belonging to Partick referred to the social practices that had been effectively formed under industrialism. This was a reflexive action and response to ontological insecurity wrought by post-industrialism. Indeed, residents also shared recognition of the processes of gentrification taking place in their neighbourhood and some were not entirely averse to this change. As Steve remarks, 'I'm happy with it, [regeneration] I like the new but you have to keep a bit of old with a bit of new, you know?' This will be explored further in chapters 4 and 5.

Levels of local attachment were not determined by age. Residents with a stronger reference to the past wanted to preserve local social practices, but not exclusively so. I was a little surprised to hear Darren reject London in favour of Partick:

> When I've lived in Partick it's kind of been the centre of my life, going to school. It's somewhere I've had a strong affinity for, I don't know why.

This was perhaps because the majority of people interviewed reported that they *currently* belonged to a close knit community, contra to Savage et al.'s (2005) and Blokland's (2001) suggestion that residents often bemoan the loss of cohesive communities which never really existed:

> Betty: It's quite a close knit community. Everybody knows everybody. I don't know what that's like for the young ones.

This was, in fact, something enjoyed by the younger residents:

> Gordon: See, Partick they're very friendly. It's just got a real good strong community, a big sense of it. People always know everyone and there's no hassle. I go to work and I'm just saying hello to everyone. It's just dead vibrant.

Younger residents like Gordon also used the phrase 'I belong tae Partick'. Although not identifying with being working-class directly, he claimed to always be a 'Partick boy', and he took comfort from that, saying 'it's like a pair of old slippers'. Local attachment offered a familiarity, a self-affirmation that provided an ontological security for younger and older generations, although not everyone experienced this. Steve jokingly complained that 'everyone knows everyone' which meant that you 'cannae get away with nothing, nosey, nosey, nosey' and Kathleen no longer wanted to live in Partick because she felt judged by locals.

'Local' residents' orientation towards place could be described as elective belonging, where their place of residence is congruent with their life story (Savage et al., 2005). Yet the articulation of attachment through historical recollections were not exclusive to 'locals', 'outsiders' authentically shared in this recollection as it resonated past cultural formations which related to the wider city. Contra to Savage et al.'s account, 'locals' exerted some moral supremacy in their attachment to place. Those 'local' to other areas in Glasgow made clear they were not claiming Partick 'born and bred' status. Brian said that Partickonians were protective of the fact they were born and brought up in the neighbourhood:

> [...] it's not just Partick, that is any district in Glasgow, I'm an Anderston buddy even though I haven't hung around there for 40 years. [Anderston only being about a mile east of Partick]

Rhonda said she was an 'immigrant', as she came from neighbouring Yorkhill. Angie, coming from Ibrox, remarked that those local to Partick seemed keen to stay in the neighbourhood:

> One thing I've noticed though is people from Partick tend to stay in Partick. They're not trying to get out. I see the same faces all the time. See my mother, I didn't know until we moved here, she was born in Mansfield street, she moved when she was three so this is her really coming back.

But there was a resonance that 'incomers' could be 'locals' through generational connections. Angie moved to Partick because her mother, who originated from the neighbourhood, gravitated back there. This shaped Angie's own attachment to the area:

> Angie: It's a feeling. I feel like I've stayed here for longer. This feels like home. Why Partick? It was a better class of living I thought, better for my mother. More shops, more going on. I wanted life to be better for her.

Partick has a magnetic pull for people. Gary, Sonny and David all referred to it as a 'Mecca':

> Gary: People gravitate towards it because they have family networks here. They have been dispersed from the '60s and the slum clearances and out of the likes of Partick and Anderston, they all got moved to Castlemilk, Drumchapel, Pollok, Knightswood. So that is why you still get people coming. There wasn't any amenities and social networks so they come back for the pubs and shops. Drumchapel was just housing. Put everyone out there, nice houses, no community. I think they were having a bloody laugh. Partick has got everything. If you want to go shopping, you don't need to leave Partick. High amenities, transport, social life, if you want it, and good housing.

So, for 'incomers' to Partick, the move there was congruent with their biography. It often expressed a return to the neighbourhood and an articulation of their working-class biography.

Similarly, the notion of 'local' identity was complex. Many 'born and bred' residents had lived elsewhere, including abroad, and had returned to Partick after extended time away so they were not 'local' or 'born and bred', in a pure sense. 'Local' and 'born and bred' are, therefore, unstable referents.

Table 3.3   Locals' residential biography with tenure

'Born and bred' residents	Age	Currently living	Lived anywhere else	Tenure
Betty	49	Partick	Australia	PHA
Leona	37	Partick	Australia, 3 years	PHA
Mary	67	Partick	London, 5 years	Private
Bea	62	Partick	No	Homeowner
Loretta	42	Partick	Southside, Glasgow, 5 years	Homeowner
Gary	37	Kelvindale	Kelvindale, currently	Private rent
Gordon	24	Partick	Southside, Glasgow (moving to Australia)	With parents – Homeowners
Kathleen	33	Clydebank	Drumchapel	Social housing
Danny	51	Partick	No	PHA
Agnes	69	Maryhill	Maryhill, currently	PHA
Bilal	37	Partick	Birmingham, 12 years	With parents – Homeowners
Darren	25	Partick	London, 2 years	With parents – Homeowners
Dylan	19	Partick	No	With parents – PHA
Rosa	54	Partick	No	PHA
Robert	73	Hyndland	Southside, Glasgow, 20 years	Unsure
Rachael	49	Partick	No	PHA
Alice	37	East Kilbride	East Kilbride, currently	Homeowner

In some cases, 'locals' were from migrant families, like Darren, Gary, Betty, Bilal and Lisa. Unlike connotations in older community studies, 'born and bred' and 'local' are not racial referents. As discussed in the previous chapter, expressing your belonging to Partick was not ethnically bound. It expressed cosmopolitanism rather than being racialised, as it is within urban policy, as 'white' and the abject limit to modernisation (Haylett, 2001, 2003). Comments from Bilal and Tim in the previous chapter expressed how ethnicity, class and place-attachment formed an interconnected subjectivity. Bilal very proudly associated with this 'local' identity which expressed a working-class cosmopolitanism: being the Other and having solidarity with the Other. So did Lisa as a second-generation Italian immigrant. Her ethnicity intersected with her attachment to the area:

> Lisa: Partick is very multicultural. It's always had that crossover […] I'm really proud of Partick, of being from Partick. Don't know how it manifests itself. It's a feeling, like you go into the butchers and you chat away, have a natter. Folk

stop, talk say hello. I cannae walk from my house to the pub without meeting somebody – "How you doing? Not seen you for a bit". You don't know their names but you know their coupons [*sic* – faces] ... I'm part of Partick, a lot of Partick punters don't see me like that. They're all born and bred. I feel part of this area and it's got a rich cultural history, with Irish immigrants and the Italian immigrants, the Highlanders.

Within the neighbourhood, Lisa was differentiated as being born outside Partick rather than being Italian. Bilal considered himself typically Partick, 'born and bred'. He had meaningful, historical, family attachments to Partick. It was where his father and uncles built up their business when they first moved to the UK as part of Commonwealth immigration in the 1960s. This underpinned his identification with the neighbourhood.

By contrast, 'incomers' to the neighbourhood who were middle-class displayed a different kind of attachment to the area, which did not demonstrate elective belonging. Angus, Stuart and John clearly differentiated themselves from 'locals'. Angus perceived and articulated the cultural polarity between old working-class groups and new middle-class groups, which he felt part of, in the neighbourhood. Stuart displayed some elective belonging to the area. Originally from Aberdeen, he described his experience of moving to Partick after graduating from Edinburgh University:

> Stuart: [...] this one time I was early meeting a friend in the Clyde Valley pub and I was standing at the bar with a pint, minding my own business. And this guy came up to me and said "Hey big man, how you doing? Why you here? What you up to?". And I'm thinking what does this guy want, you know? But that's what it's like here, it's like the polar opposite to London. Partick recognised me when I was a stranger and I think they would do that to anyone [...] That's the kind of stuff that you really like. You're pleased that it's a traditional working-class community and a stable working-class community, especially coming from Edinburgh.

Stuart does not see himself as part of this local working-class culture, but he does enjoy it. However, in praising the area, he is culturally differentiating himself from it. He told me that at work, in the city marketing bureau, he discussed how fitting he thought the 'Glasgow: Scotland with Style' slogan was for the city as it encapsulated the 'typical' Glaswegian, with their 'trashy glamour'; 'dressed up to the nines but no jacket'. He saw this as typical of Partick, recalling the night bus home from town, where you 'get some sights and a good sing-song'. Stuart said this as an expression of fondness but it was, nonetheless, Othering, attaching disgust to 'local' subjects. Not only did these residents clearly differentiate themselves from 'locals', their locational biographies were distinct, demonstrating greater power and choice. They did not share in the collective experience of the neighbourhood, because they had no ontological or material necessity to do so. This is at odds with

Savage et al.'s (2005) understanding of the elective belonging; these residents did not have stronger attachment simply because they have elected to live in their neighbourhood.

Therefore, elective belonging was not just the proclivity of incoming groups, 'locals' experienced it too. Indeed, it was middle-class respondents who were less likely to articulate elective belonging and it was, instead, more salient for working-class respondents, who experience more ontological insecurity under restructuring. Places can be both historical residues of the local and sites chosen by particular social groups to announce their identity. The two are not incongruent. To differentiate them is to suggest that there is no meaningful social identity to be claimed from relating to residual culture. Local belonging related to a sense of ownership, not in the material sense of homeownership, on the contrary, the majority of these residents were social renters. Elective belonging seemed to speak of an attachment to the residual industrial culture. It expressed agency in the face of changing social relations. This ownership related to an emotional and personal investment in the neighbourhood. There are not essential differences between 'incomers' and 'local' residents' attachment. 'Locals' displayed elective belonging, commonly associated with incoming middle-class groups. However, being working-class, they were unlikely to have much power or choice to elect a neighbourhood in the same way as middle-class residents and faced the prospect of being denigrated for doing so, which I will discuss further shortly.

Place as a Proxy for Class

This orientation to place was class-based. Some residents needed to stay and be fixed in the area; it was not that they were fixed there beyond their choice but rather being fixed in the neighbourhood provided networks and coping strategies. Most of the 'locals' were locally embedded in neighbourhood life. Gordon, Leona, Bea, Bilal, Rosa and Loretta all worked in the neighbourhood. Steve rarely even left the area. He had been unemployed for a few years, drifting in and out of casual labour that he picked up from people he met at his local pub. He relied on his parents, who helped look after his son as well as him. He went to them three or four nights a week for dinner. This was out of necessity, rather than a social call:

> Steve: [laughs] I borrow. And sometimes I steal [laughs] you've got to [...] I make sure I pay my bills and have enough to treat the wean [*sic* – child]. I have some for messages but I'm spoiled and go to my mum's for dinner so I don't need to buy messages [food shopping], that saves me. You do what you've got to do. I'm skint this week and next week. Feck it ... *I could be trapped in my house for a couple of days*. [My emphasis]

Similar to Bauman's (1998) interpretation, Steve is firmly fixed in place; he relies on local support but sometimes it confines him and he is rendered immobile. But it was more beneficial for him to live in Partick than other neighbourhoods. Having family and friends close by was a crucial strategy in dealing with poverty and in getting through daily routines like accessing childcare to get to work. In many of the informal or home-working employment strategies that women undertook, spatial proximity was essential. Notably, all local residents interviewed, except Kathleen, had family members living in the neighbourhood. Some had only their immediate family, parents, children and siblings, while others like, Darren and Gary, Loretta, Bilal and Mary had aunts, uncles and cousins in the neighbourhood. Those with family also had weekly contact with them – this varied from socialising to carrying out caring roles. Gordon, 24, had a very strong relationship with his family, so much so that he went out with his parents for a last orders drink two or three nights a week. Loretta was one of only two 'local' homeowners. She was financially better off than all the other 'locals' interviewed, as she made a living from owning properties and had more control over whether she stayed in the area or not. Her capital and livelihood was locally invested and contingent. She had just bought into an ironmongers business and used goods and labour from there to help in the maintenance of her properties.

Residents recognised the importance of having solidarity in relation to socio-economic inequality:

> Bea: [...] neighbourly spirit has gone because we are not all in the same boat. You have to be in the same boat. They're not going to discuss it [hardships] because they are not in the same boat.

> Fi: People don't talk. If people don't have money now they don't talk about it. I mean we'd be like, "I've only got a pound" [...] we were all poor so it wasn't that bad. When I moved here it wasn't an issue, *everyone was like me*, we didn't have any money. *I never felt inferior* because I had to go to the pawn or get a meat parcel [the cheapest cuts of meat from the butcher]. Jean Murphy used to always have money and her man gave it to her on Wednesdays, and she would give us this fiver and we could pay it back whenever. [My emphasis]

The idea of 'being in the same boat' provided material, social and emotional support. Inequality was a commonly shared experience amongst 'incomers' and 'locals'. Janey, who moved to Partick in 1980 aged 18, invokes a similar motif:

> Partick had a real responsibility to each other, the poor need the poor. Now the big difference is between the "haves" and the "have nots".

Elective belonging via collective experience is a powerful resource, especially for women. Knowing other people were 'in the same boat' meant that residents were not Othered. It had social and psychological benefits as well as providing a material resource, based on local networks. Golden Friends offered a place in Partick for current and former residents to come together to support each other and recall the past. The solidarity, 'we are in it together' through this time of change, indicates that some class identification existed and it facilitated redistributive actions amongst residents. Lisa was working for the then Department of Social Security at the time:

> Thatcher came in '79 and the transition from Supplementary Benefits to the Social Fund and all that. I saw it all happening first hand and we knew anyone with half a brain or in the union knew what was going on. There was nothing, again, that we could do. And I watched that impact on the community as well what was happening to elderly people – utterly confused, distressed, what to do? They've lost their heating allowance, dietary allowance. It used to be great [whispers] we used to let them pile them up – heating allowances – [mock conversation]:
>
> "You've got high ceilings haven't you?"
>
> "No".
>
> "Aye you have".
>
> "You've got problems with your diet".
>
> "Not really".
>
> "Aye you have".
>
> It put people's money up but that all went by the wayside. You couldn't do that anymore and that impacted upon a lot of people.

The shared experience of inequality was an essential resource for residents. Residents' drew from a 'sameness': the notion of a shared experience of hardship and inequalities, which offered a material and social form of support. Lisa explained that this solidarity gave her affirmation which she did not experience living as a working-class teenager in the middle-class neighbourhood of Hyndland after her father was promoted to a manager in a steel work factory:

> Lisa: [...] I'm still friends to this day with people, clients. You were having impromptu benefit meetings in the pub getting them sorted out. I eventually turned from gamekeeper to poacher and went into welfare rights. I became a punter, if you like, because I socialised here. I have more empathy for people here than I did up there [Hyndland].

Part of the reason behind this bonding was that they were brought together as the Other in the face of the restructuring and denigration of traditional working-class identities. Janey noted that the problem lay in the fact that there were increasingly more 'haves' in the neighbourhood than 'have nots', who are threatened with displacement, which she herself has experienced, now living in a town outside Glasgow:

> Janey: [...] and that is the biggest difference between the "haves" and the "have nots", the people who have grown up there all their lives and they can't afford to stay there.

Increasing 'social mix' in the neighbourhood compounds the experience of inequalities. Middle-class residents, or 'haves', are unlikely to participate in elaborate, quotidian networks of support or empathise with the experience of inequality. They do not share this standpoint with working-class residents in a material or phenomenological sense. Using terms like the 'haves' and 'have nots' shows that the differences that mattered amongst residents were material, rather than only cultural.

That said, local attachment was not just a functional, economic necessity. Partick was a chosen location that expressed working-class identity. Like 'locals', 'incomers' most commonly shared an attachment to the area because they viewed it as being traditionally working-class. Janey made sense of Partick as a worker. She spoke passionately about what Partick represented and meant to her moving there from Chicago. She felt this bond and attachment was locally defined, but essentially related to class identity:

> Janey: I belong to Partick and the wider West End in general but definitely Partick. I like it because it's regular, it's not toffy, it's not up itself [...], *because I am regular*, I don't think I'm all that, I have confidence in myself but I'm not interested in blowing my own horn or being super rich. That doesn't appeal to me. What matters to me is that I'm happy that my kids are happy and my community they know our kids and we grow up and make a difference, keep it open and friendly and that is what Glasgow was like, Partick in particular. [My emphasis]

Her perception of the area in the 1980s was as a staunchly political and working-class neighbourhood:

> [...] work ethic but no work. Everybody was on the dole when I came here. We were all fighting the poll tax and there was seven year olds telling us to "get to 'France'" because they knew we [USA] had cruise missiles. It was quite interesting. Little kids. I think that's what made me stay. Little kids knew more about world politics than me. I was an 18 or 19 year old girl, well, woman.

Janey had some reservation in recognising herself as working-class as she perceived it to be a distinctly British phenomenon, but she explained what class meant to her at the end of our conversation:

> Class first strikes me as the economic, but what it means to me is that you are willing to work towards something to make things better. There's more social awareness and social responsibility to everyone and their community and Partick had that for me and that is why I think I'm cut from the same cloth and *am a Partick person*. I'm more Partick than I am American, and it was because of the way it enveloped me. [My emphasis]

For Alison, who had experienced social mobility, her elective belonging represented ontological security in the face of liminality and discomfort in her new middle-class status. Alison first spoke about being working-class when we began our conversation. She lectured part-time at a university but had grown up on a housing scheme in Northern Ireland. She was also a political activist and a local Socialist Party candidate. Her working-class upbringing attracted her to Partick. She liked the diversity, being 'in amongst it all':

> Alison: I mean it [to live in Partick] was quite important to me with the whole kind of class make up kind of thing. It's a strange thing because in a way I'm typical of how Partick is changing and I feel people might be like are you one of these people; professional folk in Partick type thing. But it was important for me to live somewhere diverse do you know what I mean? Like where I live, I live on Gardener Street. It's kind of like you feel like you're on the edge of lots of different concepts, if that makes sense. It's like you've got Byres Road really close, Dumbarton Road then you've got Highburgh Road. So I quite liked that aspect of it, like there were lots of different people living in quite close proximity. It wasn't homogenous in that sense. It seems to be a place that's almost fighting to keep its identity. Kind of holding on to Dumbarton Road.

Where she lived – on the edge of different concepts and types of people – expresses the liminality she feels personally. Alison embodies the contest and change occurring in Partick. Just as she acknowledged her working-class upbringing, she was equally aware of her newly emergent middle-class status. Alison spoke of the increasing gentrification in the area:

> I'm going "oh this is terrible" but at the same time, as someone who has parachuted into the community, am I part of that? Am I part of that change in the class make up? And then the whole class make up thing is incredibly complicated because I would see myself as working-class, because I have a working-class background, but, then again, a lot of people would say wait a minute here, you're a university lecturer, you're pretty well paid, you're professional. It's a complicated thing.

Elective Belonging and Fixity to Place 111

She was getting to have her cake and eat it too, because she, a university lecturer and living in Partick, thinks of herself as working-class and enjoys the neighbourhood culture. Yet Alison actively opposed gentrification and privatisation, particularly around protecting a local school being closed down in favour of building a new Public–Private Partnership 'super-school'. For Janey and Alison, their neighbourhood attachment was highly politicised. They actively sought out Partick; their orientation towards it was based on it being a working-class neighbourhood. It was a reflexive acknowledgement and expression of their class position similar to that of 'locals'.

This class connotation in local attachment was sometimes negatively experienced. Class was not something Leona was comfortable expressing. There was a real sense of dissatisfaction in her tone in what seemed like a confession to being working-class, when I asked her what living in Partick meant to her:

> Leona: [...] everywhere I go I feel that someone knows me, I'm old Partick. I guess that's working-class, I go to work and socialise in Partick. Partick's my life.

'Local' residents' proclivity to live in different places demonstrated ambivalence to the locale and being 'local', rather than elective belonging. Local attachment can have positive and negative class based connotations – this was contingent upon whether individuals could express physical mobility. 'Locals' Gordon and Leona said they belonged to the neighbourhood but simultaneously expressed ambivalence towards it. When I asked if they saw themselves staying in the area, Gordon said, 'I suppose I do, that's the problem', yet he is trying, unsuccessfully, to secure a PHA flat. Both he and Leona declared there was 'more to life than Partick', believing that staying in the neighbourhood would limit their freedom dreams (Weis, 2004). Being 'born and bred' was a sign of lower status and backwardness. Nick as an 'incomer' to the area 25 years earlier, expressed this idea. He enjoyed the fact his tenement block consisted predominantly of owner-occupiers rather than 'born and bred', social renters. This is a coded, derogatory way of talking about class. He equates the 'typicality' of the Partick mother's unrespectable, 'coarse' behaviour, with Partick overall:

> Nick: Partick was not the best. It was a downmarket Hyndland. It had lots of old-fashioned shops, a big pawnshop. I knew it from when I was young, I loved it as a child.
>
> Kirsteen: So why did you end up ...
>
> Nick: Well it wasn't that bad. I checked the type of residents at PHA and they were nice, decent, families so we knew it was ok.

Nick could make distinctions between what was 'bad' working class and what was 'good' working class. He vetted the area before he moved in to make sure the people were 'decent' enough.

However, Gary, a 'born and bred' resident, had no reluctance in being seen as so. This was because Gary grew up in Partick but was briefly homeless and now lives outside the neighbourhood. He would love to be 'local' as he cannot afford accommodation in Partick and has been on the housing allocation list, to no avail. So he privately rents in nearby Kelvindale, where the rental market is cheaper:

> Kirsteen: Why in particular do you want to move back to Partick?
>
> Gary: Social and family networks … amenities and transport. I like socialising there.
>
> Kirsteen: I suppose Kelvindale is just that wee bit far out.
>
> Gary: It's too posh for me. I'm used to Partick, Yoker and housing schemes. High-rise flats. I'm used to that. Partick, ideally. I would live there in a minute but the prices, £100,000 starting off.

This suggested that the ability to control one's fixity to place and movement is based on power and control. Those who were 'born and bred' and living the neighbourhood felt that they had not demonstrated physical mobility. Nick does not mind that Partick might be seen as rough as he was not born there, he has demonstrated mobility, whereas Leona and Gordon feel inhibited by living there. But those who cannot come back in, or even move there in the first place, see the neighbourhood in a more positive way and moving there is a sign that they have made it.

Transforming Class through Location

Most people I spoke to articulated the idea that their residence and class position were inextricably linked. Lisa knew Partick through her job with the DSS and began socialising in the area. She revealed her explanation for having such attachment to Partick and local residents:

> I was seeing them every day, I was in their houses. We became friends. I never had friends up there [Hyndland]. I had some but I didn't fit in with them. That was because of my upbringing [accent becomes broad] 'cause I'm fae Barmulloch originally. I came from a working-class housing scheme area and that stays with you.

Lisa thinks that, ultimately, she cannot escape her class and as a result was unable to fit in with residents in affluent Hyndland, where she moved to from working-class Barmulloch as a child. Her father was a manager in a steel works, which she said meant 'there was no denying he was middle-class', which reflects that her father's income was large enough to move to an affluent area but she felt phenomenologically working-class thus identifying with Partick and being a 'punter'. Location is more easily negotiated than class position, and it seems that residents perceive that physical mobility is a reflection of social mobility.

The perception that Partick was a step-up and a respectable neighbourhood was quite common amongst working-class respondents. It fed into residents' freedom dreams (Weis, 2004). Natasha joked to me that her partner Jimmy had done well for himself moving to Partick with her, a Londoner, as he was from Drumchapel. People perceived that moving to Partick could change their social destiny. Sylvie is desperate to keep living in Partick after moving there to live with her gran when she was 10 years old to ensure a 'better life'. She was sent to school in the West End, away from the perceived dangers for teenagers growing up in Ibrox:

Kirsteen: So would you say that you feel you have a fair deal in life?

Sylvie: Aye definitely. I've turned alright considering that I'm from Govan. I go over there to visit and I see folk from primary school and they are heroin addicts. I'm like, "My God!".

Kirsteen: I see that when I go home too. It makes me think how come they are like that and I'm not?

Sylvie: Oh my God, totally, it's like they stayed in the next close, [tenement block of flats] you know? But my mum she knew what she was doing, where she could see me. She got me out of there. If I'd stayed there a few more years though I might have changed. I had started drinking and stuff as teenagers do, when I moved to Partick. But if I was doing that in Govan then who is to say? That was a big impact.

Physical mobility is equated with social mobility, so that Sylvie attributes the neighbourhood she stays in with the life chances she has. She went on to recount the trouble that she got into as a teenager in Partick, underage drinking and hanging out with the children in a residential care home, which challenges the idea that the move into the area improved her circumstances. Rather it seems to have had a psychological effect, that by moving, her behaviour would alter accordingly, which it, eventually, did.

Fi recounts the unusual and lucky circumstances that bought her to Partick:

Fi: I'm from the Southside originally. My granny brought us up, 13 of us. We were there to 1960 and we moved to Castlemilk because of the redevelopment,

> which nobody could have lived in anyway [because it had few amenities] but we moved as a family and my granny died, and left us the house and Castlemilk was getting quite bad, you know, so that way we looked over here. I mean, this is early '60s, working-class people didn't buy houses, you know? Do you know what I mean? Maybe it sounds stupid. The reason we got this is a big story. My granny had a sister who married a Swiss man in 1917 [...] his family was chocolate makers in Switzerland. They lived there and then went to America and when he died it [the money] went to her, and there was seven sisters left and my granny got £1000, which was a lot of money, and I got the money 'cause I was the youngest, and with that money I bought this house.

With this windfall, Fi and her sister were able to, unusually for working-class women, purchase a house in Partick. However, not all residents translated her previous neighbourhood of Castlemilk favourably:

> Fi: It wasn't hard as an outsider as I wasn't an outsider, because that's the way it worked. I was working-class. Only because we came from Castlemilk, the folk in the close came and told us what days we put out the clothes in the green [sic – garden] and this is how we wash our close, and I was like, well I do it my way, so we'll just go for that.

There was a hierarchical territoriality, where people ranked different neighbourhoods to reflect class and respectability. In reality, this is a reflection of structural inequality, particularly the effects of uneven development and housing policies. Nick commented that it was easier for his wife to move to Partick than it was for him because there was a territorial translation:

> My wife came from Ibrox and was used to staying in areas like Partick, whereas I was from the fields really in Clydebank.

Nick was keen to make a distinction between himself and his wife. Being from Clydebank is a signifier of being working-class, but Nick said a few times during our conversation that he was from the 'fields' which was better than the industrial part of Clydebank. Natasha and Jimmy recalled how people they know, including Jimmy's mum, deny that they are from their neighbourhood:

> Natasha: I've noticed letters for downstairs [neighbours] and they have Thornwood on them! What was it they [the kids] were calling Castlemilk the other day? Chateau au lait! [Laughs]
>
> Jimmy: My mum stays in Drumchapel and she calls it Lower Bearsden because of the road she's on. [Both laugh]. I'm like "fuck off ma, you're Drum scum!"

Jimmy's mum claims to be living in Bearsden, the affluent, suburban neighbourhood which sits cheek to jowl with the housing scheme, Drumchapel, and he corrects such illusions unequivocally. David and his wife had also come from Ibrox. She was from Partick originally and David was from the East End. They moved to Drumchapel, then Knightswood. I asked David how Ibrox and Partick compared:

> You know it's really a funny thing. See, staying over that side of the water [the River Clyde], people are different. It's strange. I never thought that could be possible because people always say that, and I've worked all over Glasgow and I didn't believe it. But people are different. It's like their outlook is different.
>
> Kirsteen: In what way?
>
> David: Eh I don't know, it's hard to put your finger on. It's a different aspect of life. I dunno it's strange [...] Cliquey ... like they blocked you out.
>
> Kirsteen: Because you weren't from there originally?
>
> David: Aye, it's territorial.

Because David had been mobile, by moving to Ibrox and then to Partick, he saw himself as different from those who were 'born and bred', who he deemed were inward-looking, territorial and the constitutive limit to what he saw as being cosmopolitan. However, he did not regard 'born and bred' Partick residents in the same way.

It seemed that residents would happily choose to live in Partick and express their social identity through this, if they had been physically mobile. That way staying in Partick was a choice, rather than circumstantial which infers that you were immobile and reveals that you are working-class. One way of being physically mobile was through travelling:

> Natasha: The kids ... we have brought them up to [travel] they have met family in London, I've brought them up to want to travel. They all aspire to travel but home would be here and that is not necessarily where mum and dad is, it's Partick. Partick would be home.

Gordon aspired to move to Australia. He had checked up on what his friends were doing with their lives on the social networking site Bebo – a salient difference to the spatial level at which relationships at Golden Friends are maintained:

> Gordon: This one guy I know, Robbie, he's been all around the world working as a fitness instructor and he was only back here for a bit. He was earning about 60 grand. He was just back after a big tour and I was looking at his pictures and I thought, jammy bastard, you know, he went off and studied in another country,

went to Australia and studied, and I thought why didn't I think of something like that? Why didn't I go off? Why didn't I think of it?

Inspired, he saw this as a promising opportunity. He heard that his current job as barman is better paid and given a superior, 'well respected' status in Australia, bolstered by credentials through on-the-job training and testing. Gordon appeared to conceive mobility through migration to Australia as a means of altering his class position. Physical mobility then reflects class position and identity in a material sense via control. The way in which residents buy into the ideology reifies place. They believe that by moving location, they can change their class position. It was easier to negotiate physical movement, such as travelling abroad than it was to alter their class position.

Being able to move, having that mobility, was a positional good and socio-spatial distinction that operated *inside* the neighbourhood. Neighbourhood spatial hierarchies were culturally distinguished but had a historical material basis. Lower Partick at Beith Street and Benalder Street was known as the 'Quarry' – the lowest area of housing before the river and Harbour was an infamously very poor and Catholic area. This distinction served to set the limits of, and bolster the status of, the skilled protestant workers, in East Partick. The fortunes have reversed slightly; the Quarry is the location of the proposed Tesco site, new luxury Western Gate housing development and the imminent West 11 development (see appendix for a fuller discussion of these developments). The distinctions are still evoked by residents as a coded way of referring to someone's religion and class. Dylan and Sylvie, as young people, knew that the particular part of Partick that you were from had some significance. This spatial distinction operated horizontally, drawn between East and West Partick. The West side was known as 'poorer' to the slightly better-off East Partick. Partickhill operates as a residential class hierarchy; the further up the hill you live the more affluent you are. Residents use location as an indicator of class status:

> Bea: We went from Dunaskin Street to Mansfield Street. I was born into Dunaskin Street, which is called the Quarry, and when I was living there I didn't know it was so poor, because we went out with our aunts and, if you went with them, we only ever went as far as Purdon Street.

Worlds were circumscribed by material inequality in such a way that even physical movement is restricted. Alice, 78, accounted how she 'did ok' in life because she was from the 'right side of the street'. She took up clerical work upon leaving school, married and left Partick for the new town, East Kilbride. I met her at the bingo; she was visiting Partick twice weekly still.

The vertical distinction was a more popular benchmark. 'Up the hill' in Partick was, and is, affluent, originally home to shipyard owners and managers, whilst workers were housed at the bottom, near the yards. Some residents in Partick

Figure 3.1   Gardener Street Partick, looking towards Hyndland

focused their residential career on being able to move 'up the hill', with the dream of owning property there. Bea lived in Partick her whole life but steadily moved up the hill:

> You learned that one side in Partick was well-off, the other side was poor. Once you crossed Dumbarton Road and Partick Cross it was poor, you won't do anything with your life. So that's why my granny then made a decision that we would move to the other side to Hyndland Street. You would pull your socks up and get on with it.

Bea believes that this move was pivotal in her life; moving changed their destiny. It was a proactive reaction against her family's material position. Moving was not easy, it was a family affair where everyone contributed to purchase the house. It aided and advanced their social reproduction:

> Bea: When my daughter got married, here I am this wee lassie from the Quarry, standing in this posh hotel. The first one's wedding, it cost thousands of pounds so we have come a long way.

Mhairi, an 'incomer' to the area in the 1980s, from Clydebank, learned quickly about this once she settled into the neighbourhood. She bought her flat after her first year in teaching:

> Mhairi: You know it goes on the pecking order: Partickhill was the dearest; that was beyond me. But Caird Drive was just that wee bit further down and I could afford it. It's still like that to this day ... There's a big divide – folk up the hill, people buying, and poorer folk on benefits [further down the hill].

Nick had explained the class distinction in relation to the hill:

> Kirsteen: Do you consider yourself to be working-class?
>
> Nick: Yes, yes.
>
> Kirsteen: Don't you stay up the hill though?
>
> Nick: [laughs] Yes but I'm in the middle [of the hill]! I used to work in engineering [laughs].

Nick's location on the hill mirrors his class position as a skilled worker; a central location on the hill – not affluent middle-class but not lower-skilled working-class. The Other were characterised by their lack of spatial mobility. Whether through internal or external movements, residents activated the 'area-effects' thesis by reifying place as the core determinant of poverty and inequality and therefore being able to move physically provided a way of resisting or denying class position. Working-class residents are never simply immobile or static – they can be both – the crucial distinction is the amount of power they have to control this movement in their own terms.

Elective Fixity

Middle-class residents appeared to have less elective belonging but more control over their residential movement. Angus and Stuart were planning to move out of Partick in the year that followed, John had already moved to new luxury flats on the other side of the river from Glasgow Harbour. Partick was the first and temporary rung in their housing 'career' from which they would upgrade to more upmarket neighbourhoods. Angus was planning to move to Pollokshields and I tell him that I lived there and it is being extensively gentrified with the development of luxury flats around the industrial estates. He grins at me and tells me that he knows, indicating that this informed his choice. These residents spend much less time in the neighbourhood compared to the other respondents. Indeed, their idea of what constitutes 'Partick' is profoundly different. Stuart claims to spend time in the area, listing places he goes for brunch and dinner, which local residents would not identify as Partick:

> Stuart: One of the best things is I can be a middle-class wealthy professional and not have to own a car. The West End on your doorstep, restaurants, bars, and the city centre and the airport are a stone's throw away. It's the best neighbourhood in Glasgow.

At the end of our conversation, John dismissively remarked, 'I'd never move back, one thing though Partick is a great place for getting drugs' and gives me a wink. These residents experience the neighbourhood in a different way, reminiscent of what Skeggs (2005a) calls asset stripping: where the middle classes consume the best part of a neighbourhood whilst being protected from any of its risks. John consumes the grimier, urban, side of life from a safe enough distance; Stuart enjoys the working-class pub, but is safely removed from other aspects of working-class neighbourhood life. They 'parachute' in and back out again, as Alison would say. Yet it must be noted that these three residents actively sought me out to participate in the research. They did so because they were concerned with the way Partick was changing. This related to their role in actively opposing the proposed Tesco development. In this respect, they were socially engaging with the neighbourhood. In doing so, Angus drew another distinction:

> You put into your area, there's not enough [of that going on] in my opinion, you should give back to your community. Like at Glasgow Harbour, they don't do that.

However, this has further ramifications in relation to the stratification of local political power. The changes they can make outlast their stay and can be contra to working-class interests and opinions on the neighbourhood. This will be discussed in the next chapter in more detail.

It would be erroneous to suggest that residents with middle-class status and homeowners were the only residents to command control over both fixity and movement. Kathleen was the only 'born and bred' resident, no longer living in Partick, who did not want to move back. She moved to Drumchapel and then to Clydebank. She did not like her new neighbourhood in Clydebank and loved staying in Drumchapel but her house was damp with a serious mould problem and she also thought her kids were at risk of becoming 'neds' if they continued to live in that area. Through tirelessly canvassing housing officers, she managed to secure a house swap, resettling in Clydebank. However, this 'exchange' was a compromise. If she had the money to or more choice or control, her new house would have been in Drumchapel. Kathleen has power as an actor to negotiate particular risks demonstrating possession of social capital, but the capacity do so is circumscribed. Similarly, Brian and Janey both recounted how they obtained PHA flats by currying favour with the staff: Brian by doing odd jobs, like securing properties from theft, for free, and Janey by going to the office everyday with her newborn baby. She wanted to put a 'human face' to the housing list and let her baby 'melt their hearts' and it worked. These actions exhibit motivation and responsibility, which this population, particularly as social renters, are said to lack.

As discussed, the most notable and explicit way that 'local' residents expressed their ambivalence was through physical mobility. Leona moved to Australia because she wanted 'to do something with her life'. As money and work dried up, she had to return and 'face up to reality', which was life back in Partick. Leona described this experience as 'horrendous', and she longed to live abroad again but she does not have the resources to realise this, currently working seven days late and early shift patterns, and, on her days off, working shifts in the pub. Her freedom dream (Weis, 2004) of travel expresses her desire to escape her current life and class position, even though she felt that she was fortunate in life, compared to some of her peers from school. Leona jokingly explained that she fiercely values her independence and privacy, so much so that she hates having people visit her flat. She recalled an incident where she asked someone she was dating to leave because he turned out the light in the hall of her flat without her permission. At 37, she only got her own PHA flat six years earlier by 'pure fluke', having been on the waiting list for eight years. She said that, without that chance, she would still be living with her parents. Yet she works hard to maintain a sense of control, by rejecting place-based attachment by travelling to Australia and yet she fiercely protects her privacy, defending her flat as her own space. In reality, Leona has little control or power over whether she could remain fixed in the neighbourhood.

While Gordon dreamt of moving to Australia to alter his class position, the reality of his ability to be mobile in Glasgow was rather limited. He had enjoyed living outside Partick but it was short-lived:

> I stayed on the Southside, me and my pal got a flat there, that was only for a few years and then I had to move back to the flat at Broomhill and then I had to move back to my mum and dad's so I'm staying there at the moment.

He had to move back to Partick to live with his sister, when her boyfriend moved out. Then they were evicted from that house in a classic process of displacement or 'winkling' (Lees, 2003) when the landlady wanted to refurbish it and increase the rent by £200 to compete in the growing rental market. Gordon's control over his mobility was highly circumscribed. Bilal too had only recently returned to Partick having lived in England for 12 years, working as a nurse. He was not employed as a nurse when I interviewed him and had moved back to Partick after his grandfather was diagnosed with a terminal illness and he was charged with temporarily running his family's post office and shop. While being 'born and bred' was a class indicator, so too was demonstrating physical mobility, and being mobile countered the fixed, immobile, traditional class connotations. However, Leona, Gordon and Bilal ricochet back to Partick and their family home and networks. They cannot permanently re-fix themselves in another location. In this way, ontological place-based attachment demonstrates class identity amidst the decline in traditional identities, but it also reveals class position in relation to physical attachment, through the degree to which someone can control their physical mobility and remain fixed into place. This foregrounds working-class residents' paradoxical relationship to place where they are simultaneously fixed and unfixed.

Conclusion

These residential biographies only scratch the surface of the highly complex relationship residents have with place. The first step in appreciating this is problematising the analytical categories of 'locals' and 'incomers' as unstable referents. For example, we see how 'born and bred' residents experienced fractured and varied locational movement *outside* of the neighbourhood. Place attachment expresses a shared memory of class and a residual industrial culture rather than merely being a nostalgic reaction to a fractured community (Blokland, 2003). This working-class orientation to place is strongly related to structural changes, industry and deindustrialisation. Remnants of networks which are rooted occupationally around industry, like Betty's family of Red Clydesiders, are still meaningful. There is a shared experience, sense of loss, social practice, economic hardship and ontological insecurity amongst people. As such, working-class 'incomers' with no previous ties to the area connect Partick to their biographical life history. Place attachment expresses working-class residents' ontological and material insecurity. It bolsters their self-identity and constancy of their social and material environment (Giddens, 1991) allowing working-class respondents to express their identity without naming it. By contrast, middle-class residents had weaker ties to Partick and differentiated themselves from 'locals'. Attachment to a residualised working-class culture was not functional or mundane; it was an expression of social identity, which was profoundly classed.

From this we could say that people used place as a proxy for class; Partick is a metaphor, which expresses class status and identity. It provides ontological and material security particularly for working-class residents. The way in which Partick is interpreted is relative to residents' class position. For 'incomers' to Partick, barring Angus, Stuart and John, it signified that they had done well in life. It was an achievement and step-up, because it was a respectable area. For the less powerful, remaining locally embedded and close to family networks and support was essential. Yet paradoxes undermine this attachment. First, 'local' is a simultaneously positive and negative referent. It is negatively experienced by those with little ability to be mobile. 'Belonging tae Partick' allowed residents to express class collectivity, solidarity and their place in the world in unclassed terms. It offers more coherence than traditional notions of working-class identity and expressions of consciousness. However, this could only fulfil a positive function if residents could demonstrate that they had the power to live elsewhere. Working-class residents who moved into Partick or were trying to move into the neighbourhood, had a positive orientation towards the area. This metaphor of movement also operated inside the neighbourhood. Residents' location within Partick reflects their class position and ability to move 'up the hill' expresses their social ascendancy. Mobility and control over mobility is a meaningful and revelatory distinction. This denotes a shift from the bourgeois predilection for fixity (Skeggs, 2005a). Mobility and fixity are both, simultaneously, positional goods; it is the control over commanding each of these that differentiates. Meanwhile, the relationship between property and propriety via homeownership endures. The working class are characterised by a paradoxical situation whereby they are fixed and unfixed to their neighbourhood. Bauman's (1998) notion of fixity to place suggests that working-class residents are firmly rooted to place with little agency to move. Yet they are far from immobile; their attachment to place is actually tenuous and unsettled: being low-income homeowners or social and private renters and increasingly jeopardised and embattled with waves of gentrification and changes in social housing provisions.

Exploring class in relation to place powerfully reinvigorates class analysis. The neighbourhood is a crucial site for observing the interrelationship between social and physical space. Residential location is a powerful identifier of who you are and reconnects the relationship between class position and identity. The notion of 'belonging tae Partick' was bound with traditional class identity and, therefore, with a certain kind of class consciousness. It demonstrates a reflexive class position. However, it is not the level of attachment or elective belonging that distinguishes people, it is their level of choice – that is why the concept of elective belonging is better understood alongside elective fixity. The kind of attachments we have to places have profoundly changed. As writers recognise (Butler and Robson, 2003; Savage et al., 2005), this is inextricably linked to wider structural and global processes, yet they do not consider how it is explicitly linked to urban restructuring and neoliberalism. When exploring the interrelationship between class, culture and place, the power of pathologising ideologies around being 'born and bred' and how this is related to state-sponsored gentrification is overlooked. The differences in place-based attachment express both cultural and material hierarchies. Gentrification, rather than regeneration, is occurring in the neighbourhood which results in people losing their fixity – in physical, social, and cultural terms. Here the term 'elective fixity' better expresses the difference between working- and middle-class groups' relationship to place. It conveys the disparity amongst residents in the power to control their physical attachment to place. The degree to which someone has control over where they live is a valuable distinction and indicator of class position. The next chapter considers, in more detail, how the processes of gentrification in Partick are received. Both positive and negative reifications of the local are essential to the successful ratification of gentrification. In order for capital to profitably re-fix in place, it has to unfix flawed consumers who are those unable to consume in the newly created spaces.

Chapter 4
Gentrifying Working-Class Subjects: Participating in Consumer Citizenship

While Chapter 2 considered how deindustrialisation relates to the restructuring of class identities, this chapter advances this by looking at how residents negotiate their identity in relation to state-led gentrification, and extends the theme of control. I refer to this as the gentrification of the working-class subject as it involves the reshaping of traditional social practices, including politics, housing and consumption, to be more congruent with neoliberal forms of flexible accumulation. This includes local governments extending participation in gentrification through promoting a more consumer-based form of citizenship (Christopherson, 1994). Accounts of working-class experiences of, and participation in, gentrification are conspicuously absent from academic and policy literature in two key ways. First, participation is commonly interpreted using either post-Foucauldian frameworks, which decontextualise class, or, as common in orthodox Marxist accounts of policy, the subject is neglected (see Clarke, 2005). Second, much writing on gentrification presupposes that only middle classes participate in this process. Working-class residents are assumed victims of gentrification, unable to negotiate processes positively and on their own terms, which inevitably results in their displacement (for if it does not the processes cannot be called gentrification) (Lambert and Boddy, 2002). Their exclusion from accounts is striking given that working-class participation in gentrification is the end goal of urban policy. Gentrification of the working-class subject is not a zero sum game. It brings both new rewards, although limited, and new injuries, which are inherently class-based. This is seen in the tension around choice. Residents are extended choice and invited to participate in local planning processes which involve gentrification but are expected, as consumer citizens, to make the 'correct' choices: those which uphold neoliberalism.

It is vital then to extend Smith's (2002) enquiry to probe the symptomatic silence of working-class experiences in gentrification processes to reveal the class politics involved. Gentrification is part of a larger political project of neoliberalism, the impacts of which are far more complex than orthodox understandings of displacement. It involves a reconfiguration of politics, which has an important local manifestation. The extension of participation and consumer citizenship signifies a shift in the traditional social contract between the state and citizens, which has negative consequences for working-class residents, relating to both grassroots and institutional forms of politics. First, middle-class gentrifiers are more powerful consumer citizens in the neighbourhood and are able to appropriate local political processes to serve their interests. This can marginalise working-class voices. Secondly, choice and participation in local political processes is extended to residents with the expectation that they will make the correct choices, which are both morally and materially productive. The gentrification of the working-class subject involves manufacturing their aspiration to be more congruent with neoliberalism. Notwithstanding, the gentrification of the working-class subject is not a determined process, it is a process of class struggle and negotiation. Working-class residents can utilise this identity and harness gentrification processes to serve their interests. In this way, consumer citizenship can also provide a means for the working class to resist gentrification processes and reshape them for their own gains.

To explore this, I look at how gentrification is implemented at the institutional level, through the case studies of Tesco, Mansfield Park, the Harbour and the promotion of homeownership (see appendix for a discussion of these developments). Each reveals the novel features of regeneration strategies, which blur and reconfigure the relationship and social contract between the state and citizens, through the expansion of participation via consumer citizenship. There is a discernible pattern in the way that people respond to and participate in gentrification, with three broad groups emerging. The first are working-class residents who are independent of community and statutory groups, and react to gentrification in highly individualised ways, expressing a neoliberal choice narrative, which reflects their experience of restructuring in general. A second group of residents are those people who are linked to more traditional, grassroots and non-statutory groups. They oppose gentrification in favour of redistributive and inclusive processes, which results in them being marginalised from local policy processes. The third group are those affiliated with or involved in statutory groups, who tend to support gentrification, which often reproduces their power. This group tends to be more middle-class and have more command over local policy processes.

Table 4.1   Residents' class identification and community participation

Name	Age	Identified as working-class	Current involvement in statutory and non-statutory groups
Loretta	42	No	STOP campaign
John	35	No	STOP campaign
Stuart	34	No	STOP campaign
Nick	68	No	PHA
Louise	41	No	PHA and the Annexe
Robert	68	Yes	PHA, PCC
Rachael	49	Unsure	PHA
Molly	37	Unsure	Voluntary groups
Rhonda	66	Yes	Statutory PHA

Name	Age	Identified as working-class	Current involvement in statutory and non-statutory groups
Angus	36	Did not ask	PHA, church groups, STOP campaign
Norma	38	Yes	PHA and the Annexe
Gareth	52	No	PHA and the Annexe
Bea	62	Yes	Grassroots, church groups
Alison	32	Yes	Grassroots and Socialist Workers Party
Rosa	54	Yes	Grassroots
Paul	41	Yes	Grassroots
Fi	65	Yes	Grassroots and voluntary work
Darren	25	No	Grassroots group
Phil	37	No	Voluntary group
Kathleen	33	Yes	Voluntary groups
Alan	41	Unsure	PCC
Janey	44	Yes	None (had been previously involved in voluntary groups)
Betty	49	Yes	None
Brian	63	No	None
Leona	37	Unsure	None
Mary	67	No	None
Lisa	48	Yes	None
Danny	51	Unsure	None
Sonny	67	Yes	None
Maggie	53	No	None
Angie	37	Yes	None
Dylan	19	Yes	None
Donna	50	Yes	None
Steve	38	No	None
Sylvie	19	Unsure	None
Bilal	37	No	None
Sean	25	No	None
Agnes	69	Yes	None
Mhairi	48	Unsure	None
Alice	78	Yes	None
Gary	37	Yes	None
Robert	73	Unsure	None
Natasha	39	Yes	None (previously involved in Save Thornwood Park)
Jimmy	42	Yes	None (previously involved in Save Thornwood Park)
Alan	41	Yes	None
Tim	43	No	None

Name	Age	Identified as working-class	Current involvement in statutory and non-statutory groups
Gordon	24	No	None
Lou	42	Yes	None
David	59	Yes	None

The Class Politics of Consumer Citizenship

While the Harbour development was the most striking symbol of gentrification in Partick's political and physical landscape, it was the proposed Tesco development that incited more controversy and resistance amongst people. GCC promoted the Tesco development as 'adding value' to the neighbourhood through jobs and retail but this was rubbished by residents. Natasha and Jimmy were insulted by this claim:

> Natasha: Well, it would be my argument that my kids aspire to more than working in Tesco, hopefully.

Rather than being interested in the jobs it would bring, she was concerned about the job losses and knock-on effect on other supermarkets and the independent shops. What bothered residents more was the slow demise of the original shops and facilities, like the butchers, rather than any new fancy shops opening. But this was problematic:

> Natasha: But it's a catch 22 anyway isn't it? Look at the shops that are there – what use are those? You can't buy anything.

However Rachael, Angie, Sylvie, Gordon welcomed it on the basis it would offer cheap clothes and goods. Some preferred it as a brand of supermarket and those who did not have a car to access other shops were glad of the plans. Angie thought it would be great to 'get wee treats, it's got good clothes'. But even with diverging opinions on it, one action that brought residents together was the demolition of the old Partick railway station on the proposed Tesco site. This became a pivot point of action, which was harnessed by the STOP (Stop Tesco Owning Partick) campaign. This group, made up of local residents and business owners, had been trying to get the building listed. Before they were able to, it was demolished one Sunday morning, without any warning. Locals felt this was underhand and there was subsequent uproar in the local press. As a local priest commented:

> An example here is Tesco, in terms of how things work or don't work. I mean that toppling of the old railway station into the river? That was just brilliant eh? 6am Sunday morning? Just flexing muscles, "peasants, behave yourself".

The act of taking away forecloses the possibility of negotiation, which is disempowering:

> Loretta: I am so angry; it's so devious, like 6 o'clock in the morning. It went behind our back and that's what bothered me. All that history just gone.

Given the strong anti-Tesco views of the respondents and the history of class action in Partick around Red Clydeside and the Rent Strikes, it was surprising to find that resistance to this centred upon a group of middle-class gentrifiers. In fact, Jimmy knew little about the campaign:

> They said they surveyed the whole place and I thought "ya lying bastards. You never bloody asked me". The only reason I even knew about the campaign was that I walked home from work the other Sunday [...] and I saw their "No Tesco" sign.

There were working-class activists and supporters of this group, including Socialist MSPs, but their petition was different – urging residents not to believe the claims about jobs or that it was going to regenerate the community. They were critical of the wider processes of gentrification, including luxury housing and the growth of public–private partnership, but their voices were more marginal to the campaign.

It became evident that the people at the core of STOP were middle-class professionals and the campaign's name somewhat of a misnomer; it was less an ideological stance against Tesco owning Partick and more NIMBY-ism. The main impetus was that the development will affect the value of their property, 'quality of life' and vista. This expressed self-interest rather than being a political or environmental issue. Stuart, John, Angus and Loretta were active in STOP. These homeowners, who lived around the development, which is mostly luxury housing, were opposed to the development because it obstructed their views and affected their property prices. This was Loretta's primary concern. She became prolific in the anti-Tesco campaign because the development threatened her property investments. The proposed building will block the view to the river from her rental flat thus devaluing the property that provided her livelihood. Indeed, Angus was the driving force behind STOP. He was concerned by the development because his house also looked onto the proposed Tesco site. As a lecturer in spatial planning, he took a keen interest in the planning policy, funding and legal frameworks involved. He noted that the proposals contravened existing GCC policies and the guidelines of the European Regeneration Fund, of which GCC were recipients. Concerned with the scale and design of the proposal, he approached the community council, who were the necessary conduit for launching objections to planning. The STOP campaign utilised the community council for this purpose. What developed was a high profile campaign, which gained much press coverage. Using his cultural capital, he was able to challenge the development on technical and legal grounds, utilising the Freedom of Information Act and the earlier city plans: City Plan and

Clyde Valley Action Plan were scrutinised for their congruence. Petitions were sent to the Scottish Government, to Downing Street and the demolition of the Partick ticket office was legally challenged.

While STOP ostensibly provided an opportunity for residents to come together to oppose this form of gentrification, it foregrounded class tensions and struggles and disparities of power. Indeed the middle-class appropriation of this campaign meant that the opinions of working-class residents were marginalised. At a public meeting at the height of the campaign, members of STOP gave presentations to the attending residents as experts in the debate. They drew from their occupational roles in urban development to speak out against Tesco's plans. This included Stuart who spoke against the environmental impacts of additional traffic. One speaker, a local business owner, suggested the fate of Dumbarton Road would be similar to Victoria Road, on the Southside, which he called 'barren' and a 'dump'. This offended a group of women in their 50s and 60s. They did not view 'Vickie Road', where they often went to shop, nor Dumbarton Road as a dump. After some grumbling and dissent, they walked out of the meeting. This occurrence was part of a wider marginalisation of working-class residents in the campaign. Alan started attending PCC meetings because he was keen to find out more about the proposal. At that time, he was undecided but after hearing the evidence, he concluded that he was in favour of the development:

> I know there was quite a lot of hostility against but I find the arguments against it a bit skewed. People have a wrong sense of the impacts it will have. Some people are against all supermarkets on an ideological level. I think there are spurious arguments that it will affect the "lovely" shops on Dumbarton Road and I don't think we have great shops on Dumbarton Road. Why I've kept going is that I thought the people that were going to community council was not representative of the ordinary people and community. It was activists, it's full of activists. I'm concerned about the level of representation of the community. My fear is that it's quite low attendance. My opinion may not be right to others but I've had the chance to make a proper decision.

He notes that his decision may not be 'right' but it is legitimate in that it is informed by his participation in institutional channels. Yet these political channels were dominated by middle-class residents.

A vocal member of STOP and long-standing community activist argued in the media that the campaign group was against the Tesco development in its entirety. The group was concerned by this claim as they did not want to give off such a strong message. Angus, as a lecturer in spatial planning, supported these kinds of development, just not in this form and not on his doorstep. The STOP campaign, unlike some working-class residents, only wanted the development scaled down. However, the person who went to the press would not back down; she was fervently opposed to Tesco and refused to be silenced. Angus strategically threatened to resign because he said that he knew the campaign would be weakened without him, which the members also knew. This sanctioned the women, who eventually backed down under pressure from other members. Angus recalled this with some amusement and failed to see that he had marginalised a local working-class resident:

> You have two different social groups who don't get on quite well. You have the Partick proper group, more working-class and the educated groups that moved in five years ago and they have never lived here before and they are coming in with ideas for the area.

He disparages 'local' residents as regressive whilst casting new educated 'incomers', like himself, as the saviours of the neighbourhood. So, these middle-class professionals with statutory affiliations, who have exhibited less elective belonging to the neighbourhood, wield more power in local political processes. They position themselves as committed to making changes that will be beneficial to Partick, but act in self-interested ways and as moral arbitrators. In a perverse way, their autonomy, conferred to them through hegemonic processes which promote middle-class inner-city settlement, was used to thwart this particular form of gentrification. This created consumer sovereignty, awarding gentrifiers more power than anticipated by the council. This was legitimatised further as it was supported by some local councillors in the run up to elections. This contradicts the notion of the role of organic intellectuals as emancipators (Gramsci, 1971). Organic intellectuals recognise their location within the dominant ideology and use their position to cultivate strategies to help the wider community to develop organic consciousness. They fill the void left by collective action that characterised industrial times but do so in their own interests which preserves their property value – acting within the hegemony of consumer citizenship. Within the context of neoliberalism, promotion of market principles, individualisation, commodification and the construction of the more affluent user, participation reproduces class relations and inequalities. These residents act as urban entrepreneurs rather than organic intellectuals. The forms of collective action evident in Partick underpinned by consumer citizenship are advantageous for more affluent groups which challenges the traditional forms of collective action associated with working-class politics:

> Fi: I sometimes think like when the miners were on strike and we were all on strike [...] and nowadays there doesn't seem to be these big debates about it. We're not really doing it. Don't get me wrong, there are some but there's not people saying you know, this is what we are going to say and do and people you know, might then take notice of it, I don't know, I just put everything down to apathy. I'd like to see Partick the way that it was but I don't think I ever will see that again.

Fi highlights how there is little working-class collective organisation or public debate against gentrification. As demonstrated in Chapter 2, responses to restructuring are class based but individualised. Residents' individualised responses, whereby they disassociate with class, partly relate to the denigration of working-class practices. Ideologies of aspiration seek to cultivate more responsible citizens and, by extension, any actions that oppose regeneration makes citizens look 'backwards'. It is a catch 22 for the working-class, as Natasha suggests.

Manufacturing Aspiration and Choice

The regeneration of Mansfield Park was less controversial and more proximate compared to Tesco. It is right on residents' doorsteps, situated just off Partick Cross, at the start of Dumbarton Road. The benefits of the park's regeneration for the community are deemed self-evident. PHA drives the regeneration of the park through a designated Wider Action Officer, using various statutory and third sector funding and, by contrast, the redevelopment of the park put community participation at the heart of the planning process. The park consists of a red blaes football pitch, with a concrete and grassy area with some benches at the bottom end. A local football tournament has been running there for almost 20 years. From what I observed, it was steadily and regularly used for football and as a general run-around space for kids, known by some as the 'spare G' or 'the cage' and by a group who drank at the benches. It has become popular recently for hosting the West-End favourite Farmers' Organic Market, every second Saturday. It is in an important geographical location, adjacent to the PHA office and the new West 11 development. It is a kind of gateway to the rest of the neighbourhood. The plan for regenerating the park carves the space up to perform multiple functions for a variety of groups, with a focus on consumption. The foot of the park is to be 'Partick civic square'; a market place to facilitate the Farmer's Market, as well as a café, kiosk and an eco-play area for toddlers. There was also to be a bandstand available for hire, a meditation labyrinth, a fitness plaza and a shelter for teenagers. Most statutory affiliated groups and individuals, including local councillors that I spoke to celebrated the redevelopment. GCC agreed to a 99-year lease of the park to PHA, which effectively gives Partick community ownership. According to the respondents, there was nothing particularly 'wrong' with the park's current condition, but its amenities were quite basic. It still had a use value for different groups at different times, with diverse social groups sharing this space but, it was not productive or profitable.

Helen, the director of PHA at that time, asked me what I had found the community in Partick were saying about their neighbourhood. I did not disclose their concerns about the park directly but instead reported that many respondents said they would like to have a community centre. She seemed slightly annoyed that this was the consensus and asked where I had found these particular people. I thought that she did not think I was fairly representing the community's opinion but it became clear that her irritation was not with me, it was the wider Partick community:

Helen: If you look at the park, what you have is a real amazing opportunity for people to shape an outdoor community centre. And what have they done? They have not engaged with it. Now, my view is that if we went out with a bulldozer one day they would be "save the park!" and we'd have 60,000 people there.

Kirsteen: So you're saying people didn't engage with the park [regeneration and consultation] process?

Helen: There were people who engaged as part of the formal consultation process but there's not that dynamic thing about it. What is that about?

Rachael:[1] We've been doing things like we opened a shop and had people writing in books and they were writing things like "leave it alone, it's ok". You've seen the state of it? They say they don't want it [...] What is wrong?

Helen: It's almost an aspirational thing [...] I was staggered by the comments I read from these people. What reasons are people in this [neighbourhood] are not aspiring to something dynamic and vibrant and wonderful here and they have the opportunity to do so? Now is that a vision thing, making a kind of – I don't know – an external comment that they don't think they should get it? Where is the vision? There were comments that were positive but not as much as I would have hoped for. Why is that? Is it because they have been on the receiving end of not having these opportunities? I don't know.

Helen and Rachael cannot understand why anyone would have another opinion. Helen was disheartened that residents were not engaging in the way she thought they should. They were given an opportunity and, not only were they not suitably dynamic, they were negative. Defending the park against bulldozers would be a nostalgic response and act of preservation. She suggests that the act of 'taking away' would elicit more response from residents than the redevelopment of it ever could. Redevelopment is deemed progressive and residents' opposition to it is anti-modern. Helen's bemusement at residents' recalcitrance signifies that she accepts the neoliberal hegemony. Helen connects residents' lack of engagement with the park regeneration processes with an unwillingness she can only explain as lack of self-worth. Rachael's suggestion that something is 'wrong' implies that this response is deviant. Her thinking resonates with Clarke's critique:

> Responsible citizens make reasonable choices and therefore "bad choices" result from the wilfulness of irresponsible people, rather than the structural distribution of resources, capacities and opportunities. (Clarke, 2005: 541)

---

1 Rachael is a local resident and member of the PHA Board of Directors. She attended my meeting with the Director.

Rejection of regeneration is not accepted as a valid or legitimate choice. It is couched in terms of 'right' and 'wrong' rather than being accepted as an active, autonomous act. 'Right' in this instance is being part of the neoliberal consensus. If you think alternatively about it, or uphold values and practices deemed residual, like municipalism, you cannot participate. Helen believes residents' 'bad choices' result from their lack of aspiration, due to poverty. She said that poverty was a self-fulfilling prophecy and preferred that I did not refer to the neighbourhood as having pockets of poverty, as low self-worth and aspiration beget poverty. This is because she believes local residents embody the negative experience of having a lower income (it is likely that she is referring to social renters, her customer group whom she engages with daily). If residents do not know they are in poverty they might not feel so bad and aspire to achieve more.

This view is not only relevant to the Mansfield Park development; it underpins the approach to changes in social housing in general. Helen recommended I read the latest housing research from the Chartered Institute of Housing,[2] which proposes the social housing sector is diminishing because of the changing characteristics and lifestyles of social renters. Helen said that this research suggests that society is more prosperous and so homeownership is an increasingly attainable option. This is part of the political strategy of hegemony. Such research is disseminated to housing associations, who then promote it as a new set of ideas. Thus, it is further legitimated:

> Helen: It's about that word "aspiration". If you watch the TV, as people do, it's about lifestyle choices. And whatever the whole thing about your aspiration, if you read the New Haven research you'll see the traditional, you know, the social renter and renting, they say, has become an inferior good in economic terms and what they mean by that is it becomes what margarine is to butter. It was so, in fact, in the past, people ate margarine but now because of increases in wealth, margarine has become the inferior good. So now what they are saying is that social rent has become an inferior good. Now that's not our experience of it because we still have high demand, but if you look at it nationally, what the statistics reveal, of the profile of people who will be social renters in the future will quite dramatically change. It will be that it is a staging post rather than a tenure choice for life, which has all sorts of impacts.

Helen not only supports the idea that the need and desire for social rented accommodation will decline and homeownership will increase, she actively promotes it, as a social housing provider. This is compounded by the gentrification or reprivatisation of social housing (Rudolph, 1993) which involves the selling of stock, the promotion of homeownership schemes, but she does not acknowledge this. While Helen talks of butter versus margarine, this can be more pertinently

---

2   Helen was referring to a general trend in research rather than mentioning a specific document.

expressed as chicken versus egg. Housing associations tailor their services accordingly, thus it is not poverty that becomes a self-fulfilling prophecy: it is the forecasts of expert discourses that support gentrification and the effective end of social housing. Indeed, Helen was at pains to point out that PHA now referred to tenants as customers. The desired tenant was not just a good consumer, they were active and responsible, as their mission statement highlights:

> We believe in people's potential to improve their circumstances in partnership with us. Together we will ensure that Partick and other areas in which we work become vibrant sustainable city neighbourhoods. We will ensure that all who can and should contribute to this vision do so. (PHA, 2009)

Local working-class residents are implicated in their own decline and therefore responsible for their own regeneration. The closing sentence in the statement suggests, PHA 'customers' have a responsibility to be active citizens, but 'those who can' infers that some cannot, or are incapable. This resonates with the theoretical underpinning of the underclass discourse, which pathologises the poor as feckless, beyond help and at odds with the desired neoliberal citizen (Haylett, 2001). This differentiation is a powerful motivational tool. Increased choice does not necessarily translate into having the means to make any *real* choices. Helen's suggestion that buying a home is a lifestyle choice fails to acknowledge that some people cannot afford to, or may prefer to, buy margarine rather than butter, that is, socially rent rather than own their home. There is a material barrier to residents' participation in the consumption of homeownership, which will be captured in the next chapter. Interestingly, Helen concedes her own experience of housing demand differs from that presented in the research but this discourse exerts expert and moral authority.

The expectations around responsibility and making the 'right choice' are placed on community groups as well as individuals. Some community workers used a distinctly bureaucratic, business lexicon, speaking of steering committees, tendering, auditing and so on. I attended some meetings of the newly created West Area Community Planning Partnership (CPP). One involved a lengthy discussion of the structure, form and aims of CPPs and how these had altered from the previous Social Inclusion Partnerships (SIPs) area funding orthodoxy, as there was little clarity amongst members. The rest of the meeting focused on how funding would be allocated and ended on a presentation from a representative on the benefits of social auditing – how to make your community group operate like an effective business. While training is given to the community to help them participate, it is often done to better fit them within existing parameters (Gosling, 2008). At the summation, one woman representing a community organisation confessed to not having understood most of what had been said in the meeting, saying 'I don't speak that same jargon talk as you'. I did not see this woman again in the following meetings. If community groups do not play by the neoliberal rules of the game, they not only miss out on funding, they lose their voice in local political processes. Those operating within privatised urban governance view dissenting voices as resentment and ineptitude rather than legitimate. I spoke to the Wider Action Officer about the plans to charge for services in the park:

> Craig: People complain about having to be charged for these facilities. But my feelings that if people have a group then it's easy to raise money, even a small budget for a couple of hundred pounds to rent a room. It's easy. These groups like the Annexe you know they have to pay their way. You have to charge for the services […] if people want space they can just apply for grants, committee grants they can get thousands of pounds. I mean that is so easy to get. *It's just a question of getting off your backside and doing it*. It's only a three page grant and that what it's there for. Even the churches don't offer free meeting space. [My emphasis]

Craig overestimates the resources and knowledge to which small groups and individuals have access. This filters out groups as non-legitimate. Golden Friends were holding their bi-annual fish tea dance. To do so they needed more chairs. This posed an insurmountable problem for Bea who turned to me for help. She thought I had connections with the council who she thought were responsible for such provisions. She clearly was not part of, or familiar with, the complex funding regimes. I suggested that she contact the Annexe or Partick Burgh Halls and ask to borrow their chairs, but she said even if they agreed, she had no transport to get the chairs to the church, only 600 metres away. For Craig, they should have got off their backsides and applied for a grant. This was would have been utterly bemusing to Bea. There is disparity between old and new funding regimes and bureaucracy which excluded groups like this who are relatively self-sufficient and independent. The privatisation of social welfare is divisive creating a 'haves' and 'have nots' hierarchy whereby groups are battling over scarce resources. There were those groups who were financially supported through the business, private finance model and then there were the grassroots groups and charities who relied exclusively on public grants and funding to get by. These latter organisations are Othered as being naive and antagonistic. They cannot formally participate in regeneration processes unless they conform to the neoliberal model. It then becomes a competition for the survival of the fittest community groups. Some groups, like the Annexe, are supported by private and statutory finance and so uphold the neoliberal ideology, which informs what they support and who they work with in the community. When neoliberalism is introduced it is difficult to escape. If anything, neoliberalism becomes a self-fulfilling prophecy, not poverty. It transpired that Mansfield Park had been earmarked to be sold to a private property developer. A public–private partnership led redevelopment saved it from this fate. The redevelopment was an intervention which retained the park as a community asset. This information affected Nick's decision regarding the park. He was not happy with the development and felt that the FoMP board was dominated by a group of people who were pursuing their own interest, rather than that of the wider community:

> Nick: Some ideas have got so bad [...] the park was basically going to get sold off to developers, if it wasn't developed in this public-private development, and turned back into housing, so Elspeth [the local councillor] was keen to push the park through. I'm just happy that didn't happen.

He did not challenge the development plans because he believed what was in envisaged was better than having it developed as luxury housing. He ratifies gentrification because as a statutory worker he is all too familiar with the increasing privatisation and obsolescence of public provisions and state welfare. Gentrification is successful because privatisation begets further privatisation. It irrevocably changes the provision from being a public, common good to a private, consumable entity. For example, the cutbacks in the state's financial support of social housing leads to housing associations having to generate their own funds. This, by extension, elicits support for upgrading the park to create revenue for community groups affiliated with PHA. They get other community groups involved who would financially benefit from generating revenue from it. Alliances are created amongst community groups, who support neoliberalism out of financial necessity. The support for privatisation then becomes self-perpetuating. This creates a domino rather than a trickle-down effect. It leads to competition for resources and unequal distribution of power. Being in receipt of statutory funding may influence the stance that community groups take. This created divisions amongst community groups; to be a successfully funded community group you had to play by the neoliberal rules of the game.

A Tale of Two Parks: Resistance through Consumer Citizenship

The design for Mansfield Park was the result of a process of community consultation. Designers tendered for the contract and then presented the designs in 3D model in a shop, converted for such use over a one-week period. The Wider Action officer reported that the local councillor declared it to be to most consulted project she had ever worked on. However, Rosa informed me that there had been a competition for the design of the park but the winning proposal was, latterly, rejected and instead a committee, Friends of Mansfield Park (FoMP), was set up to oversee the development. The role of general members of the FoMP group is to oversee the development and nominate and elect the directors at the AGM. In this group of 10 people, there were six members of the PHA board or affiliated groups: Westworks, Partick United Residents Group, Partick Community Association, and there was a solicitor and a cinematographer and two people who did not live in Partick. Two of those I interviewed, Louise and Rhonda, sat on the FoMP board. Louise works in the Annexe, which was earmarked as the provider of the café service in the park. Rhonda was closely aligned to PHA, often appearing in their newsletter. In August 2007, this decision was 'called-in' for scrutiny by a newly elected SNP councillor who was concerned with the way in which the plans had changed from the original decisions (these were overseen by the FoMP board). The Labour councillor attacked this for potentially threatening the go-ahead of the scheme as it could have overturned the executive council decision on the lease. The councillor commented on her blog:

> I just can't work out why anyone would want to threaten a multi-million pound investment in their ward – over half of the £2 million pounds [*sic*] has been secured (and wouldn't be available for a plan B as it's tied to this plan) and if the Lottery bid is successful will be a major cause for celebration in Partick.

It is important to mention that the regeneration of the park has not been completed. The development halted but this is not due to political intervention, rather, the recession has meant that the project lost some of its financial backing. The park has been subject to very minimal surfacing and upgrading – none of the aforementioned facilities materialised. It brings to the fore the efficacy of trickle-down regeneration.

The involvement and functions of the FoMP group rendered the development a consulted, consensual one, achieved with the wishes and participation of the 'community' despite clear conflicts of interests of board members. Thus, it was not an extension of participation, but a denial of it because these different views threatened a multi-million-pound investment. Local residents' interventions would threaten the profitability of the project. Again, the right choice is a profitable one.

Many respondents were concerned about the plans. Bea was worried about the women at Golden Friends, whose access to the club is where a proposed skate ramp was to be, would be intimidated by the teenagers hanging around and bothered by noise the ramp would make. She was canvassing for the ramp to be located at the lower end of the park. She went to the office where they held the plans for public inspection to voice her concerns. She relays how difficult it was to get involved in the planning process:

> Bea: [...] took me easily months finding out committees. For instance, when I went into Partick Housing to say "do you know who Friends of the Park are?" and they said "no" [...] So I went somewhere else to find out because Friends of the Park were the ones making these decisions and they all came from Partick Housing but I didn't know that at the time. I had to sit through meetings at the Burgh Halls and wait and listen to find this, for this stuff to come out and I find out in the meeting that it's at 10 Mansfield Street [PHA offices].

Bea felt she had been given the run around. She was exasperated by this process and angered because her grandmother had played a central role as part of the philanthropic group, Partick Society, which helped establish PHA. Its primary

Figure 4.1   Mansfield Park, unfinished redevelopment, 2009
Note: This is where the bandstand, civic square and eco-play area were to be developed.

function is a charitable housing organisation, which it still ultimately is, but it is compromised by privatisation. This park was being regenerated on business principles; transformed into public–private space and a profit-making entity. The exclusion of other opinions has a material justification. It is likely that Bea's request that the skate ramp be moved to the other side will not be accommodated since it is used by the Farmer's market which raises revenue. This is the end goal, whether or not the community consent. Paul attended the early consultation meeting although he said it was difficult as they became increasingly elusive and he felt he was been excluded from the discussion:

> Paul: I don't remember from any meeting or consultation I attended any ground swell of people saying "we want a business-led plan" but we're getting a business-led plan, we're getting a park that's going to be open on the basis of profit. That's utter nonsense.

Lisa was also concerned that the Park redevelopment symbolised PHA's reconfigured role as a business rather than charitable organisation:

> Lisa: I think that park is a big bloody monument to Partick Housing Association, big bloody grandiose Stalinesque monument saying "look what we have done".

> Sorry, that doesn't wash with me. To me, "look what we've done" is build more houses, more opportunities, training jobs for young people. I want to see Partick Housing Association be intrinsically 100 per cent across the board involved with the community, in the schools, in the hospitals, sorry I'm going off on one here. I want them involved in every level of society in this area. It's a charitable organisation […] I just don't think there's enough discourse with people. They get their missive out and their glossy magazine, what they've done this year, blah blah blah.

Some residents felt that the regeneration that PHA implemented was driven by profit rather than being in the best interest of the community. This privatisation altered the rules of engagement:

> Fi: We wanted the regeneration so it would be useful for Partick. From the first meeting that was all signed. It's like anything, it's signed long before we had the meeting to give us a choice.

> Molly: There's absolutely no doubt that this space needs investment, it's run down. But, do we really need another bloody cafe here? The place is full of cafés for the latte mob, with their wee cakes.

As Lou pointed out, 'who the hell in Partick asked for a meditation labyrinth?', questioning who in the neighbourhood would know what it was, let alone want it. Natasha expressed this pithily: 'It's not for us'. Many residents will be effectively priced out of participation:

> Paul: There isn't a mass use of the facilities provided because they can't afford it and if they do they can find that they are not necessarily welcome in the places run by these interest groups.

Not only do the plans for the park assume homogeneity and fail to acknowledge the difference between representation of *a* local community and representation from local *communities* (Gosling, 2008), views that do not fit with the end goal are discounted. So there was a material premise to this cultural differentiation which marginalised working-class residents. Steve suggests that the regenerated Mansfield Park will be targeted by the local gang, the Partick Young Team. Steve explains that this is not mindless vandalism:

> The question is … will the Young Team destroy it? Spray paint and that. It's simple wee things. It's 'cause there's nae governor on it. It's Partick Housing or Glasgow City Council, it's not local people that are running it, you know? If it was going to be locals running it they [the Young Team] would have respect. No, it's going to get ruined.

Figure 4.2 View of Mansfield Park looking towards the upgraded, but downsized, sports court with bin with graffiti in the foreground

Steve believes that the Partick Young Team will not respect the park because they can see there is no local ownership over it. Since it is not there to serve their interests, they will vandalise it as an act of resistance. In doing so, they defy the regulation the park will impose around consumer citizenship. Their marginalisation and anonymity means they have little fear of being identified as, and reprimanded for, being working-class. They were excluded as underclass, but included themselves in regeneration, in their own way.

Fi was concerned about what action the community could take to oppose this. She felt helpless:

> Fi: Who do you put in? Not Labour or Conservatives. What do we do? Do we go about and do it ourselves? How do we get regeneration for us in the community? Who can we put in government instead? Do we do it like these refugees are doing: SOS, we don't want to be here? This is what is going to happen to Partick. People are moving in and buying houses but it does nothing, nothing. Spending money, it's not worth it because there's nothing in Partick. But regeneration is a vital part for a community to be together.

Figure 4.3 Graffiti on Glasgow Harbour promotional board
Source: Courtesy of Tom Brogan.

However, a possible strategy of resistance lay within gentrification process. Residents utilised consumer citizenship as a means of *resisting* developments. This is demonstrated through the politics around another park in Partick. Thornwood Park lies at the other end of Partick and was threatened with becoming a car park and private flats. Some local residents formed Friends of Thornwood Park's 'Save Our Park' campaign to challenge the development:

> Paul: The park was awarded to the community to be held in trust and managed by the council. So that's why we had a problem with them making decisions. […] The community was presented with a fate accompli basically we're going to build 50 houses and spend some money on you whether you like it or not. You're not going to get a say in the design or the houses or how long the work will take, what facilities they provide. The council don't spend money on our community but they want to make complaints about the kids, about antisocial neighbours' behaviour, about all these negative aspects of the views of our community but they don't want to put the even smallest effort or money in to make any material effects on changing that or help the community take control of their community.

What emerged was a very different type of community campaign. This grassroots group set up weekly consultation stalls and knocked on doors to inform locals about what was going on and elicit their opinion and views. It was grassroots based and run because it aimed to gain a range of opinions and shape the park that way rather than persuade the community of an idea:

> Paul: You have to come at from the different point of view, that it's you that's trying to get people's views, you are trying to elicit something or trying to get people involved so it's incumbent on you to go out and get views and give people the forum to get in and say what they want. You give people the chance to get involved in things and they do. People do identify themselves with each other, they do want to stand up and get involved and know that something is there, between them, by in large they know they are from the same place and have a desire for that place.

He expressed that it was vital for residents to see that plans for developments were not a 'fait accompli', even though he felt they often are. It was a highly effective strategy. The community was tirelessly canvassed, according to Paul, resulting in a 6,000 strong petition and public meetings held on a regular basis, having upwards of 100 people. Fi, Tim, Natasha, Dylan, Jimmy, Agnes, Lisa, Alison, Rosa, Sylvie, Angie and Paul, over a fifth of residents interviewed, had been involved directly or supported the campaign. Part of the park was used by developers but the community were able to retain most of it and were bequeathed £250,000 from the developers to refurbish it on their own terms. What they envisioned did not contain a meditation labyrinth and instead provided a safe, up-to-date, play area for children. It is a testimony to what can be achieved with more equitable consultation, participation and action from the community. A group of local residents worked within the confines of neoliberalism, negotiated with developers as consumer citizens. This suggests that there is an emergent form of consumer citizenship which is not a zero sum game for residents: it can bring rewards. Indeed this foregrounds the consensual side to hegemony and the agential aspects involved in implementing hegemony as a political strategy.

The Harbour: Adding Value for Whom?

The implementation of monolithic flagship regeneration projects on former industrial sites frequently do not necessitate explicit consent from the public as their value is deemed self-evident. Instead, disinvestment and discourses on decline are used to intellectually justify such projects. Redevelopment can only add value to disused sites, plus there is no displacement of situated residents in industrial areas (Lambert and Boddy, 2002). Yet, Glasgow Harbour Ltd and GCC approached Partick Community Council[3] for consultation prior to redevelopment commencing. They were not required to do so because there were no residents living in the radius stipulated to necessitate consultation but ensuring the support of the community council was a decisive step. The council represents local residents and has a consultative role in planning processes. It is the forum through which developments plans *could* be challenged. I asked the chair of the community council what the consultation had entailed:

> Nick: They invited us down and said "This is what we are going to do. We are knocking down the granary" and all the rest of it.
>
> Kirsteen: Did you have a say in it? Were you involved in the process?
>
> Nick: It was already decided. There was some complaints about the cycle path disappearing but there were no objections about the Harbour development [...] the granary was just an eyesore, full of rats and pigeons. It's making use of the space. They regenerated scrap land because it was useless right? No-one wanted it. It was all warehouses, garages. There was nothing there, no industry there now, disused. It's full of houses and cars now. So they might only last 20 years but they have made good use of the site.

The plans were presented as being in the community's interest, but not really any of their business. They were able to help plan pathways and cycle paths but could not participate in the plans for the development in general. Nick's reasoning demonstrates how disinvestment justifies neoliberal policies, which obscure the structural reasons for, and impacts of, decline. In spite of his reservations about the longevity of the development, Nick still supports it, believing that it is better to have something rather than nothing. Indeed, one of the key ways of harnessing community support at initial stages was through *specific* promises of value it would add through jobs and social and affordable housing. John and Stuart attended some of the initial consultation meetings in their capacity both as residents and urban entrepreneurs (Harvey, 1989), employed in the city marketing bureau:

> John: The presentation to Partick Community Council, they talked about what was coming, the changes, the positive things it would bring and the house prices rising. They did this beautiful PowerPoint presentation, kind of "before and after" pictures of the area. They talked about the big efforts they were going to

---

3   Community councils were created by the Local Government (Scotland) Act 1973. They form the most local tier of statutory representation in Scotland, intended to bridge the gap between local authorities and local communities and to help to make local authorities and other public bodies aware of the community's needs and problems. They do not have statutory duties or powers, and are essentially voluntary bodies but established within a statutory framework.

use to include Partick into the waterfront [...] To my mind, that has not happened at all. The most amusing thing, and I can't believe the planner said this with a straight face, he said there was going to be an element of social housing: another loaded term. But the selling point, and they said and this three or four years ago, they said that the flats were going to be between £60,000 and £80,000 and they would be accessible to ordinary people. I just looked at Stuart and we just couldn't believe it.

The average house price in Partick at that time was already upwards of £80,000. No social housing was developed but John was sure that these promises helped win over local opinion and quell any possible opposition. Those closely aligned with local politics and regeneration displayed the most scepticism towards the development. Alison, a member of the SWP, made the broader connection between gentrification and GCC's approach to schools:

I mean obviously it's a public service thing. It appeals to a hell of a lot of people. It's driven by capital. What you have going on in Glasgow is a lot of school closures. This is just about land. It seems like every square inch is being built on. What's going to happen to these sites when the schools are shut are they going to be flats which makes the community more homogeneous again [...] it seems like more and more places are just looked at as opportunities for profit, it's like what can we do here to make money. That's the society we're in and my politics are left so that's going to piss me off. It does sound like a cliché but are communities turning into commodities?

On other occasions, the potential benefits of the development were misconstrued, as Nick demonstrates when he explains to me the positive effects of the Harbour project:

Nick: Go down to the shops at Thornwood. There's more fancy designer shops. There's more fancy furniture shops, cafes and tearooms and before they were derelict.

Kirsteen: Who does that benefit?

Nick: Locals. Shopkeepers. And people are getting different kinds of groceries. They are getting more choice. There's also more charity shops opening up so that can help people get reasonable clothing.

Kirsteen: But is the charity shops opening up related to the Harbour development? I thought that might be the other way round.

Nick: Yes, well it might sound strange but if you look at the British Heart Foundation they are getting quality furniture to sell the Harbour people for about

£80. Well that might be too much for poor people to buy. They go to MFI or Habitat or something [...] Well they wouldn't spend £50 on a chest of drawers. People from the Harbour do. These charity shops get a good turnover and then that allows Partick people to be employed in the shops. Salvation Army took on some people and trained them.

Nick applies some contradictory logic, accepting that new shops would cater for the new residents and would, in turn, give residents in Partick more choice. However, this is not based on affordability. Nick expresses the urban policy ideal: that one place will bring the other 'up' through a trickle-down effect but he misconstrues the reason behind the growth in charity shops and the selling of furniture to the Harbour residents, showing a lack of experience of the real value of goods, affordability and poverty in Partick. However, he struggles to maintain support for the Harbour, given that many of the promises made did not materialise:

Nick: Yes, well, it was said to provide 400 jobs. I never saw them. In fact, to quote the Harbour in their original plans they said they were training people from Partick job centres ... to train them in apprenticeships in building work. 400 jobs. I haven't seen this, I don't know. Ideally they should have made social housing.

A few believed that the development was intended to benefit the community directly:

Maggie: Aye-aye [emphatically] ... something for the kiddies, a swimming pool or something.

For many, the effects of this development were abstract.

Jimmy: People plod on whatever happens. You know because I think people just go on with their lives. Just because people build new flats, I mean here might be gradual changes but there's no immediate changes.

As time progressed residents' ambivalence towards the development grew as the rewards did not materialise. This mostly related to the idea that the Harbour was not on their territory. The site no longer performed an economic, cultural or social function for the community as it did in the industrial heyday and the development had no shops or facilities to entice the Partick population down. The Harbour is also separated from Partick by the expressway, making it, in effect, a gated community. Another contributing factor was the name of the development: Glasgow Harbour, not Partick Harbour, or the Granary, which disassociated it from the neighbourhood:

Fi: It's not Partick Harbour, it's not linked up, it's miles away, not integrated.

For parents Natasha and Jimmy and children Ellie and Dylan, this distance was created not only by the name, it related to the people living there. Jimmy said that he would not call the area Partick, because of 'the way they are living ... it's different people'.

Distance in psychological, social and physical terms shaped residents' reaction to the gentrification of the Harbour. Given that the planning process was presented as outside their control and there are physical, social, cultural and economic barriers to their participation, this rejection offered a sense of control in the face of limited power. This was demonstrated by those who mocked people who bought properties at the Harbour for believing in the 'emperor's new clothes':

> Angie: I feel sorry for them. Those flats, it smells down there. £300,000 to sit and smell shite? I feel sorry for them, really and truly. The views of the Clyde and Govan? Hello? I think they've been conned. I do.

> Gordon: I think they are hideous man. Dead ugly, I wouldn't want to stay in them. There's nothing there you know? They're building a whole stretch of housing and I bet that in 20 years they will totally drop [in price] and then you get these idiots shelling out for these flats and they can't even get 100 grand back from them.

Janey described Partick and Glasgow as 'little America' in recognition of how the transition from Thatcherism to New Labour changed things dramatically in relation to welfare and workfare and how this greatly affects the neighbourhood and the community. She saw the Harbour development itself as a distinctly American, corporate aesthetic:

> Janey: It reminds me of America, big high developments all over the place, not very attractive. Before people took the piss out of me and my sister when we arrived [from America] and now people are more starry-eyed, "ooh American". "You are American, why move here?" and it's because it's real. That [the Harbour] is not real, that's plastic. It's not a real society or group of people. It's going plastic here [Partick], started a while back but there are still the real people.

Janey upholds the increasingly residualised culture of social housing and working-class residents which she sees as 'real' in defence of what she feared as the 'plasticness' of America developing further in Partick. That said, she thought that the Harbour development had potential positive impacts for the neighbourhood. There has been much speculation about how well the Harbour flats are selling and that GCC has acquired some of the properties, which they use as temporary accommodation:

Janey: I know that social services are using some of those flats to house asylum seekers [...] because they are not selling so the council is using it [...] I know this because social workers are going on home visits. It's an asylum seeking family with a kid with a disability. And in this world I think that can only be a good thing. I wish we had more real mix around then to represent what the wider world is like.

Janey believes that the Harbour redevelopment promotes social mix by housing asylum seekers rather than by the state's promotion of middle-class settlement. In this way, Janey believes the Harbour development can have a positive effect as it breaks up the exclusivity of the mono-class neighbourhood of residents who do not want to mix, by introducing the non-home-owning Other. It can be said that people negotiate their own forms of participation, often in subversive ways, in opposition to the way it was intended as a space for the affluent users to consume.

Sylvie and Lou admired the lifestyle associated with gentrification and urban professionals and tried to participate in it. This formed part of their freedom dream of a better life (Weis, 2004). Lou had lived in a flat at the Harbour development. After being homeless, he was able to secure privately rented accommodation at the Harbour, where his rent was paid for through housing benefits:

Lou: The Harbour was a shocker. To live in the Harbour was like, basically it was like living in a ... it was probably like a designer jail. People who tend to move into the Harbour keep themselves to themselves [...] The security is good down there. It's all coded entrances and that. A concierge can see who's coming in and out and they've got cameras inside the flats so you know who's buzzing in.

Interestingly, he explains his move to the Harbour as related to his lack of choice in housing: '[w]hen I moved into the Harbour, it wasn't through choice, it was the only thing available to me'. For those people with a record of arrears and evictions, getting on a social housing waiting list can be extremely difficult. I suspected that this was Lou's experience but I did not know for certain. In this way, he was a subversive tenant, living the lifestyle of the affluent in a luxury apartment whilst qualifying for state benefits. The Harbour appealed to Sylvie as part of her love of Partick in general. To her mind, moving there from Govan changed her life path, it offered her more choice and she enjoys the Harbour development:

Sylvie: When we were wee, we used throw stones at the granary. It's so weird to think that it's not there anymore, this great big building but I don't think about it anymore. I was down the Harbour a couple of weeks ago with boys from the college. We had a bottle of Buckfast [fortified tonic wine] in a Barrs glass bottle [for soft drinks] and we were wandering around and it was lovely. We were dead stressed because we had an exhibition at college so went there before to have a drink. They've never seen it before, they're from Hamilton so it was like showing them Glasgow and the buildings look like holidays apartments. It's dead nice.

Sylvie reminisces about the old granary building but rejects this past in favour the contemporary development. The Harbour was not designed in a way to invite down those living in Partick, especially not teenage drinkers, and it is fairly well policed. Even so, Sylvie and her friends reclaim the space in a subversive way, wandering around drinking. She is aware that doing so defies the rules as she disguises their alcohol in soft drink bottles. She proudly shows off the area which suggests that she took some sense of ownership and is staking her claim to the city.

Therefore, although the Harbour did not add value in the way that the local state proclaimed it would in relation to affordable housing and jobs, many residents still supported it. On an individual level, respondents supported regeneration as adding value to the area, which, in their opinion, was a barren, disused 'eye sore'. Interestingly, it was those least involved with statutory groups who were most supportive of the development. A small number of those I spoke to, David, Sylvie, Leona and Rachael, Lou, Jimmy, Natasha and Dylan, loved the regeneration of the Harbour and thought it was beautiful. Steve said it was 'very Mediterranean: too good for here'. It added something meaningful and positive, not just on the immediate site but to the wider neighbourhood. This was a particularly common view amongst men who experienced the sharp end of deindustrialisation, like Brian, Tim and Steve. This groups' consensus around the Harbour was not related to institutional processes, as they were the most atomised. The pre-developed site was described using pejoratives; a hangout for underage drinkers, where 'kids caused trouble', a 'wilderness', all of which are incongruent with the superlatives of regeneration; modern, vibrant, civilised and ordered. The planning process around the Harbour reveals the power that the state and their partners have to enforce such developments in a coercive way at the institutional level but residents also participated in gentrification on their own terms. Lou and Sylvie negotiate with gentrification processes to create rewards for their own lives. For Sylvie it reflects choice, for Lou lack of choice. They create rewards for themselves, as consumer citizens. They can, provided they have the means, negotiate their consumption of gentrification.

Similarly, some of those interviewed made some gains from the increased commodification of housing in the neighbourhood. Bea's grandmother deemed that buying property in Partick during the resettlement programme would be the only effective way of ensuring the extended family's successful social reproduction in the neighbourhood. At 67, Bea had some recollection of what life was like prior to the introduction of the welfare state. Subsequently, she is reluctant to rely on the council or state, believing the best way to survive is to protect yourself:

> Bea: When we realised that we were not all going to get houses [in the 1960s resettlement programme], my granny said that we are going to have to buy them as they came up to stay in Partick. It was the only way. Most of us all

did that, most of us so that we could live here rather than schemes like Arden.[4] That's where we would have ended up. It was so we could stay together. I can remember her saying "I am not going to have my family scattered to the wind".

After the policy changed to rehabilitation or 'benign gentrification', her family clubbed together to buy properties between themselves at a low price with Bea's flat costing only £200. Bea and her husband benefited from gentrification, selling their tenement home and buying a flat in a new-build development in Partick after their children left home. Bea became a gentrifier (if we take that to mean a consumer of private, purpose new built property in a predominantly social housing neighbourhood) in this respect but it was underpinned by financial imperatives; it originally saved her family from being displaced as the council tried to decant working-class families to peripheral estates. They fixed themselves to place to gain control and security. Over the years as the tenements were upgraded and the housing market improved, house prices rose. In the 10-year period from 1997 to 2007, house prices in parts of Partick have increased more than the city wide or national level.

Table 4.2 Increase in houses price sales at intermediate geography,[5] city and national levels, 1997–2007

House sales, median price	Partick	Glasgow Harbour and Partick South	Glasgow City	Scotland
1997	£47,850	£36,000	£40,000	£44,000
2007	£125,000	£172,495	£102,000	£100,000

Source: Scottish Neighbourhood Statistics (2009).

Gordon's family made substantial gains from the increase in property prices. His grandparents bought a tenement flat cheaply many years ago. This was split into two properties and was subsequently inherited by his parents:

Gordon: When my nana died we sold it for £60,000. It went up so much in 10 years. It was valued at £60,000 and now its £250,000. That's mad. That much in that time.

---

4 Arden is an SSHA (Scottish Special Housing Association) built estate on the outskirts of Glasgow designed to rehouse families from the overcrowded inner city tenements.

5 The intermediate zones are aggregations of data zones within local authorities and are designed to contain between 2,500 and 6,000 people. Partick comprises of three intermediate geography zones. Only the two listed 'Partick' and 'Glasgow Harbour and Partick South' are representative.

Fi as a homeowner in Partick since the 1960s would also gain from property price increases in theory, not that she would leave the area. Indeed her biggest complaint is that the increased prices prohibit young people in Partick from being able to stay in the neighbourhood. But it exceeded financial imperatives. For example, participating in gentrification in this way gave Bea ontological meaning, which harked back to her memories of the past. She was consuming and preserving her own history, as she bought a flat on the former site of the 'steamie' (washhouse and laundry):

> Bea: I'm living there now and I look out my kitchen window and I look across the luxury car park and I see my granny and the poorer women who were there in the "steamie" but I also see the better off ones that I even see today who are 70 years old. I see them walking about, glamorous, waiting for their new houses, waiting for telephones, it was a really exciting time. I can stand at night and dream.

This is a very different idea of 'buying into history' than that conveyed in the gentrification literature where new middle-class groups express their social distance from the working class, constructing an identity based on 'consumption as a form of investment, status symbol and means of self-expression' (Jager, 1986: 87). At the most fundamental level, Bea's participation in gentrification was an act of financial security but it was also reminiscent of the way in which Alison constructed her attachment to Partick, discussed previously. Both express an attempt to preserve their class identity or reconcile their social mobility and stabilise their identity rather than conveying post-modern sensibilities. Residents' participation in gentrification revealed reflexivity and pragmatism. Homeownership is an increasingly normalised form of investment, with a person's home being their principal financial asset (Mills, 1988), compounded by the decline in pension provisions. Buying property appealed to Brian in his quest of 'forward planning'. He recognised the financial gains to be made in the booming housing market. Years of contract work left Brian, 67, with little in the way of pension funds which is why he has been undertaking cash-in-hand work. Brian also bought property during benign gentrification processes in the 1970s and encouraged his children to do the same now to secure their future. He kept abreast of planning applications by regularly visiting the GCC's planning department:

> Brian: I looked at the planning at Boswell Street. I'm advising my granddaughter to do the same. We said she should look at Dennistoun as an up-and-coming area, good prices, fantastic houses, great ceilings. I love those properties and it's my hobby, you know, doing places up. So basically I was advising her [his daughter] to do what I had done [bought property cheaply]. She got cold feet and pulled out. She is working in the NHS just now. She's a worker, all my kids are workers.

Brian makes clear that his kids are working-class rather than middle-class gentrifiers, with a sound work ethic rather than looking to get rich quick or support privatisation of public services. Homeownership can also be lucrative if the property is successfully developed and sold. This is how Loretta made her living and what would be her pension after leaving school at 16 with no qualifications, working her way up from a tearoom assistant, to providing catering facilities for canteens at computer factories. She said that what she lacked in qualifications she made up for with 'high business acumen'. Having bought and developed property with a boyfriend, she made enough profit from the resale to create initial outlay to buy property and become a developer and landlady herself. Consuming gentrification was emancipatory for Loretta (Lees, 2004) which related to her experience of gender. Developing properties offered independence via self-sufficiency and security. From the way in which these residents participate in gentrification it is evident that flexible accumulation has not led to a post-modern consumption ethic or aspiration to be gentrifiers and demarcate differences with other (Jager, 1986), rather, there are material gains for people, security, a career and financial assets but also increased risk, insecurity and competition. Therefore, gentrification is not as it outwardly seems – as a zero sum game for working-class residents. The effects and outcomes are not black or white. The rewards that residents negotiate from gentrification processes do not necessarily correlate with policy prescriptions. They add value in their own ways, on their own terms. However, their participation and choice are highly unequal.

Conclusion

Exploring the 'rolling out' of gentrification in Partick reveals many complex and uneven political processes which are experienced in stratified ways. Middle-class residents appropriated local political processes as powerful consumer citizens and mounted the STOP campaign, benefiting directly from gentrification by moving into Partick but resisting the Tesco development as it posed a threat to their property investment and in doing so marginalised the views of working-class residents. Meanwhile the working-class subject is gentrified through manufacturing aspiration and choice in local political processes. Support for the redevelopment of Mansfield Park was expected as the 'correct' choice and dissenting views were interpreted as irresponsible, reflecting residents low aspirations and material and cultural poverty. Consumer citizenship is negotiated by community groups who challenge gentrification, in two different developments at Mansfield Park and Thornwood. The group of residents who opposed the Mansfield Park redevelopment exposes the limits to participation in local regeneration processes for those who make 'unproductive' choices. However, consumer citizenship also opens up other forms of resistance and negotiation seen in how residents challenged the gentrification of Thornwood Park. Acting as consumer citizens, they fought the development at a grassroots level, but negotiated with developers to oversee the investment of private money in this park redevelopment. Meanwhile the seeming pinnacle of gentrification, the Harbour, which was deemed to be least in the interests of the local working-class population, was negotiated by some residents in positive and subversive ways. Their reactions here were highly individualised, consuming this form of gentrification in subversive and resourceful ways which added value to their own lives. Also working-class residents, who were financially able, can be gentrifiers. While these processes of gentrification are complex and received and negotiated by different groups with different interests and different ways, we can begin to disentangle the political meaning of these processes.

We can see through this how participation is extended to residents to seek consensus for a social contract, which actually transforms their rights and responsibilities. Gentrification promotes consumer citizenship which has ramifications for policy. Paradoxically, one outcome of gentrification is that it results in the expansion of sites of consumption. Ergo, as consumer citizens, users' rights will be based on values of consumer sovereignty. The struggles that existed between working-class and middle-class groups were not just based on dissimilitude, which is a case often presented by culturalist class theorists (Skeggs, 1997); they had a strong material rational. The hegemony promoted by middle-class professionals involved with STOP was underpinned by consumer citizenship, in that it was based on protecting property values. Middle-class residents represented the dominant form of hegemony by acting as urban entrepreneurs. They were often affiliated with institutional and statutory organisations which consolidated their power to assert their own politics, which sometimes supported gentrification and sometimes opposed it, but rarely corresponded with working-class (material) interests. Grassroots organisations, consisting of working-class members, represented residual interests in the neighbourhood, fighting against the dominant culture of gentrification.

Angus, at the forefront of the STOP group, marginalised working-class residents who had opposing opinions as 'regressive'. A similar process occurs within local institutional politics, which shows the tension between statutory and grassroots groups. PHA was not only concerned with regenerating the physical environment; they were seeking to regenerate aspirations, encouraging residents to make materially and socially productive 'choices'. In doing so they were not merely being moral arbitrators, it was materially necessary that residents supported the 'right choices'. Once neoliberalism is achieved, other privatisation follows suit and so the process proliferates. The re-privatisation of social housing meant PHA had to raise revenue, which led to the privatisation of the park. It is not that participation is undemocratic per se, but the end goal is profit, which means that views which are incongruent with productivity are excluded. Again, residents who refused to make such 'choices' or who opposed regeneration plans outright were seen as recalcitrant.

This was the real catch 22 for residents: making the 'wrong choice' (opposing gentrification/regeneration) positioned them as working-class, yet the 'right choice' (supporting gentrification/regeneration) was not fundamentally in their interest as it involved privatisation, which, on a low income, they could not participate in. If a regeneration project is ostensibly adding value, like the physical upgrading of Mansfield Park, residents are vilified for opposing it, whereas if something is taken away, like the railway station, or the threat to Thornwood Park, it is palpable, ostensibly destructive and allows residents to fight against it without identifying themselves as working-class. But paradoxically, they had limited power to successfully challenge such processes. Not even the STOP campaign could prevent the demolition of the railway station. Where residents could more effectively resist was as consumers. While Fi lamented the demise of traditional forms of protest and class action in Partick, a restructured form was evident. Residents respond to the dominant culture of gentrification, opposing its effects on their residualised culture and neighbourhood way of life, by utilising gentrification processes, that is, by acting as grassroots consumer citizens, in the case of Thornwood Park. Other times, they negotiated these processes for their own benefit, becoming homeowners, for example. It is clear that responses to, and participation in, gentrification reflect the restructuring of class identities outlined in Chapter 2, as residents strive to have some sense of control, which they express through a choice narrative over these processes. Yet there is an emergent compromise and form of politics which utilises the processes of gentrification to resist processes that are not in their interest. Residents could act as consumer citizens. This was different from traditional class politics known in the area.

Of course, the power of consumer citizens is deeply stratified. Some working-class respondents became more economically affluent users by consuming homeownership, although gentrification did not alter their economic position per se, except for increasing debt. There is no perceivable improvement to the local labour market. Given the chance, residents would like to consume gentrification, but are denied the opportunity to do so. The process of cultural differentiation, which is essential to gentrification, has both psychic effects on the working-class landscape (Reay, 2005) and material consequences. The following chapter explores the process of cultural differentiation further and its material effects in displacing the working-class subject.

Chapter 5
The Paradox of Gentrification: Displacing the Working-Class Subject

While the previous chapter explored how working-class subjects may be gentrified, here I document the sharper, more punitive side, looking at how residents may be displaced by these same processes, in both cultural and material ways. State-led gentrification is not implemented with the exclusive purpose of displacing people. Rather, as the previous chapter demonstrates, it aims to civilise behaviours and manufacture aspiration. Unlike other government restructuring strategies, such as workfare, where work is redemption, in regeneration atonement is achieved through consumption of public services and provisions. Yet, as the last chapter illustrates, regeneration contributes to the privatisation of such provisions and, by extension, commodifies citizenship and so does little to improve labour market conditions and people's material situation. In this way, gentrification *simultaneously* excludes and includes working-class residents, demonstrating what Young (2007) calls a bulimic society. State-led gentrification invites people to participate but this involves private consumption and it does not provide the means to achieve this: this is its paradox. In this chapter I examine the limits to residents' choice and the stratification of control. This is revealed through both cultural and material forms of displacement. First, cultural displacement stems from the same assumptions underpinning social mix and gentrification which infer that working-class residents are essentially different from middle-class gentrifiers, with deficit desires that require valorisation. This cultural differentiation necessitates the successful ratification of gentrification and encourages consumption. Thus, working-class residents are encouraged to buy into what are deigned to be the 'right' kinds of social capital, like homeownership. Second, this can have negative material impacts. Working-class participation in processes of gentrification can be underpinned by a desire to avoid being Othered. This participation involves consumption, which can lead people into borrowing and debt, compounding inequalities for the economically less powerful. In spite of its goal to civilise populations, state-led gentrification still causes physical displacement and challenges residents' fixity to place. This is because social landlords, who have historically protected against eviction, find their more traditional social welfare-based principles are compromised by increased privatisation of their organisation. This can escalate evictions, with punitive actions taken against residents who are thought not to be materially or culturally productive.

Regeneration processes that proclaim to create choice actually stratify it: increasing choice in the neighbourhood by offering services that many residents cannot afford. This reveals the ultimate paradox in gentrification, whereby the poorest individuals are more likely to try to consume to avoid becoming Othered. Doing so creates further economic inequities. So while residents have agency and power to negotiate gentrification in their neighbourhood, the ultimate barrier, which they have little control over, is the material power to consume. Processes of cultural disrespect of working-class practices and economic inequalities (Fraser, 1998) coalesce to create different forms of displacement. The displacement of the working-class subject has both cultural and material aspects, both of which are interconnected. Operating more along business lines means there are harsher penalties for non-payment of rent. Here I identify a new four-fold typology of displacement: perverse, latent generational, strategic and spiralling. These challenge the proclaimed virtues of regeneration and social mix and suggest that such policy strategies lead to paradoxical outcomes. Thus, this fortifies the argument that the most meaningful difference between working-class and middle-class residents is a material one. It is expressed in the level of control they have in negotiating gentrification. Gentrification creates its own area effect: working-class residents are denied authorship and ownership of social capital and, therefore, economic capital. Unable to realise consumer citizenship or fixity to place, such residents cannot successfully fulfil the neoliberal identity narrative around consumption.

Social Mix, Social Capital and the Stratification of Choice

The benevolent, softer side of gentrification is said to be its capacity to deliver social mix and improve social capital, said to comprise components of shared social networks, shared social norms and high levels of trust amongst a social group (Kearns, 2003). Policy research literature casts communities who are poor in social capital as those in which people become isolated, suspicious of others, and reluctant to participate in social economic and political life, leading to a breakdown in social fabric (Kearns, 2003). Mixing is a panacea believed to mitigate potential negative area affects, such as low aspirations and low educational attainment, attract and support a higher level of local services, leisure activities and higher than average levels of disposable income, which may create additional employment opportunities for local residents (Bailey et al., 2007). Yet this agenda is based on difference. Middle-class settlement provides a means of managing situated populations, notably through improving deficient stocks of cultural values. We have seen how working-class respondents enjoy the diversity in the neighbourhood and the 'cosmopolitanism' this invoked. Paradoxically, middle-class residents, who are positioned as the vanguards of cosmopolitanism, do not desire such engagement. This was demonstrated by the separateness of Harbour residents and by the exclusionary behaviour of proximate residents living in Partick tenements. I heard many complaints against incoming middle-class residents' lack of participation and social capital, especially within the conviviality of 'the close' and daily life:

> Janey: Once the middle class began to join in it became a bloody nightmare. I think so. The middle classes, I don't know, they always want to seem better, toot their own horn and to treat people poorly. "I've worked my way into where I am and I want to be recognised". Whereas the "have nots" ... they get on with everyone.

Janey thinks that the middle class demarcate themselves and act in self-interested ways, unlike their working-class counterparts, although this may overstate working-class coherence and cohesion. Natasha and Jimmy described to me how they saw the neighbourhood changing in relation to increasing single, affluent and middle-class neighbours:

> Natasha: [...] coming in buying their own properties, keep to themselves and there is an aloofness.

Through this 'aloofness', their middle-class neighbours differentiate themselves from Natasha and Jimmy. This is a markedly different experience from their previous flat in Partick:

> Natasha: It was all housing association, all up the close and we did talk to each other whether it was "hello" or anything like that. When I moved up to this close it was bought houses and there is only one couple who speak. You know, it's very much like my kids "are cheeky", not in a right way but in a snobbery way, like "your child is too loud" or "drawing on the wall" ... I really think that is part of it, you know what I mean, the ownership? And it's not just about owning properties it's about their values and stuff obviously would be different to mine.

Natasha and Jimmy experienced a decline in social interaction and neighbourliness as they moved from a tenement of mostly social housing to one where they are the only social renters amidst homeowners. Natasha feels there is a connection between property and propriety through which, as social renters, they feel Othered in a tenement dominated by owners. But it is not only the ownership that differentiates; Natasha assumes that their values will invariably be different too. This is challenged by their relationship with a young homeowner couple in their close:

> Jimmy: They're not that affluent I've been in their house, they live like us!
>
> Natasha: [Laughs] Great!

Jimmy: Decks [music mixing decks] all over the living room, the lassie says "don't look" I said "how the hell am I going to find where I'm going to!", then I fell on his decks. They seem alright. They're great with the kids.

Jimmy and Natasha relate to this couple because they say 'they live like us'. They interact with the family, particularly with the kids, and share neighbourliness. This couple do not seek to demarcate themselves from Natasha and Jimmy's family. However, for the most part they felt differentiated. Jimmy said that those who move to Partick are mostly first-time buyers who quickly progress up the property ladder to more desirable neighbourhoods:

Natasha: It's not investing in the community [middle-class incoming residents]. It's only to take the money and move on.

Jimmy: 'Cause they won't have their families here, so they'll not. The flats here are too small.

Natasha: They will deem it as the bottom of the ladder whereas I think that I have probably made it!

Natasha suggests that Partick is the pinnacle of their housing 'career'. They wish to stay in the neighbourhood for the foreseeable future. Indeed, when I asked them where they would live, if they had the choice to live anywhere in the city, they took me to the window and showed me the fire station tower in Partick, which has been converted into flats. Subsequently, they invest socially in their neighbourhood. Natasha and Jimmy choose to live in Partick but the difference is that it is the first rung on the housing ladder for others who have more choice, for instance Stuart, John and Angus. Partick does not appeal to affluent couples who are looking to start a family, as they could afford to move to an area with bigger housing units. Contrary then to GCC's goal, middle-class groups settle in the city on a temporary basis, particularly since GCC property-led regeneration has supplied small, high-end apartments rather than family homes. Middle-class residents' choices are also constrained, but markedly less so. The brevity of middle-class settlement means that they are unlikely to invest in the area in the long-term, in the form of social networks and lobbying for changes that will improve social reproduction for all, not just for their own gain but beyond their tenure:

Mhairi: People living where I am, they see it as temporary, you can't change that. Transitory. And it makes you think, "why are you here?"

Ironically then it is middle-class incomers that do not transfer social capital within the neighbourhood:

> Jimmy: See when I was younger in Drumchapel there was loads of people that stayed round about all chipped in money so we could go to places like Irvine and beaches […] you don't get that here and if you tried it and I don't think that you would get a hand with it. I think now with the likes of the people down the stairs and those who have moved into the flats, if anything like that [the threat to Thornwood Park] happened again then I think they would be like "fair enough" whereas we don't. It's the only space we've got about here like that.

Jimmy outlines that incoming middle-classes, like those in his close, would not invest in the neighbourhood simply because they do not have to. It is not a necessity and they are not 'in the same boat' as the 'have nots' as Janey says, which can initiate mutual social and material support. However, invoking middle-class difference reifies boundaries between these groups, which do not essentially exist. Working-class residents could be equally withdrawn and privatised. Both Sonny and Stephen expressed very little desire to interact with the wider neighbourhood and led quite solitary, self-contained lives. The point is, the same behaviours exist across classes and the majority of people in Partick, working- and middle-class, want the same things for their neighbourhood, like security, community, successful social reproduction and, importantly, regeneration. The most common requests were for: better shops and services on Dumbarton Road; improvement to youth services; a publicly funded community centre; better services for the elderly; a swimming pool; and more social housing. They wanted change and choice through regeneration that was in their interest, rather than nostalgically hankering for the past. Fi expresses this succinctly:

> What Partick needs is regenerated. What that means is shops where people don't have to go to the supermarket, they've got a choice of clothes shops, fruit shops, butchers. That's good for the community. The council I think needs to play a bigger part. I think it's a bit of everything, jobs, with the shipyards being taken away. Jobs are important. But I've got this thing about kids, you've got to help kids, you've got invest in them, they are our next generation. We need to help them, give them something to put their imagination into. We've lost a generation to drugs if we don't improve this.

This sentiment was echoed by Natasha:

> I would like to be able to go to Partick and buy a pair of knickers, a coat, a pair of shoes. I don't want the other shops, second hand clothes … And I quite like the new coffee shops that have been opening up and we can say "oh let's go for a coffee, shall we?"

Regeneration is interpreted by Natasha and Fi as a process that should extend choice to those who commonly have their choices constrained. Instead, it seems to have a perverse effect. I asked Jimmy what kind of things he would like to see in the neighbourhood:

> Jimmy: Aesthetic stuff, parks, trees, but practical stuff. I mean growing up, luckily the eldest kids are alright but they have grown up with groups of people where there has been fighting and stuff and there needs to be some sort of intervention for young people so they are not labelled and not stigmatised. I mean this curfew thing that is happening in Knightswood I mean it really fucks me off.

Natasha and Jimmy rely on local public services. They are angered by the dearth of youth services and the lack of places for their kids to spend their time other than on the streets. Their son Dylan had been stabbed the previous year whilst walking home along Dumbarton Road. Luckily, he was not seriously injured. They feel that relegating young people to the streets means they are either exposed to violence or surveillance and stringent control, as seen in the curfew for young people in Knightswood. I ask about the Harbour specifically and what effect the development might have for the community. I immediately saw that this aggravated Natasha and Jimmy, who live close to the underpass that connects the two neighbourhoods:

> Jimmy: It's changing already. They've got those cameras up – specifically because of the Harbour. The tunnel has been redone, all fancy lights, trees at the side, all because they folk have forked out the money for these flats and I think that it's disgraceful. Disgraceful. We've been crying out for stuff for years and have never got it.

Security is a positional good that can be amassed by residents at the Harbour to help secure their settlement. It helps further guild their luxury ghetto, encourages middle-class settlement in the city, especially in an industrial area situated next to a working-class neighbourhood. These residents can buy safety, which Natasha and Jimmy cannot – they want security as a public good that can keep their children safe without controlling them. The middle-class gentrifiers can secure their social reproduction via purchasable and positional goods like private schooling and recreational activities for their children outside of the neighbourhood. Natasha and Jimmy were not the only residents to notice and be annoyed by the provisions of CCTV and the makeover of the tunnel bequeathed to Harbour residents:

> Fi: See that path and tunnel at the bottom of the road down there to the Harbour? Now six months ago you wouldn't go down there, you'd be dead. Now if you look down it's beautiful and its trees with lights and the tunnel is all painted with lovely wee designs. The other tunnel is a mess, smashed bottles and graffiti. And it's because of them in these new houses, don't want to look out on to a dirty tunnel. Basically down the road is new regeneration to make everything look

nice. It's like America, like New York and we're like the Bronx or the slums. But there's no input into this area, the council has put nothing in.

So while their neighbourhood is regenerated not everyone can enjoy the benefits of this. This simultaneous exclusion and inclusion, in both cultural and economic terms, is encapsulated by the following incidents recounted by Lisa and Mhairi. Lisa describes the local Organic Farmer's Market in Mansfield Park:

> It was your West End types going initially but a couple of times I've went recently there was a real mix of Partick punters and from outside the West End. I was having a conversation with this old wifey the other day about carrots she says "these carrots actually taste of carrots, it's great" you know? So folk are using it. There was initial trepidation and then curiosity got the better of people.

This 'old Partick wifey' enjoys these organic carrots over the mass produced, cheaper supermarket variety. However, as Mhairi notes, as much as local people may enjoy the organic food, they do not have the material means to consume and are excluded:

> They are trying to make the place more interesting, Polish delis and Delizique [an upmarket delicatessen] but I guess that's where the divide is up there that attracts the middle class or people with money or too lazy to cook paying through the nose. I was up there [Delizique] and there was an old lady there and she was arguing and she was saying to me "Bloody £6 for carrots! I could get those round the corner for £1.50!"

From these insights, it is clear that the differences between working classes and middle classes in the neighbourhood are not essential, they are material. They both wish for similar things for and from their local area but working-class residents have less opportunity to purchase: they are flawed consumers because they not in a powerful enough material position to participate. This is echoed by Davidson's (2008: 2,399) quip related to his study of gentrification in London neighbourhoods: 'cheap veggies lost, expensive veggies gained'. Through regeneration, residents find that choice is extended but their capacity to make choices is constrained. It fortifies the distinction between working-class and middle-class groups offered in Chapter 2, as based on control. The stratification of choice enables middle-class residents to make decisions that negatively affect working-class residents who, by contrast, are in a bulimic situation – simultaneously excluded and included. What is paradoxical is that residents can counteract being Othered or, to use policy terminology, excluded, through consumption, yet they are in a less economically powerful position to be able to do so.

Keeping Up with the Joneses

Most of the residents I interviewed lived with debt and managed it through a complex system of borrowing from friends and family, using credit cards, store cards, loans and hire purchase. This was more of a necessity rather than supporting lifestyle choices per se. This intricate network of credit arrangements existed whereby residents were 'living on the never' (Natasha) and 'robbing Peter to pay Paul' (Fi). As Fi reported, this involved grassroots borrowing amongst friends who received money on different days and who would lend to others until they got theirs. The pawnshops had been prominent in Partick in the past, with 'John the Pawn' being particularly infamous. As a child, Diane and one of her friends set up a 'business' surreptitiously returning pawned items to their housewife owners so that their husbands or neighbours, or both, did not know, although she said they mostly did. More often debt was not locally embedded. In some cases, residents required intervention to deal with it. Tim, Paul, Sean, Fi, Natasha, Jimmy, Angie, Sylvie, Rachael, James, Gordon and Lou all had sizeable debt problems in relation to rent, council tax, gas and electricity arrears and credit cards and received organisational support from places like Citizens Advice Bureau (CAB) and Westgap to help deal with it. Specifically, council tax arrears were a widespread difficulty. Tim had sizable arrears that took years to pay off. Sean was still dealing with his:

> The main problem I've had is council tax. I stay in a band C flat and at the moment I am working and I can't afford to pay any council tax because my rent is £50 a week then my electricity, a £10 loan from the Provident, that's another £10, bus fare for the week £12 so that's £82. Food maybe £20 or £30 my internet and phone bill. So I just ignore council tax. I just ignore it. I can't deal with it. It's like I have an automatic mechanism that if I see a green bill it just gets shoved in the drawer.

Sean's annual council tax in band C is £1,415.58, subject to a 25 per cent reduction (based on 2007 rates). He also has £800 rent arrears with PHA. Sean's financial difficulties were compounded by his lack of networks and nearby support. He has a difficult relationship with his family. His father lives on the Southside of the city and his mum lives outside Glasgow. He has no safety net if he is evicted, not having family or friends to take his furniture, if it came to that. Over half of CAB debt clients have monthly incomes of less than £800, and almost one quarter have incomes under £400. CAB debt clients are considerably poorer than the population of Scotland as a whole (Sharp, 2004). Even on a double income, with four children, it was nearly impossible to manage:

> Natasha: I think people think we should be ok with the jobs we've got. Yeah it is reasonable but we ended up getting into so much debt, so much, to get to this point. So you've got that to pay off. Even with reasonable wages you're living, to an extent to pay that off, living on the "never never".

This poor and insecure work and wages affected how people managed the general cost of living. Covering basic outgoings is a perennial and at times an acute problem. Natasha explains that the impacts of material hardships have a spiralling effect. As a family they have some control of their finances but the fear of punitive repercussions haunts her:

> Natasha: The fear, the fear. Sometimes the people from the finance companies who phone you up when you owe them money they put the fear of God into you, they really do. I'm intelligent and logical I say "ok what can happen here?". It's not life threatening, it's not imprisonment. I really have to tell myself what is happening here and talk myself back in so I know it's alright.

Financial difficulties affect the personal and inner world. Sean is also haunted by his debt and tries to escape the worries that it brings:

> I work during the day and then when I come home at night I've got work to do and letters to write so I keep busy, keep busy, you know. But it's hard living alone. I find it hard […] It's really hard trying to start your life I mean what have you got? Nothing. No job, no TV and you're left in this wee flat with your own thoughts.

Living with this fear is a daily reality and compounds the experience of material inequality – a psycho-social embodiment that informs people's being (Charlesworth, 2000). This echoes Allen's (2008) study of the working-class experience of housing consumption, where he found that working-class people are overwhelmed by economic demands and 'keeping the wolf from the door'. Research demonstrates that debt is a major influence in mental health problems (Mind, 2008). The emotional and psychic responses to inequalities contribute powerfully to the making of class (Reay, 2005):

> Sean: I think there's different kinds of poverty, it's not just about money, it's about feeling your life is worthless. That is poverty in itself. And to have that along with having no money, well, that is a killer combination. There's more to poverty than money.

Unlike Allen's (2008) conclusion that the working class are concerned with the practicalities rather than social significance of consumption, residents' experiences revealed a complex relationship between the material basis of class and its subjective meaning and identity. This is encapsulated by Natasha and her son Dylan's account:

> Natasha: People who are poor, right, and get their own tenancy, aspire to have brand new things … you may not have food in the cupboard but by fuck have you got a lot of gold on you!

Dylan: Aye. Aye, exactly.

Natasha: And you know what, I'm part of that as well. I make sure that my kids have all the same gear as everyone else does.

Dylan: I remember boys from school, from Hyndland and they were wearing trackies and I was like "how come you are pure rich and you still dress like 'jakes'?"[1] Know what I mean? Mind that boy from the top of the hill, long hair, dressed like a tramp?

Natasha: And it's because he doesn't need to, that is exactly what it is.

Dylan: Aye people are trying to prove a point, they are trying to say "no, I'm not poor".

Natasha : I used to sit there and say, before I had kids, oh no I won't get caught up in all that buying for your kids … now I got into debt so that my kids had exactly the same as everyone else. [My emphasis]

Dylan: Aye or you'll get bullied.

Natasha: Well I was bullied really badly because I didn't have a proper skirt so I wanted to make sure that didn't happen […] It's such a vicious circle for people. The ones who've got to get the credit cards are the poorest people. [My emphasis]

The family are fully conscious of the paradox whereby those with little money are compelled to consume more to hide this fact. Those who are poor consume in a conspicuous way when they cannot afford it, to avoid being bullied or differentiated. However, they are still Othered by the affluent, who do not need to consume to show their wealth. Dylan notes his more affluent counterpart living at the top of hill is materially secure enough not to have to display this outwardly. Dylan and Natasha consume so they are not positioned as 'being poor' while this is inadvertently the result. Even though Natasha planned eschew materialistic values to her children, the disciplinary class and male gaze on her role as a mother and the prospect of them being bullied for not having the same as others, made her reconsider. She wants to provide a caring ergo respectable role as a mother so she protects her children by providing them with the same things as other children, which contributes to them amassing debt as a family.

Indeed, this kind of consumption response to being classed was most evident amongst young people. Those under 30 were less likely to have experienced

---

1 'Jake' and 'jakey' are Scots slang derogatory terms for someone who is homeless and/or an alcoholic.

'being in the same boat' collectivity with their neighbours and local borrowing strategies and support systems as older generations reported. Indeed, their coping mechanisms for dealing with financial problems relied on institutionally-based borrowing. Young people also had a more relaxed attitude towards borrowing with seemingly boundless access to credit. Gordon believes that having the chance to work and earn money means that he has had a 'fair chance' in life:

> Gordon: I feel I've had a fair chance in life. I've always had to work for my money. From when I could work I was making my own money. I got pocket money, three quid and my mates were running around with a tenner and I didn't and I would go home at lunchtime and cook my own food. When I was 16 I started working and have made my own money since.
>
> Kirsteen: So, from a young age you were keen to be financially independent?
>
> Gordon: Aye, well I'm not now! I'm struggling! I took out a stupid loan to go on holiday and pay off my overdraft, I thought "fuck it". I took my girlfriend on holiday for her birthday and I went to Spain for the first time.

Gordon is now experiencing financial difficulties because he took out a loan to pay off his overdraft and to go on holiday. Ultimately, there is a barrier to accessing wealth, but not debt, which Gordon does not acknowledge. In addition to this debt, he has to make student loan repayments despite being unable to complete his studies. He was the victim of an armed robbery in his part-time job and the High Court case that followed caused him to fall behind in his college course work, so much so that he dropped out. Gordon had no anxiety about having student loan debt. The spread of student loans has helped to normalise debt amongst young people and give them a relaxed attitude to debt (Rainer, 2008). Nearly half of those aged 18 to 24 surveyed by the charity Rainer owed over £2,000 and one in five owed over £10,000. Rather differently to the previous notion of working-class gentrifiers, Sylvie, 19, would be more likely to knowingly put herself into debt to finance this style of life. This was expressed in her interest in living at the Harbour, as previously outlined:

> Not all the way up, maybe half way, with a wee balcony. Maybe the penthouse though!

The £700 monthly rent did not put her off even though it seemed far beyond her means. But, she was no stranger to accumulating debt in order to consume given that she was going on holiday to Barbados with her boyfriend courtesy of her credit cards, and that she was the 'best-dressed student' on her course, and hid credit cards from her mum. She announced that once she finished her course and found a job she would consider living at the Harbour. She then reigns in her ideas:

Sylvie: Maybe when I'm older and have money I would like to stay in somewhere that's a bit more extravagant not just a tenement. I guess everyone wants that.

Sylvie refuses to be excluded from the Harbour, whether by drinking down there or by renting a flat. She demonstrates a very different vision for the future compared to Brian's forward planning approach. Sylvie has a much less certain view and exercises less control but seems comfortable with this, enjoying the fact there are different possibilities and chances; it opens up freedom dreams (Weis, 2004). Young people, particularly those who are working-class, are hit the hardest by recessions, which forecasts debt and unemployment with poor chances to repay the debt – which is a very different tale to the 'fair chance' that Gordon purports to have. Even Darren who was the only young person interviewed who, not only went to university but had completed his Master's, had boomeranged back to his parents' home (Heath and Cleaver, 2003). Given that working-class graduates tend to have less opportunity in the labour market (Furlong and Cartmel, 2005), and larger student loan debt, his stay there may be longer than he would choose.

Sean appreciates that he has debt to pay off but would love to have a bike:

I had a selfish thought. With getting this audio typing job, I could save up and get myself a bike, then I thought I could use it to pay my council tax. I thought about all the stuff given to us where it comes from, the lights on the street, rubbish, water, art galleries. People taking our rubbish every day. All that comes from ... it's one big community and everyone has to put into it. If I've got the money I'll pay what I can. But I'd like the bike ... I was reading in *The Metro* [newspaper] today, some psychologist was talking about the power of advertising. I get affected by that. I feel like I want all this stuff all the time. I should just pay my council tax.

The paradox is evident in his closing comment, whereby Sean feels under pressure to consume things. Throughout our conversation, Sean expressed that he was concerned with trying to live in a way that he saw as 'right' and doing the 'right' things. A bike represents a practical, self-supporting purchase but he is compelled to pay his council tax debt. Since this is based on individuals' ability to pay, arrears become a growing problem in gentrifying areas that have a mix of social housing and expensive high-end properties. Sean does not consider two key things. First, government policies, like social mix, can exacerbate the experience of poverty thus *creating* an 'area-effect' rather than alleviating it. As middle-class practices are legitimated by the state so are working-class practices delegitimated. Consuming in this way means you can avoid being Othered, an experience which for Natasha involved being bullied. Sean tries to purchase social and cultural capital by spending economic capital but his inability to afford the bike denies him a chance of having higher social capital. In an area like Partick, situated next to the salubrious and well-to-do West End, this may be acute. Rosa succinctly compares living next to the West End as having her nose pressed up against the window of a sweetie shop, wishing to enjoy the pleasure but being excluded, only able to be a spectator. A second, connected point is that consumer citizenship and the privatisation of public services puts limitations on what people are able to consume. As mentioned, the level of social mix in Partick limits the amount of funding it receives. Therefore, having the 'Joneses' in the neighbourhood will detrimentally effect the provision of government funded services. Steve notes the decline in provisions for young people from when he grew up, like scouts and football and youth clubs, with which his mum had been involved. Indeed, one of the most repeated comments from all the people I spoke to was about the future of young people growing up in the neighbourhood and the dearth of youth services:

> Alan: Flats everywhere and now nothing to do for the youngsters.

> James: I would just want to see other people get an opportunity. Bring opportunities to the area, for youngsters growing up. Pensioners look at them and think they are little neds but they don't get it. They're bored out their heads.

> Jimmy: An "unders" disco [under 18s disco] for a start, a youth club, snooker boxing, dancing, even a café where they can sit and chat.

Steve explained that this was because there was no funding given to the neighbourhood:

> Partick is a "high amenities" area, apparently. It was one of the crackers: they [GCC] said "you've got a library". And even the football club that used to be run by the local boys, and aye, fair enough, there's a guy doing it now but that's off his own back.

The services that exist in Partick are attributed to the hard work of local people rather than government intervention, which is, again, indicative of high levels of working-class social capital. The 'Partick issue' was raised at a CPP meeting, with local community representatives complaining that Partick got less of a share of the Community Regeneration Budget. They reported that they not only have local service users with high needs, but that they serve many users who do not live in Partick, further questioning the logic behind the area-based budget provision. This concerned Natasha and her family:

> Natasha: The money is not there. It's not coming in here, it's going to Drumchapel, Easterhouse because of the mix you know, it's seen as an affluent area and there is poverty, maybe hidden.

> Dylan: There's cafes like that [social initiatives] up Scotstoun.

> Natasha: But not here. Because that's seen as a deprived area they get money. So you have to cross the boundary and then that leads to territorial fighting [amongst young people].

The 'high amenities' in question refer to the Kelvingrove Art Gallery and Museum, Sports Arena, the Transport Museum and public transport links, which justify the lack of interventionist type regeneration strategies in favour of those led by economic and property development. This reveals that a judgment is made as to what is good and bad social and cultural capital. Local community workers also rejected the 'high amenities' label:

> Louise: Aye, if you want to get drunk, bet and get crap food then aye high amenities. High amenities I would see is a swimming pool, which was shut down [...] but I don't get what high amenities are. People think that we have high amenities but we don't [...] in reality all we have is a bingo hall and pubs.

Louise, Norma and Phil's criticism of the lack of funding and poor quality services actually reifies the working class as having a deficit culture rather than recognising their role in building social capital in the community or recognising the impacts of social mix on funding and structural inequalities.

Sean described Partick as 'full of old people and drinkers'; this did not appeal to him as he has been practising Falun Gong, a form of Buddhism for four years:

> Sean: I've got loads of mixed friends now, lots of Chinese friends. Ling [...] and Chen, he is a refugee from China, here seeking asylum because of persecution [...] You know the biggest thing that I gained from moving to Partick was that. I find it fascinating that something like that can be found in a place like Partick. You have got the older generations and all the traditional things, you've still got a lot of good elements of culture because there is Partick Housing and the parade down Byres Road every year. There's so much in Partick. *It's traditional but also has good elements of culture.* [My emphasis]

Sean rejects the traditional as negative, denigrating what he perceives to be old working-class practices. He does not associate new forms of cultural practices with the working class, which relates to his class disassociation with the culture at the fish factory. Gentrification compounds the way social practices are evaluated and subsequently devalorised. The Annexe was involved in major neighbourhood activities, such as annual fetes, parades, and Christmas events. The centre has a café, holds classes ranging from African drumming, photography and fashion to the more prosaic literacy and numeracy courses. Louise, Norma and Gareth who worked there promoted values of self-improvement and active participation. For Louise, this centred on getting rid of 'negatives':

With the character here [in Partick] I can find a negative in it but I love that as I try to blast it out the water.

The negatives to which Louise referred to are pubs, smoking and the downbeat attitudes of the working-class. She assumes that these are representative of the working class and that, as such, they are devoid of any conviviality or positive aspects. Louise and Norma explained that such negative people just needed time to come round to their ideas and views of the world:

> Louise: There's things like yoga and goji berries [laughs]. There's a mix of what people want as they have asked for it and what people don't know about. It maybe takes them out and down a path to better their lives a bit. Ok, who are we to say that but that's what the Annexe is about and having a bit of fun in your life.
>
> Kirsteen: Is there an issue of getting people though the door first?
>
> Norma: There's some people in the community that have that attitude.
>
> Louise: Then you have people, who we won't mention as we're getting taped, but who are there at the start complaining but then [they are] at the reiki training. That's been a five year thing and they love it. That's what I'm saying with a slight negativity. They're scared of change. When they see things happening they try it out and they learn to enjoy it.

This shows the strategy of gaining popularity for a view by delegitimising and denigrating another, as discussed in the previous chapter. Culture is deployed here in a prescriptive and instructive way. These community workers identify certain behaviours as being good or bad, positive or negative. This results not only in cultural displacement but physical displacement too as there is a strong correlation between cultural disrespect and economic inequalities (Fraser, 1998), which I will now explore further.

Displacement: Cultural Disrespect and Economic Inequalities

Fi told me how she could no longer afford to eat at the Annexe. She and her friends used to go there for a cheap lunch, but the appointment of a former chef from a reputable Glasgow restaurant in the Annexe café saw the prices increase. Fi suggests it is now a place where doctor's wives go and recalls one woman she spoke with there:

> She's like [mock posh accent] "Oh Fi it's absolutely marvellous". I said "Not for working-class folk it's not. Folk who just want to talk about, 'I got the phone bill in' or 'my man was drunk and never gave me my money' or about your

weans not having a school uniform". I mean, I mind my kids didnae have a school uniform and I had to pass the one's who was skinny to the one that was fat. Know what I mean? You've been there! *You've nae choice, you have to.* Because that's real life. That's what we used to sit and talk about. You cannae talk about that now. Well nothing's stopping you … well you're limited to what your conversation can be because women like that cannae relate […] Someone needs to say: hold on a minute this is what we want, this is what we need. I don't want to do arts and crafts, 'cause not everybody does. [My emphasis]

Fi resents both losing a place she went to socialise and losing a space where she can be herself, or be working-class. Yet at the same time, Fi says that she regularly uses a new arts café to get supplies for her daughter who collects scraps, an activity now deemed kitsch and fashionable. This results in her bonding with the middle-class gentrifier owners:

> Fi: The women in it are lovely. And one's like … this women … it's like talking to a fairy talking to her. She goes like that [swings arms around]. I mean she's lovely but […] It's nice that it's there 'cause it's there and it brings people into Partick, which is good.

She then went on to complain that the women were all reading middle-class newspapers, *The Herald*, and no one was reading *The Sun* newspaper, although she was quick to point out to me that she did not read *The Sun* herself. Fi is aware of, and personally experiences, class displacement but, as outlined in the previous chapter, she can, and does, negotiate this.

Yet, in other ways there was less room for negotiation. Local people are excluded from a number of gentrified places, as they are non-affluent users, like the Harbour development and the range of new restaurants and bars. This was felt to be a particular problem for young people:

> Jimmy: I don't envisage that there will be many young people walking about there [the Harbour] at all, they would have polis [the police] out straight away. For young people to get down to the water from here they would have to cut through the estate, or whatever it's called, and give it 10 minutes and the polis would be on their trail.

> Dylan: Aye, exactly.

> Kirsteen: Has that ever happened? [to the kids]

> Ellie: Aye.

> Jimmy: I think just because they are so expensive and because of the people who are supposed to be staying there, I think that these young people will not be allowed down. Not allowed to walk about their own streets.
>
> Natasha: They're not allowed to walk about their own streets anyway.
>
> Jimmy: Aye I know but even more so. If you're about here you've got more chance walking up and down Dumbarton Road than they have got down there.

The granary site was a popular hangout for teenagers but the redevelopment dictated that it had to be used by the right people, with the right capital, in the correct way that corresponds to capital consumption, unlike Sylvie's subversive usage.

Steve felt gentrification had contributed to the displacement of community ties and networks:

> Steve: It [Partick] used to be well tight. The pub, the Hyndland Bar that was the gang bar.[2] It's the Rio Cafe. Every generation drank in there. We're all spread about now. Some families are banned from this one and that one. That was an institution known all over the world. It changed about 10 years ago, it's had a few different names. They tried to up-market it but it didn't work and now they've had so many owners.
>
> Kirsteen: What do you think of it now?
>
> Steve: They don't let us in [laughs]. I think they have photos of us about Partick not to let us in [laughs].
>
> Kirsteen: Really? Do you have quite a bit of trouble getting in places?
>
> Steve: Partly my fault, partly snobbery.

For Steve, it was part of 'old school' Partick's masculine, patriarchal culture. Although less catastrophic than household displacement, this still affects people in visceral and psychological ways. Men like Steve, whose identity and ontological security was undermined by deindustrialisation and Thatcherism, suffer the loss of the place once given to their social networks and are made to feel like the Other. Cultural displacement extends to cause actual physical displacement, as Marcuse (1986: 157) remarks:

---

2   The gang in question is the Partick Young Team, of various generations. This was where the hard men of Partick were said to drink.

Displacement affects many more than those actually displaced at any given moment. When a family sees its neighbourhood changing dramatically, when all their friends are leaving, when stores are going out of business and new stores for their other clientele are taking their places [...] pressure of displacement is already severe, and it's actually only a matter of time.

This cultural disrespect goes hand in hand with the increased privatisation. PHA has preserved the housing stock of around 1,700 properties, which protects against the effects of gentrification and displacement. However, the change in the role and institutional form of social housing providers has undermined this. Registered social landlord's stock levels have been decreasing each year since the 1980s.

Table 5.1   Components of new housing supply in Scotland

	Private new build	Housing assoc' new build	Local authority new build	Refurb'	Conversion	New housing supply
1996–97	17,491	2,963	241	984	1,244	22,923
2003–04	20,086	3,368	–	410	1,409	25,273
2007–08	21,618	4,097	28	389	1,417	27,549

Note: New house building: houses completed by or for housing associations, local authorities or private developers for below market rent or low cost home ownership; houses completed for market sale by private developers; Refurbishment: houses acquired by housing associations and refurbished either for rent or low cost home ownership. Refurbishment of private dwellings funded wholly or partly through the Affordable Housing Investment Programme; Conversion: new dwellings created by conversion from non-housing to housing use.
Source: Housing Statistics for Scotland (2009).

The housing supply increase since 1996 is mainly attributable to private new builds. While there has been an increase in housing association new builds, this figure does not differentiate between housing association new build for rent and for sale. The affordability of housing has been hotly contested, even when a shared equity scheme such as co-ownership is offered. A council officer presented a GCC report to the West area CPP in 2006 explaining that the council base affordability on the *Annual Survey of Hours and Earnings*, for a year, a single working person's average earnings is £21,000 p.a., giving an affordable house value of £63,000. They assume that a working couple without children would be expected to have a total income of one and a half times average earnings, or £31,500, and an affordable house value of £94,500. Using residual income calculations, a single person can afford £76, 000 and a couple can afford £146,000. There are a number of problems with this. Firstly, these figures are not representative of people with children and do not take into account other factors such as job security: short-term contract work affects the likelihood of securing mortgage loans. Secondly, a £21,000 average figure precludes those who are not in employment, which skews the representation of income of the city population. In Partick, 15 per cent of the working-age population are in receipt of JSA or DLA; in Partick South Glasgow Harbour, 16 per cent in Partick and 24 per cent in Whiteinch (falling under the locally defined boundary for Partick), are immediately excluded from homeownership, outright or shared (Scottish Neighbourhood Statistics, 2009). This does not account for those on low income. Single earners, single parents and those with a household income under £21,000, accounted for nearly half of those I interviewed. Shared equity schemes were criticised by Fi, Natasha, Jimmy, and Bea who in particular had first hand, negative experiences of it. Eleven per cent of those interviewed owned their own home, with the rest in private rented and socially rented accommodation or living with parents. Finally, added to this, the average house price in Partick largely exceeded these categories of affordability, with very few properties available in the region of £63,000.

Table 5.2   House sales median prices 1997–2007 by intermediate geography

Intermediate geography	Median price: 1997	Median price: 2007
Glasgow Harbour and Partick South	£36,000	£172,495
Partick	£47,850	£125,000
Whiteinch	£34,950	£91,500
Partickhill and Hyndland	£70,000	£187,777

Source: Scottish Neighbourhood Statistics (2009).

This suggests that that there is a clear shift in supply rather than lower demands, as the director to PHA tried to suggest. Instead, and what she had experienced in practice, there was still high demand for socially rented accommodation:

> Janey: The prices in the West End are just going up and up and pricing people out of homes so it's pushing everyone away, I'm not here and I was here for 20 years [...]. The property market is really the worst, you know. I cannot understand how a house can be valued at £65,000 but go for £140,000[3] or more

---

3   Scotland's 'offers over' system is when a stated cost is only an indication of the price that the seller is being advised to market the property at, allowing homeowners to engender competition and gain the highest price possible. This is between 5 per cent and 50 per cent over the survey price although 20 per cent has been the general rule. This means that people buy property, with loans, over the amount at which the property is valued.

than that because it's on a certain street, it's crazy it makes no sense. And that is
the biggest difference between the "haves" and the "have nots", the people who
have grown up here all their lives, and they can't afford to stay there.

In addition, PHA has turned to property development to supplement its grants and funding, using their risk isolator, DRK 2001, to build West 11 in partnership with Cruden Homes. Initial plans indicated a desire for Partick residents to take up a limited number of the flats, either as social renters or as new homeowners. It was confirmed as being overwhelmingly in favour of homeowners, with 76 flats for owner-occupation and three homes for rent. The prices are not based on affordability, starting from £175,000 and going up to £300,000. Cultural and material forms of displacement are intimately linked and relate to the wider denigration of working-class culture. Since social housing provision increasingly involves business principles, those who are not morally or materially productive are in danger of being 'unfixed' to place. I elaborate this in following sections, which identify four novel typologies of displacement which relate to the privatisation of social housing.

Perverse Displacement

The key change in community housing providers, from a primary concern with social well-being to a neoliberal model, through the partial re-privatisation of associations (Randolph, 1993), alters the role of social housing providers as safeguards against displacement. By developing property, PHA contributes to gentrification in the area, which has a domino effect on shops and services, what Marcuse (1985) calls 'displacement pressure'. The development increases the number of luxury houses in the area, which attracts more affluent groups, which subsequently alters the local demographic composition, whereby working-class residents become the minority. I suggest that when this process is initiated by a social landlord, the term perverse displacement is more befitting. This occurs when the social housing provider, in an effort to financially support themselves, inadvertently increases gentrification in the area, which affects the housing opportunities of social renters. In 2002, there were 208 applicants on the Partick housing waiting list; by 2005 this was 225, and by 2006 it was almost 400. In this time, PHA have barely built any new properties in the area, acquiring only 16 properties. Yet during this time they helped commission the building of private apartments at West 11. Ironically, as PHA undertakes increasing self-financing projects, residents' – their customers – housing opportunities are curtailed.

This can lead to displacement through lack of choice or availability of suitable stock. Living in socially rented accommodation, Janey faced a dilemma as her family size increased:

Janey: Space; we needed more space. We put in for a bigger flat and it was like how long is a piece of string? Nice people get bigger flats and they don't move out.

She had to move out of Partick, and Glasgow, to neighbouring Dumbarton. She accounts for why she did this:

Kirsteen: Are you renting?

Janey: [Quietens voice] It's a bought house, it's bought. It was my mum's. She sold it to us for a very reasonable price. We could never have afforded it, we had a five-year plan. Just after Logan was born my mum said she would sell it to us, which was great as I wasn't working. Michael was, but not an amazing job. I wish I could move it to the West End.

Kirsteen: Would you like to move back?

Janey: God yeah, if I won the lottery, or if my dad left me loads of money. I would, I would. It is the best area in Glasgow.

Kirsteen: How does living in Dumbarton compare?

Janey: Oh it doesn't, it doesn't. We have to come to Glasgow for everything ... swimming lessons. There's nothing except cheaper and bigger housing.

Similarly, Agnes also took a larger, socially rented family home outside Partick 20 years earlier when it was clear she would have to wait on the list for a long time to get suitable accommodation. Now that her family have grown up, moved out and into Partick themselves, she could not return to the neighbourhood and was stuck with the family home. Therefore, this community housing association's new entrepreneurial endeavours, not only offer little returns to the social renters, they have a negative effect. The poor supply of new social housing not only limits housing choices, but coupled with increased private housing, working-class residents are outnumbered by middle-class renters, which creates political displacement, seen in Chapter 4, and cultural displacement. The full effects of this are latent; the process is only just occurring and has serious ramifications for young people leaving home.

Latent Generational Displacement

There has been a marked increase in young people shifting from owner occupation to the private rental sector (Heath, 2008). Working-class youth transitions in housing incur more risks and fewer choices than similar middle-class transitions. They are at the forefront of changes in social attitudes, especially towards housing, contributes to the remaking of class identities from a theoretical perspective. This builds from culturalist class theorists' oppositional account of class that places emphasis on difference, to include the material realities of the hierarchical nature of class and inequalities and the material basis of culture. However, the conceptual language needed to explore this further is limited. Indeed, Savage (2000: 19–20), suggests the lack of conceptual resources is the key impediment to class analysis:

> [...] the conceptual cupboard of classical class theory looks dusty. To those not socialized into its particular interests, the problem is not that the cupboard is bare, but rather that the items inside seem out of date.

I suggest that we already have these resources, they just require adjustment.

First, the revival of the place-based, community studies tradition offers rich resources (Savage et al., 2005, 2005a; Allen, 2008; Blokland, 2005, 2003). However, Savage et al. (2005a) suggest that the term community should be cast off as it carries baggage from the past, connoting homogeneity and face-to-face interactions. Habitus is said to better convey the varied biographies, lifestyles and autonomy of individuals and community 'sifting' where similar people flock together (Savage et al., 2005). While a Bourdieusian framework and the concept of habitus have been a popular way of reviving place-based community studies it has limited capabilities when it comes to understanding urban restructuring. Since habitus is a fixed concept it does not capture the powerful dynamics of transition and contestation or the material processes that this involves, whereas a hegemonic framework explicates processes of change over time and critiques the value judgments on working-class practices and capital which can be inadvertently reified becoming disempowering. If, as Gramsci (1971) said, Fordist hegemony is born in the factory then it can be said that neoliberal hegemony is born in the neighbourhood. In the context of the neighbourhood, community is a keyword albeit in a restructured way, which helps elucidate the political and structural aspects of hegemony as well as the lived and fought for culture. Regeneration and urban policies are implemented and ratified through community planning and consultation processes, as outlined in Chapter 4. The reconfiguration of politics and citizenship occurs at the level of local community politics. Thus, community is an object and instrument of urban policy (Imrie and Raco, 2003) as well as providing a medium through which citizens can bargain with the state via participation processes. Second, the term community helps us understand class based social relations in industrial working-class neighbourhoods. While in some respects neighbourhoods like Partick have lost their traditional raison d'être, the immediacy and intimacy of relationships and the conviviality around tenement living, we also know this nostalgic picture of community cohesion is illusory. Neighbourhood communities are not homogenous and are characterised by a socially mixed demographic more than ever (Mooney and Danson, 1997; Lees, 2003). As demonstrated in Chapter 3, the neighbourhood population was not fixed but mobile and comprised a range of individuals from various backgrounds and

and processes of individualisation and class. Owner-occupation is the normalised choice but is increasingly beyond their means, whilst the decline in the availability of social housing further reduces their housing options (Heath, 2008). They display strong 'choice narratives' (Heath and Kenyon, 2001) but are more financially vulnerable. Latent displacement refers to the experiences of young people, who in their first move from the parental home, are unable to afford to buy or rent privately or secure socially rented accommodation in the area and have no choice but to leave the neighbourhood.

Studies have found that access to affordable housing in the private rented sector is often curtailed by landlords' preferences to rent to students, which seems a likely explanation of why Gordon and his sister were evicted from Broomhill. Gordon is living with his parents and has his name registered on numerous housing lists including PHA. He notes the irony whereby he is teased by workmates for being 'posh' because he comes from the West End but cannot afford to live in the neighbourhood in which he was born:

> Gordon: When I worked in the city centre and they would say you're from the West End and I'd be like I'm from Partick! It just bothers me because you know I can't get anywhere to stay around where I live now. I can't afford it and that's something that annoys me because the prices are so expensive, I guess that's like everywhere now.

Fi, whose son had a similar experience to Gordon, echoed this:

> It's a big issue. I can't get my son a house but other people do. A whole generation of people can't get a house, you can't buy. They are with their mothers.

This latent generational displacement worries Bea. She sees young people as the ones with their 'neck on the block' with mortgages. She berates the homeownership – through a co-ownership scheme with PHA:

> It didn't help people, it put them more into poverty. Because PHA didn't explain co-ownership to people; what was happening to them. They were like this is great, I'm going to get half the house, half the house is bought but they didn't tell them the problem […] in the very small print of the title deeds, which they kept […] it said the second part of the house can only be yours when you buy the second part at today's prices. So in 20 years the second part is worth £90,000. So the house they bought at £45,000 and they paid £20,000 odds towards it, they got a mortgage to pay that other half is £90,000. They don't even try and get a mortgage to pay for that half. So ownership is a no-no for young people. They can't get out of it, the only way they could is if they buy the first half and then some great aunt dies and leaves them a fortune.

Bea believes that the shared equity schemes penalise and prey on the young, who have less capital and who are keen to get on the ladder.

Gary had been affected by the deficit in affordable housing in Partick. He was in the problematic and common, peripheral position where he is eligible for only a few housing allocation points yet does not earn enough to buy a property in Partick. He could not get a PHA flat when he was leaving home for the first time. He privately rented then went through the homeless system. Now he is displaced and cannot return to the neighbourhood:

> Kirsteen: Would you like to live in Partick again or are you happy where you are?

> Gary: (slowly to emphasise) *I would love to stay in Partick*. I looked at the Homestake in Partick Housing Association scheme with Communities Scotland and it was only opened to Partick residents, Housing Association residents. You take on 70 per cent they take on 30 per cent but the prices started at £180,000, so how is that affordable housing? Especially working-class residents, on an average income.

Darren was in this situation too. Coming back to Partick from London, he wanted to buy a house in the area, but could not afford to do so. He did not qualify for social housing, and found rent too expensive in the area so moved in with his parents. The process may seem less like displacement to young respondents: as Heath and Cleaver (2003) point out, they express a choice narrative, which suggests that this is a lifestyle preference, rather than a choice dictated by circumstances.

Strategic Displacement

Ironically, whilst urban policies valorise location in relation to middle-class settlement, this same reification of place denigrates local attachment. This was compounded by the negative treatment of local connections within housing policy. The Local Connections policy, which awarded residents points on the housing list on the basis that they were from the area originally or that they had family in the area, was scrapped. Residents did not welcome this change: there was much bitterness and resentment about not being given recognition on the housing list. The PHA previously used the slogan 'Partick homes for Partick people', where priority was given to local residents with local family connections in the allocation process. Now, it follows a sensitive allocation approach:

> In accordance with the association's aim of achieving a balanced community, and to take account of the needs of other residents, there may be occasions when it is not considered appropriate to allocate a property to the person with the highest points total. Such an allocation would require to be authorised, with

supporting evidence by the Customer Services Coordinator or another senior officer. (PHA, 2009)

This was part of equal opportunities legislation. This constituted 25 per cent transfers; 40 per cent housing list applicants; 4 per cent Home Mobility scheme; 19 per cent nominations (statutory homeless); 6 per cent referrals from supported agencies; 5 per cent 'aspirational moves'; 1 per cent reciprocal. PHA record and monitor relevant information to 'identify trends, and take appropriate action to try to redress imbalances' (PHA, 2009) which means they can introduce more desirable residents if they think it is necessary.

While it has the potential for racial bias, removing recognition of local connections has a punitive effect, especially on those for whom proximity is a necessity. Various arguments exist around the costs and benefits of such a policy. Either way, a process of social selection takes place, outside of the local community's control:

> Fi: You can't just go down and say "Can I get a house, I stay in Partick". The Housing has to do this pick outside and family members are not getting the choice of living in Partick […] They sent round cards to everyone […] You were to go down to the office for a house. Put your name down. I went down and said that I was there for my daughter because she was at work and we queued and queued and queued and she was 1,009th on the list. What they do is give you points. That was all changing. People were saying "here wait a minute we're not getting houses here". The women down the street, her son stays out way past Rutherglen. He was brought up here he was in the Boys Brigade and everything and his family are not getting brought up in the community that his dad and his granny did. And because "Joe Bloggs" from Springburn's mum is battering them they have to move.

Fi, herself an 'outsider', is against 'incomers' receiving priority in housing allocations in Partick over 'born and bred' residents. She is not opposed to outsiders coming in but rather the displacement it results in for local families. Residents want the right to stay fixed in their area, for their family not to be dispersed. Molly described her long wait on the housing list: 'I was born here basically and still not entitled to anything'.

Some incoming residents were surprised at how quickly they were housed by PHA and perceived that their suitability as tenants was rewarded. Norma, Gareth and Louise were community workers at the Annexe and PHA tenants. Norma had lived in Partick for 14 years, before which she had lived in the West End as a student but originally came from Ayrshire. She likes the mix of people who go to the community centre and commented:

> Norma: So me who's not from Partick can come into it and meet other people from Partick, that's why it's good. My neighbours in the close are old Partick people, they've stayed here all their life. I get on with them. My upstairs

neighbour commented to me that Partick Housing Association policy was to get lots of new people in. So his friend couldn't get a place to live here when he's from Partick. I think there's a bit of resentment in some people as their brother, cousins, what have you, couldn't get a flat.

Louise has lived in Partick for 12 years, moving from her parent's flat in Hyndland after she had her first child:

> Louise: I was told I would have to wait a while for a house but it was really, really quick.
>
> Norma: I waited three months.
>
> Louise: Well I was a few weeks. Seriously. I phoned up and it was like "here's the keys".
>
> Gareth: I agree. I found that out of all the associations I applied to PHA were more sympathetic to people's needs ...
>
> Louise: And Gareth's got a lovely house and all, it's beautiful. It's above the PHA office, it's got a balcony and everything hasn't it? He can watch what's going on, looking onto the market. See I didn't realise it, you know, about class, 'til I moved down here. People got a bit miffed about working class, middle class and that.
>
> Kirsteen: And that was not something significant when you were growing up?
>
> Louise: No, because I didn't notice it as a problem. I thought it more as open and closed. I like people in any shape or form, take them as they are and I didn't get the whole class thing. My neighbours they gave me a hard time. I think it was about me getting the flat.
>
> Gareth: People have said that to me. How did you get that flat? In some ways I was made to feel guilty. I had to tell myself that I do deserve it. It's better now I know I'm a well kenned [*sic* – known] face.
>
> Norma: Yeah, we're all classed as the community now, but loads of people have grown up here.

Later in our conversation, Louise describes class as a negative disposition of people who blame the world for their problems, rather than being self-motivated. Class is a negativity, which she takes great pleasure in 'blasting out the water' in her work at the Annexe. She does not perceive class to be a problem in her life, or indeed recognise it at all, growing up in affluent Hyndland. She cannot believe that the government provides social welfare, 'I can't believe they just give you a house and a giro, a house and money for nothing. I just can't believe that'. She does not appreciate the difficult circumstances people find themselves in that would require such support, even though she draws from these provisions herself. While I cannot comment on their precise circumstances, not knowing the situation under which they were allocated accommodation, it is clear that these residents fit the policy profile of the ideal citizen and resident. They have New Labour values, do not believe in class, are aspirational and self-motivated. This compounds the idea that being 'born and bred' in the area is a negative, and ill-regarded, while more educated, motivated incomers are the welcomed demographic.

Some respondents who had low incomes or were reliant on benefits lived in fear of eviction for missing payments on rent:

> Sean: I'm just worried about my rent arrears. Partick Housing have threatened to take me to court a few times. I've got all my furniture in that flat, if I was to lose that flat I would have nowhere to put that stuff.

Steve found himself threatened with eviction by PHA for rent arrears.

> That was happening with me. I got this letter from Partick Housing Association. They do this traffic light thing; three strikes and you're out. I'm on amber. But surely you're entitled to a couple of hundred pounds [arrears]? I went to Shelter. They've been great; these housing associations are laws unto themselves … I mean it's not the greatest of wee flats I've got but it's a roof over my head and I need it.

Rent arrears are a significant problem for housing associations since the 1988 Housing Act required them to use a proportion of private finance in their building projects (Sprigings, 2002). Steve risked being evicted from his flat for having a couple of hundred pounds rent arrears. He said that he was not given the opportunity to make arrangements to pay this. Sprigings (2002) comments that these are often easily resolved but the processes are overly bureaucratic involving little face-to-face communication. Steve recalled his girlfriend's experience:

> Steve: She is from Springburn [in the North of Glasgow] but she had to go through Hamish Allen[4] [in the city centre]. She got evicted from Maryhill Housing Association for rent arrears I couldn't believe it. Her dad went down with a cheque, they said "no, we want her out".

The direct cheque payment was rejected and she was evicted. Sprigings (2002) notes that it is bad business sense since, if evicted, the association would foreclose

---

4 The Hamish Allen Centre is run by GCC. It is where people who find themselves homeless go to officially present themselves in order to receive temporary accommodation, a homelessness case-worker and to enter into the process of being re-housed.

any chance of collecting monies owed and would treat it as a 'write off'. He notes that money would also be lost in the time between evictions and re-letting, probably around one month's rent, and that standard re-let repairs cost around £500 to £1,000, which is not cost effective.

'Notice of proceedings'[5] have increased over the same period that gentrification has increased, and concurrent changes in re-privatisation of social housing, which confirms what I heard from respondents.

Table 5.3   **'Notice of proceedings', court actions and housing recovery undertaken by PHA 2005–2008**

	2004–2005	2005–2006	2006–2007	2007–2008
Notice of proceedings	50	58	108	61
Court action initiated	28	13	41	9
Recovery of possession grants	4	5	7	5

Source: The Scottish Housing Regulator (2009).

The number of 'Notice of proceedings' issued to tenants doubled in the 2005–2007 period, which was also the peak of the housing boom. This raises the question as to whether profit is more desirable than social welfare and whether housing associations are increasingly policing residents, especially those who are flawed consumers, in favour of creating aspirational residents in the neighbourhood. Charged with the responsibility of monitoring the balance and mix in the area, PHA can intervene in the selection of housing applicants to secure this balance. This can result in the selection of socially and financially productive tenants and de-selection of those who are not. PHA's tactical mixing and its quest for profit could result in strategic evictions, whereby residents with rent arrears are treated less sympathetically and more punitively:

> Steve: Someone was really wanting me out cause they weren't backing down on it, they [PHA] were trying to evict me. Kait [at Westgap] was going to go to the paper and that made them back down.

It can be argued that working-class residents without the 'correct' capital credentials can be unfixed from place, in order for it to be more profitable.

---

5   The process is as follows: first, a 'notice of proceedings' is sent, followed by legal proceedings and tenants will be sent a summons telling them when their case will be heard at court. When the case goes to courts the sheriff can grant a decree for eviction. Sheriff officers will be sent to remove tenants from the property. They are entitled to use reasonable force to enter the home and remove tenants and their possessions.

Spiralling Displacement

The effects of these different forms of displacement are not limited to the immediate neighbourhood. Gentrification has a spiralling effect. Gordon ricochets back to his parents from other areas, including a neighbourhood in the Southside as it underwent gentrification and became too expensive:

> If you get on the waiting list and wait seven years, you might get one but I wouldn't bank on it. I've put my name down every year, Partick and Yorkhill as well. But I'm putting my name down for Ibrox. Apparently they're trying to regenerate the area and they have kicked out the junkies and the troublemakers and they're giving the houses out *to people*. So people who have been working in a job for two or three years have a good chance of getting a house [...] A few folk who have done it, a couple who come in here [the pub]. It's only £120 a month or £150 for a studio or one bedroom, it's cheap, cheap as fuck [...] I went to the Southside before because it was cheaper but it got as bad as round here, £475, £500 a month [for a one bedroom apartment]. [My emphasis]

Although a 'Partick boy' and 'posh totty', Gordon sees the potential in moving to 'up and coming' Ibrox, despite being seen as a less respectable neighbourhood by Partickonians. This becomes an acceptable move for respectable people. So the working class in Partick position themselves as respectable in comparison to other working-class neighbourhoods. Gordon differentiates junkies and troublemakers from 'people' in general. His reading of regeneration involves displacing 'problem' residents in Ibrox to make way for respectable people, like himself, which differs from Janey's belief in the community's solidarity. He does not see this process happening in Partick, where he positions himself as 'a norm' but the perceptions of gentrifiers and policy-makers position him as the Other. Sylvie's uncle is an Ibrox resident. He is being threatened by displacement as his house is due to be demolished in the redevelopment process. GCC had served him with a compulsory purchase order so they could obtain the land his property is on for redevelopment. His neighbours accepted their offers from the council on their properties but he was resisting:

> Sylvie: My uncle Joe, his house is coming down in Ibrox and the only place he wants to move to is Partick. So he's not taking money for his house, he's not moving or anything so they won't pull it down. He won't move 'til he gets Partick.

Ironically, he refuses to leave until he can be sure that he will be re-housed in Partick, where his mother, sister and niece live. This shows just how complex the locational movements created by gentrification processes are.

Conclusion

Gentrification seeks to create space for the more affluent user and, as I have argued throughout, the more affluent user within a financial and moral economy. The paradox is that working-class participation in gentrification is encouraged but it compounds class inequality. It creates a bulimic situation where respondents are simultaneously included and excluded in gentrification processes. The improvements that are generated through gentrification come from the retreat of state provisions and increased privatisation of services. Nowhere was there an improvement to the labour market, earnings and material conditions of residents. Rather, the upgrading of the neighbourhood, including housing, shops, services and environment are often privately funded. Participating in gentrification then comes at a cost. This cost is compounded by the policy thinking that holds that neighbourhoods requiring regeneration are socially and economically deficient. Subsequently, working-class participation in gentrification is redemptive: a way of avoiding being differentiated as the Other or as a means of 'keeping up with the Joneses'. This action resulted in negative, material consequences relating to debt. Paradoxically, if working-class respondents' local practices appear to be more socially productive than their middle-class counterparts which fundamentally challenges the logic underpinning social mix policy. What all these complex processes reveal is the productive value in displacing the working-class subject, which extends beyond issues of culture and can, in some instances, result in their physical displacement.

What I want to emphasise is that not only are residents simultaneously included and excluded, their exclusion has cultural and material dimensions which are inextricably linked. This is because social practices are commodified, expressed in the terminology of 'social capital' and the logic of value. This foregrounds the relationship between cultural disrespect and economic inequalities. The delegitimation of working-class practices could result in physical displacement like Steve's hang-out at the Hyndland Bar, or Fi's lunch dates at the Annexe. The working-class subject is displaced in both cultural and physical ways. Class distinction is based not only on dissimulation but on unequal terms, which is often overlooked by culturalist class theorists. Conceptualisations of social capital, whether in policy prescriptions, Putnam (2000), or contemporary class analyses which draw from Bourdieu's (1984, 1986, 1987) tend to underplay the material basis of differentiation. The problem is that hierarchical accounts of cultural distinction and metaphoric capital can inadvertently legitimise the value of the dominant culture of gentrification and neoliberalism. Working-class practices are always cast as inferior and culturally deficient to begin with. I suggest that distinctions between groups are over emphasised and are too tightly delineated, which homogenises and fixes class categories. Instead heterogeneity is evident in the way in which working-class residents identify Others. The working-class are seen as having deficit social capital stocks and therefore not able to make distinctions, but they do. There is a domino effect. Working-class residents can be colonisers, displacers, gentrifiers. They can differentiate and denigrate Other groups. This is heavily circumscribed and stratified: not on the same par as the middle-class' differentiation. It is actually borne out of the restriction of choice (meanwhile maintaining the seeming illusion of greater choice).

This restriction of choice is evident in the commodification, and subsequent contraction of social housing. While PHA undertook self-financing projects, residents simultaneously had their housing choices circumscribed and made more tenuous. Social housing associations, borne out of working-class struggles against housing problems last century, are now complicit in promoting gentrification within the neighbourhood and displacing residents, evident in the use of Compulsory Purchase Orders and crystallising with the recent 'Bedroom Tax'. Since gentrification is driven by profit, working-class groups will be unfixed from place so that capital (and more socially and materially productive residents) can more profitably refix to that place. This new typology of displacement elucidates the complex ways that this is realised. This leads to the physical displacement of the working-class subject. The fundamental paradox is that despite being invited to participate, the working class are denied the means to do so and their fixity to place is weakened. So, again, we are alerted to the fact that the cultural differences that are said to exist between middle and working-class groups are overstated. The real differentiation that exists between these groups is seen in the degree of control they have over fixity to place. This underlines too the significance of understanding place as a key intersection in class analysis.

Conclusions:
Reinvigorating Urban Class Analysis

In the introduction, I used the keyword 'restructuring' to encapsulate the essence of the processes being examined in this book: gentrification as experienced by the working class. Throughout, I have attempted to understand how urban restructuring affects, and is affected by, working-class communities, presenting a new sociological perspective of gentrification from a working-class standpoint. The hope is to have demonstrated that gentrification is integral to the process of restructuring towards flexible forms of accumulation and neoliberalism. As such it is part of a hegemonic project driven by the state and the market, although not exclusively, as it involves middle-class gentrifiers, urban entrepreneurs and public and private agencies who form alliances which coalesce to create a hegemonic bloc. In this context, gentrification is all at once an economic, cultural and moral project that necessitates the reorganisation of class, identity and neighbourhoods associated with industrial Fordist production. I have sought to demonstrate how gentrification helps create a space for the affluent user but also, more significantly, cultivates a more affluent user within a moral and financial economy and how this is a negotiable rather than determined process. Part of this political project involves a shift in the relationship between the state and the citizen, redefined through the expansion of participation via consumer citizenship. Through this restructured form of citizenship, working-class people negotiated with processes of gentrification that were not outwardly in their interest or advantageous to them. In doing this I also hope that I have managed to convey how residents with both first-hand and generational industrial working-class histories adapted their identities to fit with the post-industrial neoliberal hegemony. These restructured identities were classed, but not in the traditional sense. Instead, they displayed neoliberal characteristics through narratives of choice. Restructuring, then, provides new pleasures and rewards, as a well as inequalities and injuries for people. This intimates a dialectical process whereby urban restructuring and working-class communities are intimately and inextricably interrelated. This is not only dialectical in relation to the politicisation of community vis-à-vis participation and partnerships, but also in the way consumer citizenship and choice narratives become common characteristics of working-class neighbourhood life over more classic forms of collectivism. Yet, these new characteristics still allowed people to act in collective ways to oppose gentrification and neoliberalism.

I will elaborate this new sociological perspective on gentrification in more detail by discussing three major themes. The first considers what this new perspective tells us about the use of gentrification as a strategy of restructuring and what effects it has on those it targets. The second theme focuses on how to analytically and conceptually recharge working-class analysis through place-based community research and by appropriating conceptual language reserved for middle-class groups. Finally, if restructuring is the keyword of this book, the keyword, and third theme, of this concluding chapter is control. To reiterate, keywords emphasise changing social relations, political contests, and prospects of possibility for the present and the future (Williams, 1983). Residents' individualised responses to restructuring are an act of control. The concept of control is useful in differentiating the stratified experiences of gentrification amongst working-class and middle-class groups. It is analytically useful for differentiating class inequalities and distinguishing experiences of displacement from elective movements. The concept of control also helps elucidate how gentrification operates as a hegemonic project. I consider how these issues discussed may be taken forward to reinvigorate urban class analysis.

The New Theoretical Lens on Gentrification and Displacement

The definition of gentrification employed informs how its effects are conceived. Using a framework of hegemony allowed me to surpass orthodox accounts of gentrification. It enabled a broader empirical enquiry which helped generate new insights into both gentrification and displacement and the workings of hegemony within a current project. It also generated further research questions. Research into gentrification has been impeded by arguments that the concept does not grasp the processes that people use it to describe; 'gentrification is almost too quaint and small scale a concept to capture the process at work' (Boddy, 2007: 103). Alone and without a clear theoretical framework, it is true that the concept of gentrification cannot explain all the processes at work. Hegemony can help attend to the shortcomings in gentrification research outlined by Slater (2006). Certainly, other political projects and strategies are involved in post-industrial restructuring and there are many other regeneration initiatives implemented by the state. What is particularly significant about the use of gentrification to achieve restructuring is that it expresses the two aspects of hegemony. It relates to the social structure and the political project involved in making the social structure cohesive. In Partick, gentrification is a crucial strategy in the hegemonic shift towards post-industrial neoliberalism. Ostensibly, Partick is gentrified via the Harbour redevelopment, where disused industrial land in this prime location has been transformed into luxury flats. This space is altered to facilitate consumption and is, therefore, geared towards more affluent users. Neoliberalism is also 'rolled out' to the wider neighbourhood. This involves the re-privatisation of social housing and the privatisation of public space and services, as Alison suggested, thereby turning the community into a commodity. This is not only a spatial fix; gentrification also transforms social processes so that they correspond to productive relations. As part of a hegemonic project, gentrification has cultural and moral imperatives. It is used to gentrify the subject by shaping social practices to be more congruent with neoliberalism and flexible forms of accumulation. In this way, gentrification not only turned communities into commodities, it turned the subject, through the notion of human capital into a commodity, which is evident in the discussions in Chapter 5.

It is worth saying more on this. The social capital model is paradoxical and neoliberal. The model is used throughout government policy, implemented through strategies that seek to cultivate 'valuable' capital within communities which are deemed to have 'devalued'. Regeneration policy on social mix evaluates cultural practices in terms of capital which signifies their moral and material value. The scale for measuring this is constructed by the state, based on their vision for what a community needs and should be like. In the context of policy, 'valuable' social capital is reflected in shared social networks, shared social norms and high levels of trust amongst a social group (Kearns, 2003). Working-class capital is deemed to lack these qualities and is, instead, without worth or value. Yet it was clear, particularly in chapters 4 and 5, that working-class residents had 'valuable' social capital in a policy sense of shared networks, norms and trust, in relation to Putnam's (2000) interpretation which bridges and bonds, and in relation to Bourdieu (1986, 1987) where it constitutes a persons' social status in the sense that Partick residents were proud to be so. While Bourdieu's model of metaphoric capital is infinitely more critical than both Putnam's and policy models since it acknowledges the hierarchical material nature of capital, using the metaphor of capital imposes an evaluation on practices. Even in Bourdieu's account the working-class habitus as the 'choice of the necessary' (Bourdieu, 1984: 372–96) which Watt (2006) points out is effectively a deficit model in which the working class are treated as an absence, lacking both cultural and economic capital and therefore incapable of making distinctions. This was shown not to be the case in the last chapter as Partick residents denigrated and displaced Others in neighbouring Ibrox. What the use of metaphors of capital do not get to is an appreciation of intricate relationship between the (de)valuing and (im)moralising of cultural capital and land value and capital. The devaluing of behaviour, practices and ways of life in formerly industrial neighbourhoods, towns, correlates with gentrification processes in fact they are the often essential to this hegemonic process. Devaluation of people and places not only contributes to the creation of a viable rent gap it also legitimates the use of gentrification as regeneration as being redemptive for these people and places and those who oppose find themselves pathologised and stigmatised further. So what starts as consensual is undergirded by coercion.

While metaphors of capital are useful in conceptualising some of these processes, they cannot explain the way in which cultural forms are negotiated and the new cultural forms that emerge. Williams's (1977) language is more useful here. The concepts of dominant, residual and emergent culture are analytically powerful. Part of the success of the hegemonic project involves residualising prevalent culture practices, in this case, working-class support for social housing, state welfarism, collective bargaining and action. The effects of this are evident in residents' rejection of a working-class identity, demonstrated in Chapter 2. Understanding working-class culture in these terms recognises that it is valid and legitimate and something that is not fixed and is, rather, fought for and negotiated. It is essential that culture is understood within a framework that does not fix or bound it since it is, essentially, subject to change and blurring. This is captured by Young's (2007) notion of bulimic society where people are simultaneously part of different cultural spaces, the meaning of which I will consider more in the following sections. Understanding gentrification as a hegemonic process problematises the interplay between structure and agency and puts working-class actions, rarely considered in gentrification research, at the heart of the enquiry. This led to an important insight: working-class residents are not merely victims of the processes of gentrification in Partick. Rather, they actively negotiate gentrification. They do so as owners of new-build developments like Bea, or as subversive consumers like Lou who was socially renting a flat in Glasgow Harbour. The hegemonic project is successful because it actually invites working-class people to participate in gentrification. This makes gentrification more consensual rather than forcefully imposed. In this respect, I suggest that hegemony would be better analytically understood as comprising three aspects rather than two (Joseph, 2002). In addition to the structural hegemony and the actual surface level political projects, hegemony also refers to an emergent, lived experience, which is the outcome of negotiation and compromise. This aspect is important since it is the outcome of the interplay between urban restructuring processes and the agency of working-class people. Aspects of this emergent lived stage of hegemony have been presented throughout all the empirical chapters in this book. For those with only generational working-class histories like Sylvie, Dylan, Darren and Sean, the notion of an emergent culture is especially resonant. Too young to have experienced much of what had become the residualised culture in Partick, relating to Fordist–Keynesian relations and the imagery of Red Clydeside, they come of age at a time where capitalist production corresponds to flexible forms of accumulation and neoliberalism which they see as the norm and as a way of life.

Another strength of the new theoretical perspective on gentrification is that it opens up a space from which we can discern new forms of displacement. This emphasises the coercive rather than consensual elements of the new emergent culture of consumer citizenship in Partick. Displacement comprises different degrees, ranging from cultural residualisation which had phenomenological impacts on people, seen in their rejection of class identity in Chapter 5, to economic costs caused by increased privatisation and the desire to be the same and 'keep up with the Joneses' seen in Chapter 4, and, ultimately, in some cases, eviction. The new forms of displacement that emerge are conditional to the specific form of state-led gentrification. The privatisation of social housing involves the introduction of business principles, which have a punitive effect on those tenants who are not materially or socially productive. If people do not act productively as residents or, indeed, customers they are unfixed to place. This manifested itself with four new types of displacement: perverse, latent generational, strategic and spiralling. The case study approach undertaken in this book was essential in uncovering these types. These insights are critical given how widespread these changes are throughout the housing sector in the UK. The changes initiated by gentrification proffer a prescient but retro research trajectory. The emergent housing situation has many echoes of private landlordism that was prevalent at the beginning of the twentieth century. The boom in new build gentrification, which has culminated in a growth of buy to rent properties, and the decline in social housing suggests we are witnessing a return to this. Since undertaking this research there has been a toxic combination of events: the global financial crisis; economic recession; a change in government; and further conditionality on welfare. Most significantly the introduction of the under-occupancy penalty for tenants in social housing aka the 'Bedroom Tax' represents the most coercive edge in gentrification process. Leading to the removal or penalisation of those who do not become more flexible housing consumers, it is, essentially, state enshrined revanchism. All in all, these processes underline the need to continue research into contemporary working-class lives.

Restructuring Class: Understanding New Working-class Identities

The experiences of people living in Partick represented in this book testify to the fact that class is far from a zombie category (Beck, 2004). However we require conceptual resources to advance contemporary class analysis. The continued relevance of class as a material position was not under scrutiny here. Rather, my interest was with how one's material position relates to phenomenological and cultural aspects of class. Modern Britain is thought to be a less class-conscious society, with people having poorly articulated views about membership or a clear sense of their place in the class structure (Savage, 2000). However, the experiences of people living in Partick showed this to be to the contrary. They may not name it as class but they know their place and have a sense of membership and consciousness, from Sylvie's experience of being classed by middle-class university students while sitting in the park, or when her freedom dreams did not come to pass; to Fi's encounter with the doctor's wife at the Annexe; or Steve being displaced from the pub. People demonstrated a reflexive awareness of their class position and are conscious of how urban restructuring has shaped this but they do not fully connect their personal situation and experiences with being working-class. In Mills's (1959) terms, they recognise public issues but do not connect these with their private troubles. This denotes the fragility and complexity of consciousness under the new social and economic conditions which requires conceptual language with enough finesse to capture this. One of the major insights generated from the people that I spoke to has been the impact of neoliberal ideology on working-class identity in relation to individualisation and choice narratives. Processes of individualisation have a material basis related to urban restructuring which neighbourhoods, some from outside of Glasgow and Scotland. Yet it was shown that respondents used the term community to describe their social relations. The one thing that most people had in common, amidst this diversity, was a shared sense of belonging to Partick. They used the term community to describe this sense of attachment, solidarity and membership. In this way, being part of the neighbourhood community expressed that they were working-class. While contemporary place-based communities studies acknowledge how residential space can usefully express one's social identity (Savage et al., 2005, 2005a; Blokland, 2003, 2005), we can extend this further.

Place based community is an important proxy for class because it has both material and phenomenological meanings. Residents express neighbourhood collectivity through the 'haves' and 'have nots' and 'in the same boat' sentiments. In doing so, they expressed solidarity with those they share a material position with. Claims to place and territory are highly classed but are not stratified – by which I mean they are not merely limited to middle-class subjectivities and identity making (Allen, 2008; Savage et al., 2005; Butler and Robson, 2003). Place-attachment is just as meaningful, if not more so, for working-class communities living in places previously defined by work and class which have become gentrified. Their ways of life, family and social networks and, in the worst case scenario, their own home are under threat. The neighbourhood community was also a key vehicle through which resistance occurred, echoing Castells (1983) assertion that the new social movements are profoundly urban. In Chapter 4 I showed how people resisted through local mechanisms, like the STOP campaign, the community council, or Save Thornwood Park. The act of taking away became an important pivot-point, invoking consciousness and initiating action from residents, illustrated by the reaction to the destruction of the old railway station. Regeneration processes appear to add value and so people may be hesitant about opposing these processes, fearing they would appear ungrateful or recalcitrant. As Natasha remarked, it is often a catch 22 for working-class residents.

Second, there is a range of conceptual resources for analysing contemporary working-class identities that have thus so far been reserved to describe middle-class experiences. The declining interest in the working class within sociology is evident in the lack of social characters and conceptual figures used to describe this social group. Whereas middle-class groups are depicted as gentrifiers, cosmopolitans, edge workers, to name but a few, the working class are not socially differentiated which suggests that their behaviour is not deemed to have value or distinguishing attributes of social interest. They are referred to as a homogeneous fixed category (Young, 2007). Yet the respondents were not devoid of the traits thought to be middle-class proclivities. This recalls Kathy Newman's (1999: ix–x) dawning realisation when she first ventured into Harlem:

> Standing at the bus shelters were lines of women and men dressed for work, holding the hands of their children on their way to day care and the local schools. Black men in mechanic overalls, women in suits – drinking coffee from Dunkin'

Donut cups, reading the New York Post, fussing with their children's backpacks – tapped their feet on the ground, waiting for the buses trying to manoeuvre towards them, caught in the same maddening traffic. The portals of the subways were swallowing up hoards of commuters who had given up on their buses. Meanwhile people walking purposefully to work were moving down the sidewalks flowing around the bus shelters, avoiding the outstretched arm of the occasional beggar, and ignoring the insistent calls of the street vendors selling clothing and videotapes from tables set up along the edge of the sidewalk. It was Monday morning in Harlem, and as far as the eye could see, thousands of people were on their way to work.

Similarly to Newman, the representation of working-class lives presented here challenges the idea that differences between social groups are essential. By over emphasising and too tightly delineating cultural differences we are in danger of actually compounding the distinctions of 'us and them'. These become reified as discrete categories which perpetuate their existence and create the imperative for the outsider to be brought inside, the excluded to be included and so on (Young, 2007). This led to material disadvantages as residents tried to 'keep up with the Joneses'. This partly relates to the cultivation of aspirational traits of gentrifiers and cosmopolitans amongst working-class groups. Working-class people can be gentrifiers as I outlined in Chapter 5. They can also be cosmopolitans since, as Binnie and Skeggs (2004) argue, it is not an essential possession of the privileged. While residents have a very localised understanding of class identity, limited by a kind of neighbourhood nationalism, being from Partick was a referent for being working class which was inclusive of different ethnic and racial identification. Thus, it was not ethnically bound. This challenges the ideology within neoliberal neighbourhood-based policy and attests to the idea of the working-class cosmopolitan (Werbner, 1999), who is both Othered and willing to engage with the Other. While this suggests solidarity at the neighbourhood level, this raises the questions of whether they would recognise solidarity of working-class experiences across the UK and beyond, or whether consciousness remains undeveloped and restricted by place. Neighbourhood case studies are useful if taken as building blocks in a wider set of studies. Without comparative frames, gentrification can become reified and detached from other wider processes that deal with the relationship between stratification and the political economy. I will consider this in more detail in the following section.

Therefore, I suggest that from this research we can ascertain that key differences between social groups were material rather than cultural. Respondents exhibited practices that expressed their efforts to take control of processes that were restructuring their lives. These processes brought new pleasures and new inequalities. The key differential in the binary is the degree of control residents held. Middle-class residents displayed more control over their movement in and out of the neighbourhood. They did not need to invest in the area; they could afford to secure activities to ensure their social reproduction and lifestyles outside of the neighbourhood. Working-class residents have less control and, therefore, less choice. That is not to deny that they have any choice, they did, and often attached their social identity to their chosen location but, as Chapter 3 showed, they had less control over their fixity to place. Again, the appropriation of the concept of elective belonging (Savage et al., 2005), reserved for middle-class groups can be reworked to consider working-class people's physical and ontological attachment to place. I used the term elective fixity to refer to the degree of control people had over their residential location, which ensures that they continue to live in their neighbourhood. Working-class attachment was more tenuous and, paradoxically, more socially and materially meaningful as their neighbourhood transitions from being industrial to post-industrial. Whilst tensions between the working and the middle-classes have a long drawn out history in British culture, the struggle between these groups was indicative of the neoliberal culture of neighbourhoods. The material differences are foregrounded in the way state-led gentrification promotes aspiration and differentiation. The accentuation of differences between the working class and the middle class is essential to the ratification of the neoliberal hegemony. Acknowledging this adds a critical material dimension to theories of cultural differentiation. Differences are not based on dissimulation between groups; their promotion has a material rationale. This is not to undermine the centrality of the conflict between capital and labour as the key mechanism behind class inequality. Control over fixity to place is a key conceptual resource for understanding class in a way that brings together the issues of capital and labour alongside property and culture. In this sense, working-class communities can become a topic and resource of the social sciences.

Control

> *Between equal rights, force decides.*
>
> (Marx, 1996: 243)

I have chosen control as a keyword in this final chapter over displacement. I do not want to undermine the gravity of displacement and the devastation it can bring. As Slater (2006: 748) suggests:

> Displacement is and always should be vital to an understanding of gentrification, in terms of retaining definitional coherence and of retaining critical perspectives on the process.

However, orthodox understandings of displacement do not convey the complexity involved in these processes. For example, in Chapter 5 we saw how young residents like Gordon, who was displaced from living in the Southside with his friend and then from his West End flat, before boomeranging back to his parent's home (Heath and Cleaver, 2003), did not interpret this move as displacement. This was deemed a relatively normal housing trajectory for a young person: fragmented and nonlinear (Heath and Cleaver, 2003). Janey too had to leave Partick in order to get a house big enough to accommodate her growing family. She bought her mother's house at a low price in a nearby town. She both loses and gains from this experience. The notion of agency in displacement has not been problematised in orthodox literature yet is critical to understanding this process. Deeming that residents have been displaced by gentrification can disempower them. It supposes that they have no power in gentrification processes or that they will always be negative. As outlined, above working-class residents could benefit from gentrification processes. Again, it is with care that I suggest this. Displacement is a very real process with devastating ramifications for people and, as I have alluded to, far graver today in its state-led from via evictions caused by the 'Bedroom Tax' and other restrictions on housing benefits. In this endeavour, the concept of control becomes a particularly meaningful operative. Control means both to have power and to limit power. The concept of control enables us to consider the degree of power people have over their housing situation.

This is evident in residents' choice narratives. The very premise of consumer citizenship and the new social contract are based on choice. Neoliberalism, projected through gentrification in the neighbourhood, extends choice, which infers that there is individual freedom to select between a number of options. Residents acted in a seemingly individual fashion to negotiate dislocations. They deemed that their ability to do so is their choice. Expressing choice was a way of expressing control over processes of restructuring. This involved rejecting the constraints associated with being working-class. However working-class residents' physical attachment to place expresses the lack of choice and control they have over their location. Elective fixity expresses the difference between working and middle-class groups' relationship to place. The power to control this fix is a key class indicator. The real disparity amongst residents is evident in the power to control one's physical attachment to place. Choice denotes an individual freedom in forms of citizenship that relates to a marketised system. So while choice is extended, it is also limited. Working-class residents are encouraged to act individually, be entrepreneurial, pursue their freedom dreams but they are materially constrained. Thus, in a system of neoliberalism choice is ostensibly extended to all but, as the above quote from Marx indicates, force decides. The force of material circumstances is a coercive process that ensures hegemony. Just as consent and coercion are two sides of the same coin, so too are (freedom of) choice and control. Control becomes a key concept in differentiating between middle-class and working-class groups and also in understanding how hegemony is successful.

Of course, control also means to manage or rule. This is relevant to how gentrification is used to govern in the neighbourhood as a political strategy of hegemony. The manufacturing of aspiration and denigration of working-class practices are political strategies used as a means of ratifying gentrification and reproducing the ruling class and social structures. Residents are expected to make the 'right' choice by making decisions that support entrepreneurialism and neoliberalism. The 'right' choice is both morally correct and rational. In this, residents' consent for the privatisation of public and social provisions was generated by proxy. That is, urban policy initiatives and the social housing provider, PHA, sought to cultivate aspiration, particularly around privatised forms of consumption. Choice and participation in local political processes are extended to residents with the expectation that they will make morally and materially productive choices. The gentrification of the working-class subject involves manufacturing aspiration to be more congruent with neoliberalism. They are coerced through the fear that they will be Othered if they oppose what is presented to them as a positive change. Opposing these processes is deemed a deviant or illegitimate 'choice'.

This reveals the ultimate paradox: residents often support gentrification because they conceive that they have a choice in being a consumer in the process. Consumer citizenship does not confer working-class people with any additional rights or means necessary to participate. There are moral and material constraints to actually making such choices. This reveals the coercive edge of hegemony. Gentrification is not always ratified in a consensual way but is decided by the force of material circumstance. Working-class people are ultimately excluded from the process if they cannot afford to consume. People try to restructure their own position by exchanging their (limited) economic capital for perceivably more valuable social capital. The paradox is that they were already socially and culturally rich; it is that their stock is misrecognised, maligned and devalued by political ideology. The power of the political project of hegemony is that it is realised through consent rather than force. Because of this insight the coercive aspects of hegemony can be overlooked. Consent of the governed is based on idea that all people are created equal – not only are they not, hegemony requires social divisions in order for it to be effective. Hegemonic processes then exacerbate differences in power by compounding the power of those who already hold it: 'The boundary between consent and non consent is contested in relation to issues of differential power, coercion and deception' (Waites, 2005: 8). As Gramsci (1971) asserts, consent is armoured by coercion. It is essential that we bear in mind that consent and coercion are two sides of the same coin. It is this aspect that makes hegemony a valuable concept for exploring social classes in relation to economic change and the shifting shape of contemporary housing and welfare. It is the coercive elements of hegemony articulated through people's lack of control that reveal the hidden injuries in processes of restructuring.

The Way Forward

The economic downturn has had a pronounced effect on housing. The legacy of gentrification in Partick is a surfeit of private stock, transferred to the rental market and the demise in social housing stock. Social housing has hit a 50-year low in Scotland (Shelter, 2009). In 2001 there were 3.9 people on council waiting lists for

Figure 6.1 Abandoned promotional sign on the Glasgow Harbour site at South Street, September 2009

every let. This rose to 6.6 people per let in 2008 (Shelter, 2009). This suggests that the full effects of gentrification and the extent of displacement are only beginning to fully manifest and latent generational displacement will begin to come to the fore. Further, it indicates a return to private landlordism which characterised the early part of the twentieth century and was fought against during the Rent Strike. This resulted in a legislative change in rent controls, which eventually resulted in the creation of PHA. Now, this organisation promotes gentrification in the neighbourhood whilst simultaneously buying back land from Glasgow Harbour for social housing, albeit a limited amount. Young people are at the sharp end of these changes in housing but such changes are normalised by the hegemony of gentrification. They expressed stronger choice narratives, yet had less choice and more insecurity. Unlike the women at Golden Friends, this generation are highly unlikely to find themselves living in close proximity or even in contact with people they grew up with. Their long-term housing transitions are unknown and perhaps the most interesting. Young people displayed less class consciousness and attachment to the residualised culture. This raises a range of questions about the relationship between class identity and consciousness and place attachment (both physical and ontological) and, indeed, that of the wider cross section of residents. This case study captures a set of social processes at a certain time and place. Further research is necessary to ascertain whether the consciousness that was evident was limited to place, in the context of Partick, or constrained by time, in the context of the relatively prosperous economic times in which this research was undertaken.

Mapping a geography of class and gentrification will allow us to explore the relationship between location, identity and consciousness in relation to working-class claims to place in more detail. Researching regenerated neighbourhoods in cities with similar and different trajectories can uncover broader socio-spatial relations of territoriality. This can extend the inquiry into how identity making and class formation might relate to urban restructuring, regional political economy and history and policies in different locations. This also inverts the wider interest in middle-class place-making and territoriality (Savage et al., 2005). The strength of this book lies in its ethnographic case study approach. What I began with resembled a historical materialist ontology, using an orthodox account of gentrification but an investigative inquiry using situated knowledge, challenged the notion of determination. Looking at the interplay between structure and agency challenged the efficacy of categorisations and constructions. An ethnographic, investigative approach, challenges the heuristic value of traditional understandings of class and gentrification. By framing standpoints through locational narratives, we can understand what shared or diverse experiences exist. The uneven nature of urban restructuring affects neighbourhoods in different ways, which demands exploration of the broader socio-spatial relationship to foreground affinities or differences in how people claim space in different geographical locations. This has helped generate a new perspective of gentrification, which has been taken forward in this book to explore contemporary class relations and identity. This theory and insights can be used in cross-comparative frames to test whether these processes are exclusive to Partick or express wider global trends of gentrification (Atkinson and Bridge, 2005). This cross-comparative element is important as a tool for understanding both the shared experience and the cultural differences of the working class in different places and times (Russo and Linkon, 2005). In doing this, a new sociological perspective on gentrification and class can be advanced which connects public and private issues across space and time, reinvigorating urban sociological research.

Appendix:
Cases of Gentrification

Listed here are processes that were occurring in the Partick which I identified as gentrification based on how they rolled out neoliberalism and that they met Hackworth's (2002) definition: shaping urban space for the more affluent user.

Glasgow Harbour

Glasgow Harbour is the name given to the redevelopment of the former shipyards, docks, warehouses and granaries on the River Clyde into a mixed-use development of retail, leisure, residential and business aspects. The development, which began 2001, is characterised by the 2,500-unit residential development of luxury flats, homes for an estimated 5,000 new residents. It covers 49 hectares and over 3 km of waterfront. Glasgow Harbour began as a joint venture between Clydeport Plc and Bank of Scotland but was acquired by Peel Holding Plc in 2003. The land has been purchased by Glasgow Harbour Ltd, a private sector company and wholly-owned subsidiary of Clydeport and part of Peel property and transport group. The development was privately funded by investment, although it receives funding from the European Union through the European Regional Development Fund (ERDF) and Scottish Enterprise. Despite being a privatised entity, Glasgow Harbour is one of six key areas that Clyde Waterfront is focusing on for regeneration. GCC envisage the project as having 'hugely beneficial economic, tourist and social implications for both Glasgow and Scotland' (Clyde Waterfront, 2007). There are, at the time of writing, there are no shops, services or amenities on site, only luxury flats. It creates a wealthy ghetto, contra to policy goals of social mix.

Glasgow Harbour Ltd and GCC are the lead partners but work alongside Scottish Enterprise Glasgow and Strathclyde European Partnership. Their aim follows that: 'The £1.2 billion Glasgow Harbour is a world class regeneration project which will spearhead the revitalisation of the river in this area' (Clyde Waterfront, 2007). Such hyperbolic statements mask the ambiguity around how they might actually attain such ends. There is no project manager or officer designated to work holistically to ensure the project fulfils the stated goals. In reality, by overseeing the sale of land to Glasgow Harbour, GCC have foreclosed any intervention into the future trajectory of the development. It is at least explicit in one goal: to bring the middle class back to live in the city. Glasgow Harbour Ltd (2007) conceives itself as the vanguard creating this elusive 'liveability':

Glasgow has a lack of premium quality housing, a need that Glasgow Harbour is addressing. We are bringing people back to live in the city once again, and providing the quality of environment and facilities they require. Once again, the city benefits, this time directly from the council tax payments they will receive.

Tesco

Shortly after the waterfront site was secured by Glasgow Harbour, Tesco speculatively purchased land on a site on Beith Street, the former 'Quarry' vicinity of the neighbourhood most of which was demolished during the 'slum clearances'. It has become a disused brownfield site with a ripe rent-gap value. After securing the land, Tesco submitted a proposal to GCC in December 2005 for a 9,950 square metre superstore plus student accommodation for 1,315 bed spaces, leisure and student union facilities, private residential flats and car parking for 620 spaces. This was to offer 350 full- and part-time jobs and a Tesco spokesperson announced it would transform a derelict brownfield site into a 'multi-purpose centre for the Partick community' (Planning Resource, 2009). Local councils find it difficult to refuse such developments and, consequently, the stated regeneration goals are compromised in favour of a piecemeal approach which sells off land to private entities. It is highly lucrative if it leads to such mammoths as Tesco and Glasgow Harbour going head-to-head over the land and proposed developments. These companies carve up the land between themselves and negotiate deals with GCC, like Glasgow Harbour's £25 million package of road works and infrastructure improvements on the Clydeside Expressway. In doing so, GCC hands over the burden of infrastructure costs and maintenance.

Tesco claimed after conducting a consultation process that they had support from 80 per cent of the local population. However, some local residents formed STOP (Stop Tesco Owning Partick), to challenge the development on many different grounds, including environmental impact of extra cars; the change of road infrastructure; and the scale and design. The proposal has since gone through successive application phases due to this opposition and the plans have been modified. Access to the student flats was intended to be from a new roundabout built on an area of land owned by GCC at Beith Street. Glasgow Harbour secured this piece of land, outbidding Tesco's £4.1 million. While Tesco was appealing the plans for their store, Glasgow Harbour tried to out-manoeuvre them. They announced plans for an on-site 130,000 square foot supermarket at the west end of their 130-acre regeneration project, with 252 apartments, specialist shops, a café and a landscaped public square, with a new pontoon on the River Clyde (Glasgow Harbour, 2007). However, the Tesco plan was eventually given the go-ahead after the Scottish Government appointed a Public Local Inquiry Reporter to chair a two-week probe into the plans. Despite more than 2,400 objections, he moved to let the development proceed. Tesco then resubmitted two plans: one for a large-scale development with a 7,435 square metre superstore, 653 student flats, 220 private flats and the other for a stand-alone superstore. The larger, more controversial 'Tesco Town' plan was passed. However, without the necessary land, now owned by Glasgow Harbour, it is unlikely the superstore and flats can be built. However, if an agreement can be reached with Glasgow Harbour, the proposed Tesco could go ahead.

The Re-privatisation of Social Housing

Since the mid-1990s, the City Council, in partnership with Communities Scotland has promoted the introduction of 'middle market' homes for owner occupation, especially in areas of disadvantage. Homeownership is promoted in the social rental sector through the Right-to-Buy and part-ownership schemes such as 'grow grants' for households on a low income to purchase private properties. This is a reversal of municipalism and is an important component of restructuring. This manifests in a variety of complex ways but principally involves gentrification, in that it seeks to create space for the affluent user. Municipal housing has declined and since 2003 homeownership has risen faster in Scotland than anywhere else in the UK (*The Scotsman*, 2008). No real steps have been taken to replenish the stock subsumed into the private market. Therefore, a freeze on further sales was implemented to preserve the remaining stock. PHA has conserved the area but the decline and public money and rise in privatisation means the association has to generate its own funds if it wants to build additional – and much needed – housing stock in the area.

Privatisation in social housing is encapsulated by the Housing Stock Transfer, 'the largest public sector modernisation project in Europe' (Scottish Executive, 2003). Scottish Executive proposed that GCC wholesale transfer the control of its 81,000 council homes over to a not-for-profit, Glasgow Housing Association (GHA). In return, GHA will service the council's huge housing debt and assist in securing £1.2 to £1.6 billion worth of investment to tackle Glasgow's housing crisis. As a charitable Industrial and Provident Society and a registered social landlord, PHA is regulated by the Scottish Housing Regulator. It is also a member of the Scottish Federation of Housing Associations. It has not been transferred over to GHA as it was not council-run, however, it is still affected by this changing framework for housing provision and does not receive share in the GHA investment. Since 2000, PHA have lost 138 properties through residents exercising their Right-to-Buy; 26, in 2001; tapering off to just 12 in 2006. The new funding regime requires creative funding techniques. In order to generate funds to build additional housing, PHA has become a parent company to other subsidiary groups Partick Homes Ltd and Partick Works Ltd (PWL). PWL set up another subsidiary group, Patrick DRK 2001, in partnership with property developers Cruden Estates. This is a risk isolator and it allows PHA to generate funds and develop property without taking any financial risk or jeopardising tenancies and, at the end, has their full investment returned. DRK 2001 was responsible for building West 11, a luxury residential development on Dumbarton Road:

> Homebuyers will soon be able to view this top-notch property and envisage living in a swanky new home, in the heart of one of the city's most thriving residential districts ... Situated at the foot of Byres Road, cosmopolitan chic [...] Particularly appealing to today's young urbanites [...]. (Cruden Homes, 2007)

Economic restructuring which promotes neoliberal policies cascades down, restructuring the supply of housing, the role of housing associations, the tenure within neighbourhoods and individuals – from social renters to owners. There was some concern around the percentage at which this development would provide further socially rented accommodation in the area. The director suggested that Partick residents may be preferred tenants of the flats when they were made available. It has been confirmed overwhelmingly in favour of homeowners with 76 flats for owner occupation, three homes for rent and six workspaces for PWL. Therefore, under the present funding regime social housing providers can actually become the initiators of gentrification. Of particular importance to this broad role of social housing is 'Wider Action', a term used to describe programmes and projects implemented by Registered Social Landlords that go beyond the simple remit of housing. This continues and extends the historical use of housing policies as a civilising enterprise (Johnstone, 1992; Damer, 1990). Funds are given to Registered Social Landlords to help bring about economic, social and environmental improvements. The types of housing-linked projects include: employment and training opportunities; improved traffic and pedestrian safety measures; better access for disabled people; and additional community facilities. Thus, it not only creates space for the more affluent user, it seeks to create the more affluent user. This is in financial terms as a homeowner but also in a moral sense, as a more responsible actor.

Privatisation of Public Space: Mansfield Park

GCC's Park and Open Spaces Strategic Best Value Review (2005) seeks to enhance and develop facilities and amenities in Glasgow's parks. Through this the council can ease the burden of maintenance and public spending by using private partnerships and devolving responsibility to 'Friends of Parks' groups. Their park strategy for the city involves a 'best value' approach to 'examine the viability and prepare plans for the franchising or leasing of suitable facilities' (GCC, 2005). Mansfield Park, situated near the end of Byres Road and the start of Dumbarton Road, became the focus of a 'Wider Action' development, led by PWL. It is being regenerated as part of £2.3 million project after being awarded city park status. It was formerly tenements, some of the very few that were demolished during the CDA. The site was thereafter incorporated into the public realm as common good land.[1] The park redevelopment expresses the increasing trend towards the privatisation of public goods and services whereby GCC sell or franchise public land to developers or businesses, who create revenue by privatising the space.

The council agreed to contribute £500,000 from the City Growth Fund and another £300,000 from the Land and Environmental Services Park Development Programme's capital budget. Communities Scotland is contributing £190,000 and the Big Lottery were also a major funder, whilst Glasgow Harbour Ltd added a couple of thousand pounds to the pot. A PHA worker has been seconded to this 'Wider Action Project' and receives a small percentage retainer of the over-all costs. The redevelopment of the park partly alters its function. It changes from being primarily public good space, that is, democratic consumption, not based on property rights to a privatised consumer space. It was though that the park could be a cash cow for PHA, generating revenue through ticketed events, leasing of rooms, and so on. These would finance future ventures and are especially crucial since PHA is not in receipt of LHO or GCC funding. However, the change in the economic climate meant that they lost some of this funding. While initial work was undertaken, the park redevelopment could not be completed. They eventually managed to receive additional money from Big Lottery in 2009 but it looks likely that they will have to look elsewhere and find another self-financing project for the rest.

---

1 Common good land and property is administered by local authorities in a manner that respects the rights of the inhabitants of the local area to which the common good originally related (Wightman and Perman, 2005). This concept dates back to the fifteenth century and is unique to Scotland. It represents land and property held for all the people of that burgh. The burghs are now gone and title has passed to the local authorities but the rights associated with those original burghs still remain (Wightman and Perman, 2005).

Bibliography

Adkins, L. (1995) *Gendered Work: Sexuality, Family and the Labour Market*. Buckingham: Open University Press.

Aglietta, M. (1987) *A Theory of Capitalist Regulation: The US Experience*. London: Verso.

Allen, C. (2008) *Housing Market Renewal and Social Class*. London: Routledge.

Althusser, L. (1971) 'Ideology and the ideological state apparatuses', in L. Althusser *Lenin and Philosophy and Other Essays*. London: New Left Books.

Anderson, P. (1976) 'The antimonies of Antonio Gramsci', *New Left Review* 100: 5–78.

Anthias F. (2005) 'Social stratification and social inequality: Models of intersectionality and identity', in F. Devine, M. Savage, J. Scott and R. Crompton (eds) *Rethinking Class: Culture, Identities and Lifestyle*. Basingstoke: Palgrave Macmillan.

Arnstein, S. (1969) 'A ladder of citizen participation', *Journal of the American Institute of Planners* 35(4): 216–24.

Atkinson, R. (2003) 'Introduction: Misunderstood saviour or vengeful wrecker? The many meanings and problems of gentrification', *Urban Studies* 40(12): 2343–50.

Atkinson, R. (2004) 'The evidence on the impact of gentrification: New lessons for the urban renaissance?' *European Journal of Housing Policy* 4(1): 107–31.

Atkinson, R. and Bridge, G. (eds) (2005) *Gentrification in a Global Context: The New Urban Colonialism*. London: Routledge.

Bagguley, P., Mark-Lawson, J., Shapiro, D., et al. (1990) *Restructuring: Place, Class and Gender*. London: Sage.

Bailey, N. and Robertson, D. (1997) 'Housing renewal, urban policy and gentrification', *Urban Studies* 34(4): 561–78.

Bailey, N., Haworth, A., Manzi, T., et al. (2007) *Creating and Sustaining Mixed Income Communities in Scotland*. Chartered Institute of Housing Scotland, Edinburgh: Joseph Rowntree Foundation.

Bates, I. (1984) *Schooling for the Dole? The new vocationalism*. London: Palgrave Macmillan.

Bakshi, P., Goodwin, M., Painter, J. and Southern, A. (1995) 'Gender, race and class in the local welfare state: Moving beyond regulation theory in analysing the transition from Fordism', *Environment and Planning A* 27: 1539–54.

Bauman, Z. (1998) *Work, Consumerism and the New Poor*. Buckingham: Open University Press.

Beck, U. (1992) *Risk Society: Towards a New Modernity*. London: Sage.

Beck, U. (2004) *Ulrich Beck – Johannes Willms: Conversations with Ulrich Beck*, trans. M. Pollak. London: Polity Press.
Beck, U. (2006) *The Cosmopolitan Vision.* Cambridge: Polity Press.
Berman, M. (1982) *All That is Solid Melts into Air: The Experience of Modernity.* London: Verso.
Binnie, J. and Skeggs, B. (2004) 'Cosmopolitan knowledge and the production and consumption of sexualized space: Manchester's gay village', *Sociological Review* 52: 39–61.
Blokland, T. (2001) 'Bricks, mortar, memories: Neighbourhood and networks in collective acts of remembering', *International Journal of Urban and Regional Research* 25(2): 268–83.
Blokland, T. (2003) *Urban Bonds: Social Relations in an Inner City Neighborhood.* Cambridge: Polity Press.
Blokland, T. (2005) 'Memory magic: How a working class neighbourhood became an imagined community and class started to matter when it lost its base', in F. Devine, M. Savage, J. Scott and R. Crompton (eds) *Rethinking Class: Cultures, Identities and Lifestyle*. Basingstoke: Palgrave Macmillan.
Boddy, M. (2007) 'Designer neighbourhoods: New-build residential development in nonmetropolitan UK cities, the case of Bristol', *Environment and Planning A* 39: 86–105.
Bondi, L. (1999) 'Gender, class and gentrification: Enriching the debate', *Environment and Planning D: Society and Space* 17: 261–82.
Bondi, L. and Rose, D. (2003) 'Constructing gender, constructing the urban: A review of Anglo-American feminist urban geography', *Gender, Place and Culture: A Journal of Feminist Geography* 10(3): 229–45.
Bourdieu, P. (1984) *Distinction: A Social Critique of the Judgment of Taste.* London: Routledge.
Bourdieu, P. (1986) 'The forms of capital', in J.G. Richardson (ed.) *Handbook for Theory and Research for the Sociology of Education*. New York: Greenwood.
Bourdieu, P. (1987) 'What makes a social class? On the theoretical and practical existence of groups', *Berkeley Journal of Sociology* 32: 1–17.
Bourdieu, P., et al. (1999) *The Weight of the World: Social Suffering in Contemporary Society*, trans. Priscilla Parkhurst Ferguson. Oxford: Polity Press.
Bottero, W. (2004) 'Class identities and the identity of class', *Sociology* 38(5): 985–1003.
Bottero, W. (2005) *Stratification: Social Division and Inequality*. London: Routledge.
Boyle, M. and Hughes, G. (1994) 'The politics of urban entrepreneurialism in Glasgow', *Geoforum* 25(4): 453–70.
Boyle. M., McWilliams, C. and Rice, G. (2008) 'The spatialities of actually existing neoliberalism in Glasgow, 1977 to present', *Geografiska Annaler Series B: Human Geography* 90(4): 313–25.

Bridge, G. (2001) 'Bourdieu, rational action and the time-space strategy of gentrification', *Transactions of the Institute of British Geographers* 26(2): 205–16.
Burawoy, M. (1979) *Manufacturing Consent: Changes in the Labor Process under Monopoly Capitalism.* Chicago: University of Chicago Press.
Burawoy, M. (1991) 'Reconstructing social theories', in M. Burawoy, A. Burton, A. Amett Ferguson, et al. (eds) *Ethnography Unbound: Power and Resistance in the Modern Metropolis.* Berkeley: University of California Press.
Butler, T. (2007) 'For gentrification?' *Environment and Planning A* 39: 162–81.
Butler, T. and Robson, G. (2001) 'Social capital, gentrification and neighbourhood change in London: A comparison of three South London neighbourhoods' *Urban Studies* 38: 2145–62.
Butler, T. and Robson, G. (2003) *London Calling: The Middle Classes and the Remaking of Inner London.* Oxford: Berg.
Byrne, D. (2005) 'Class culture and identity: A reflection on absences against presences', *Sociology* 39(5): 807–16.
Castells, M. (1983) *The City and the Grassroots: A Cross-Cultural Theory of Urban Social Movements.* Berkeley: University of California Press.
Cattell, V. (2004) 'Having a laugh and mucking in together: Using social capital to explore dynamics between structure and agency in the context of declining and regenerated neighbourhoods', *Sociology* 38(5): 945–63.
Caulfield, J. (1994) *City Form and Everyday Life: Toronto's Gentrification and Critical Social Practice.* Toronto: University of Toronto Press.
Charlesworth, S. (2000) *The Phenomenology of the Working Class Experience.* Cambridge: Cambridge University Press.
Chase, M. and Shaw, C. (1989) 'The dimensions of nostalgia', in M. Chase and C. Shaw (eds) *The Imagined Past: History and Nostalgia.* Manchester: Manchester University Press.
Christopherson, S. (1994) 'Fortress city: Privatised spaces, consumer citizenship', in A. Amin (ed.) *Post-Fordism: A Reader.* Oxford: Blackwell.
Clarke, J. (2005) 'New Labour's citizens: Activated, empowered, responsibilized, abandoned?' *Critical Social Policy* 25(4): 447–63.
Clyde Waterfront (2007) www.clydewaterfront.com, accessed 27 March 2007.
Cochrane, A. (1986) 'Community politics and democracy', in D. Held and C. Pollitt (eds) *New Forms of Democracy.* London: Sage.
Cochrane, A. (2001) 'New Labour, new urban policy?' in H. Dean, R. Sykes and R. Woods (eds) *Social Policy Review*, 12. Newcastle: Social Policy Association.
Cochrane, A. (2007) *Understanding Urban Policy: A Critical Approach.* Oxford: Blackwell.
Cockburn, C. (1997) 'The local state: Management of cities and people', *Race and Class* 18(4): 363–76.
Coffield, F., Borrill, C. and Marshall, S. (1986) *Growing Up at the Margins: Young Adults in the North East.* Milton Keynes: Open University Press.
Connell, R.W. (2005) *Masculinities.* Cambridge: Polity Press.

Cooke, E.P. (1982) 'Class practices as regional markers: A contribution to labour geography', in D. Gregory and J. Urry (eds) *Social Relations and Spatial Structures*. Basingstoke: Palgrave Macmillan.

Communities Scotland (2007) *Scottish Registered Social Landlord Statistics 2005/06*. Edinburgh: Communities Scotland.

Communities Scotland (2008) www.communitiesscotland.gov.uk, accessed 10 April 2008.

Cox, K.R. and Mair, A. (1989) 'Locality and community in the politics of local economic development', *Annals of the Association of American Geographers* 78: 307–25.

Crompton, R. (1993) *Class and Stratification: An Introduction to Current Debates*. Cambridge: Polity Press.

Crompton, R. and Scott, J. (2005) 'Class analysis: Beyond the cultural turn', in F. Devine, M. Savage, J. Scott and R. Crompton (eds) *Rethinking Class: Culture, Identities and Lifestyle*. Basingstoke: Palgrave.

Cruden Homes (2007) www.cruden-homes.co.uk, accessed 24 October 2007.

Cruikshank, B. (1999) *The Will to Empower: Democratic Citizens and Other Subjects*. Ithaca: Cornell University Press.

CWCS (Centre for Working Class Studies) (2008) www.cwcs.ysu.edu, accessed 20 January 2008.

Damer, S. (1990) *Glasgow: Going for a Song*. London: Lawrence and Wishart Ltd.

Davidson, M. (2008) 'Spoiled mixture – where does state-led "positive" gentrification end?' *Urban Studies* 45: 2385–405.

Davidson, M. and Lees, L. (2005) 'New build "gentrification" and London's riverside renaissance', *Environment and Planning A* 37(7): 1165–90.

Dean, M. (1999) *Governmentality: Power and Rule in Modern Society*. London: Sage.

Dupuis, A. and Thorns, D.C. (1998) 'Home, home ownership, and the search for ontological security', *Sociological Review* 46(1): 24–47.

Dennis, N., Henriques, F. and Slaughter, C. (1956) *Coal is Our Life: An Analysis of a Yorkshire Mining Community*. London: Tavistock.

Devine, F. (2004) 'Talking about class in Britain', in F. Devine and M. Walters (eds) *Social Inequalities in Comparative Perspective*. Oxford: Blackwell.

Ekers, M., Loftus, A., Hart, G. and Kipfer, S. (eds) (2012) *Gramsci: Space, Nature and Politics*. Malden, MA: Wiley-Blackwell.

Evening Times, The (1956) 'Partick's Shopping Bonanza', *The Evening Times* from www.partick.eveningtimes.co.uk/area/particks-shopping-bonanza.html, accessed 12 January 2010.

Featherstone, M. (1991) *Consumer Culture and Postmodernism*. London: Sage.

Flint, J. (2003) 'Housing and ethopolitics: Constructing identities of active consumption and responsible community', *Economy and Society* 32(4): 611–29.

Flint, J. (2006) 'Housing and the new governance of conduct', in J. Flint (ed.) *Housing, Urban Governance and Anti-Social Behaviour*. Bristol: Policy Press.

Flint, J. and Rowlands, R. (2003) 'Commodification, normalisation and intervention: Cultural, social and symbolic capital in housing consumption and governance', *Journal of Housing and the Built Environment* 18(3): 213–32.
Foucault, M. (1980) *Power/Knowledge: Selected Interviews and Other Writings 1972–1977* (ed.) C. Gordon. Brighton: Harvester.
Foucault, M. (2003) 'Governmentality', in P. Rabinow and N. Rose (eds) *The Essential Foucault: Selections from Essential Works of Foucault 1954–1984*. London: The New Press.
Fowler, B. (1997) *Pierre Bourdieu and Cultural Theory: Critical Investigations*. London: Sage.
Fraser, N. (1998) 'Social justice in the age of identity politics: Redistribution, recognition and participation', in G. Peterson (ed.) *The Tanner Lectures on Human Values*, XIX. University of Utah Press: Salt Lake City.
Freeman, L. (2006) *There Goes the 'Hood: Views of Gentrification from the Ground Up*. Philadelphia: Temple University Press.
Furlong, A. and Cartmel, F. (2005) *Graduates from Disadvantaged Families: Early Labour Market Experiences*. Bristol: Policy Press.
Furlong, A. and Cartmel, F. (2006) *Young People and Social Change: New Perspectives*. Buckingham: Open University Press.
Gallagher, W. (1987) *Revolt on the Clyde*. London: Lawrence and Wishart Ltd.
GCC (2003) *City Plan Review*. Glasgow: Glasgow City Council.
GCC (2003a) *Metropolitan Glasgow*. Glasgow: Glasgow City Council.
GCC (2005) *Park and Open Spaces Strategic Best Value Review*. Glasgow: Glasgow City Council.
GCC and Scottish Enterprise Glasgow (2001) Glasgow Economic Monitor, Glasgow, Glasgow City Council: Development and Regeneration Services and Scottish Enterprise Glasgow.
Giddens, A. (1984) *The Constitution of Society*. Oxford: Polity Press.
Giddens, A. (1991) *Modernity and Self-Identity: Self and Society in the Late Modern Age*. Cambridge: Polity.
Giddens, A. (1998) *The Third Way*. Cambridge: Policy Press.
Glasgow Harbour (2007) www.glasgowharbour.com, accessed 27 March 2007.
Glasgow Women's Studies Group (collective eds) (1982) *Uncharted Lives: Extracts from Scottish Women's Experiences 1850–1982*. Glasgow: Pressgang.
Glass, R. (1964) 'Introduction: Aspects of change', in Centre for Urban Studies (ed.) *London: Aspects of Change*. London: MacGibbon and Kee.
Gledhill, J. (2004) 'Neoliberalism', in D. Nugent and J. Vincent (eds) *A Companion to the Anthropology of Politics*. Malden: Blackwell.
Goldthorpe, J.H., Lockwood, D., Bechhofer, F. and Platt, J. (1968) *The Affluent Worker: Industrial Attitudes and Behaviour*. Cambridge: Cambridge University Press.
Gordon, E. and Nair, G. (2003) *Public Lives: Women, Family and Society in Victorian Britain*. London: Yale University Press.

Gosling, V.K. (2008) 'Regenerating communities: Women's experiences of social exclusion and urban regeneration', *Urban Studies* 45(7): 607–26.

Gramsci, A. (1971) *Selections from the Prison Notebooks*, ed. and trans. Q. Hoare and G. Nowell-Smith. London: Lawrence and Wishart Ltd.

Hackworth, J. (2002) 'Post-recession gentrification in New York City', *Urban Affairs Review* 37: 815–43.

Hall, S. (1986) 'Gramsci's relevance for the study of race and ethnicity', *Journal Community Inquiry* 10(2): 5–27.

Hall, S. and Jacques, M. (eds) (1989) *New Times: The Changing Face of Politics in the 1990s*. London: Lawrence and Wishart Ltd.

Hall, T. and Hubbard, P. (1996) 'The entrepreneurial city: New politics, new urban geographies', *Progress in Human Geography* 20: 153–74.

Hall, T. and Hubbard, P. (1998) *The Entrepreneurial City: Geographies, Politics, Regime and Representation*. Chichester: John Wiley and Sons.

Hamnett, C. (2003) 'Gentrification and the middle-class remaking of inner London', *Urban Studies* 40(12): 2401–26.

Hannerz, U. (1990) 'Cosmopolitans and locals in world culture', in M. Featherstone (ed.) *Global Culture: Nationalism, Globalization and Modernity*. London: Sage.

Hannerz, U. (1992) *Cultural Complexity: Studies in the Social Organisation of Meaning*. New York: Columbia University Press.

Harvey, D. (1973) *Social Justice and the City*. Baltimore: Johns Hopkins University Press.

Harvey, D. (1975) 'The geography of capitalist accumulation: A reconstruction of the Marxian theory', *Antipode* 2(S): 9–21.

Harvey, D. (1982) *The Limits to Capital*. Oxford: Blackwell.

Harvey, D. (1989) 'From managerialism to entrepreneurialism: The transformation in urban governance in late capitalism', *Geografiska Annaler* 71B(1): 3–17.

Harvey, D. (1990) *The Condition of Postmodernity*. Oxford: Blackwell.

Harvey, D. (2005) *A Brief History of Neoliberalism*. Oxford: Oxford University Press.

Hastings, A. (2003) 'Strategic, multilevel neighbourhood regeneration: An outward looking approach', in R. Imrie and M. Raco (eds) *Urban Renaissance: New Labour Community and Urban Policy*. Bristol: Policy Press.

Haylett, C. (2001) 'Illegitimate subjects? Abject whites, neo-liberal modernisation and middle class multiculturalism' *Environment and Planning D: Society and Space* 19(3): 351–70.

Haylett, C. (2003) 'Culture, class and urban policy: Reconsidering equality', *Antipode* 35(1): 33–55.

Healy, P. (2003) 'Collaborative planning in perspective', *Planning and Theory* 2(2): 101–23.

Heath, S. (2008) *Housing Choices and Issues for Young People in the UK*. York: Joseph Rowntree Foundation.

Heath, S. and Cleaver, E. (2003) *Young, Free and Single: Twenty-Somethings and Household Change*. Basingstoke: Palgrave Macmillan.

Heath, S. and Kenyon, E. (2001) 'Young adults and shared household living: Achieving independence through the (re)negotiation of peer relationships', in H. Helve and C. Wallace (eds) *Youth, Citizenship and Empowerment*. Aldershot: Ashgate.

Helms, G. and Cumbers, A. (2006) 'Regulating the new urban poor: Local labour market control in an old industrial city', *Space and Polity* 10: 67–86.

Hermes, J. (1995) *Reading Women's Magazines*. Cambridge: Polity Press.

Hudson, R. (1989) *Wrecking a Region: State Policies, Party Politics and Regional Change in North East England*. London: Pion.

Hunt, A. (1997) 'Moral regulation and making-up the new person: Putting Gramsci to work', *Theoretical Criminology* 1(3): 275–301.

Imrie, R. and Raco, M. (2003) 'Community and the changing nature of urban policy', in R. Imrie and M. Raco (eds) *Urban Renaissance?: New Labour Community and Urban Policy*. Bristol: Policy Press.

Jackson, B. (1968) *Working-Class Community*. London: Routledge.

Jager, M. (1986) 'Class definition and the aesthetics of gentrification: Victoriana in Melbourne', in N. Smith and P. Williams (eds) *Gentrification of the City*. Sydney: Allen and Unwin.

Jessop, B. (1990) *State Theory: Putting the Capitalist State in its Place*. Cambridge: Polity.

Jessop, B. (1989) 'Conservative regimes and the transition to post-Fordism: The cases of Great Britain and West Germany', in M. Gottdiener and N. Komninos (eds) *Capitalist Development and Crisis Theory: Accumulation, Regulation and Spatial Restructuring*. London: Palgrave Macmillan.

Jonas, A. (1996) 'Local labour market control regimes: Uneven development and the social regulation of production', *Regional Studies* 30: 323–38.

Joseph, J. (2002) *Hegemony: A Realist Analysis*. London: Routledge.

Kearns, A. (2003) 'Social capital, regeneration and urban policy', in R. Imrie and M. Raco (eds) *Urban Renaissance?: New Labour, Community and Urban Policy*. Bristol: Policy Press.

Keating, M. (1988) *The City that Refused to Die: Glasgow: The Politics of Urban Regeneration*. Aberdeen: Aberdeen University Press.

Kintrea, K., Bannister, J., Pickering, J., et al. (2008) *Young People and Territoriality in British Cities*. York: Joseph Rowntree Foundation.

Knox, W. (1999) *Industrial Nation: Work, Culture and Society in Scotland, 1800–Present*. Edinburgh: Edinburgh University Press.

Kumar, K. (1995) *From Post-Industrial to Post-Modern Society*. Oxford: Blackwell Publishers.

Lambert, C. and Boddy, M. (2002) *Transforming the City: Post-Recession Gentrification and Re-Urbanism*. CNR Paper 6, Bristol: ESRC Centre for Neighbourhood Research.

Lash, S. and Urry, J. (1987) *The End of Organized Capitalism*. Madison: University of Wisconsin Press.

Lash, S. and Urry, J. (1994) *Economies of Signs and Space*. London: Sage.

Law, A. and Mooney, G. (2006) 'We've never had it so good: the "problem" of the working class in devolved Scotland' *Critical Social Policy* 26(3): 523–42.

Lawler, S. (2000) *Mothering the Self: Mothers, Daughter, Subjects*. London: Routledge.

Leckie, S. (1995) *When Push Comes to Shove: Forced Evictions and Human Rights*. Utrecht: Habitat International Coalition.

Lees, L. (1994) 'Rethinking gentrification: Beyond the positions of economics and culture' *Progress in Human Geography* 18(2): 137–50.

Lees, L. (1998) 'Urban Renaissance and the Street: Spaces of control and contestation', in N. Fyfe (ed.) *Images of the Street: Planning, Identity and Control in Public Space*. London: Routledge.

Lees, L. (2003) 'Visions of "urban renaissance" the Urban Task Force report and the Urban White Paper', in R. Imrie and M. Raco (eds) *Urban Renaissance?: New Labour Community and Urban Policy*. Bristol: Policy Press.

Lees, L. (ed.) (2004) *The Emancipatory City: Paradoxes and Possibilities?* Sage: London.

Lees, L. and Ley, D. (2008) 'Introduction to a special issue on gentrification and public policy', *Urban Studies* 45(12): 2379–84.

Ley, D. (1996) *The New Middle Class and the Re-Making of the Central City*. Oxford: Oxford University Press.

Ley, D. (1986) 'Alternative explanations for inner-city gentrification: A Canadian assessment', *Annals of the Association of American Geographers* 76(4): 521–35.

Lipitez, A. (1986) 'New tendencies of the international division of labour: Regimes of accumulation and modes of regulation', in A. Scott and M. Storper (eds) *Production, Work, Territory: The Geographical Anatomy of Industrial Capitalism*. London: Allen and Unwin.

Lister, R. 'Gender and the analysis of social policy', in G. Lewis, S. Gerwitz and J. Clark (eds) *Rethinking Social Policy*. London: Sage.

Lockwood, D. (1958) *The Blackcoated Worker: a study in class consciousness*. London: Allen and Unwin.

Lockwood, D. (1966) 'Sources of variation in working class images of society', *Sociological Review* 14: 249–63.

Logan, J. and Molotch, H. (1987) *Urban Fortunes: The Political Economy of Place*. Los Angeles: University of California Press.

Lovering, J. (2007) 'The relationship between urban regeneration and neoliberalism: Two presumptuous theories and a research agenda', *International Planning Studies* 12(4): 343–66.

Lyng, S. (ed.) (2005) *Edgework: The Sociology of Risk Taking*. Abingdon: Routledge.

MacInnes, D. (1995) 'The de-industrialisation of Glasgow', *Scottish Affairs* 11: 73–95.

MacLean, I. (1983) *The Legend of Red Clydeside*. Edinburgh: J. Donald.
MacLeod, G. (2002) 'From urban entrepreneurialism to a "revanchist city?" On the spatial injustices of Glasgow's renaissance', *Antipode* 34(3): 602–24.
Magee, B. (2003) 'Peel Holdings faces pressure to make Glasgow Harbour pledge; MSP demands guarantee that original plans remain intact', *The Sunday Herald*.
Mark-Lawson, Savage, M. and Warde, A. (1985) 'Gender and local politics: Struggles over welfare policies 1918–39', in Lancaster Regionalism Group (eds) *Localities, Class and Gender*. London: Pion.
Martin, J. (1997) 'Hegemony and the crisis of legitimacy in Gramsci', *History of the Human Sciences* 10(1): 37–56.
Marcuse, P. (1985) 'Gentrification, abandonment and displacement: Connections, causes and policy responses in New York City', *Journal of Urban and Contemporary Law* 28: 195–240.
Marcuse, P. (1986) 'Abandonment, gentrification and displacement: The linkages in New York City', in N. Smith and P. Williams (eds) *Gentrification of the City*. London: Unwin Hyman.
Marx, K. (1996) *Capital, Volume One*. London: Lawrence and Wishart Ltd.
Massey, D. (1984) *Social Divisions of Labour: Social Structures and the Geography of Production*. London: Palgrave Macmillan.
Massey, D. (1988) *Global Restructuring, Local Responses*. Worcester: Graduate School of Geography Clark University.
Massey, D. (1993) 'Power-geometry and a progressive sense of place', in J. Bird (ed.) *Mapping the Futures: Local Cultures, Global Change*. London: Routledge.
Mayer, M. (1994) 'Post Fordist city politics', in A. Amin (ed.) *Post-Fordism: A Reader*. Oxford: Blackwell.
McCrone, D. (2001) *Understanding Scotland: The Sociology of a Stateless Nation*. London: Routledge.
McDowell, L. (1991) 'Father and Ford revisited: Gender, class and employment change in the new millennium', *Transactions of the Institute of British Geographers* 26: 448–64.
McDowell, L. (2002) 'Masculine discourses and dissonances: Strutting "lads", protest masculinity, and domestic respectability', *Environment and Planning D: Society and Space* 20: 97–119.
McKee, K. (2008) 'Community ownership of social housing in Glasgow: Building more sustainable, cohesive communities?' *People, Place and Policy Online* 2(2): 101–11.
McKeganey, N.P. and Barnard, M.A. (1992) 'Selling sex: Female street prostitution and HIV risk behaviour in Glasgow', *AIDS Care* 4(4): 395–408.
McLennan, D. and Gibb, A. (1988) *Glasgow: No Mean City to Miles Better*. Glasgow: Centre for Housing Research, University of Glasgow.
McRobbie, A. (2005) *The Use of Cultural Studies: A Textbook*. London: Sage.
Miles, R. and Dunlop, A. (1987) 'Racism in Britain: The Scottish dimension', in P. Jackson (ed.) *Race and Racism*. London: Allen and Unwin.

Mills, C. (1988) 'Life on the upslope: The postmodern landscape of gentrification', *Environment and Planning D: Society and Space* 6: 169–89.

Mills, C.W. (1959) *Sociological Imagination*. New York: Grove Press.

Mind (2008) *In the Red: Debt and Mental Health*, from www.mind.org.uk, accessed 17 August 2009.

Mitchell, I.R. (2005) *This City Now: Glasgow and its Working-Class Past*. Edinburgh: Luath Press.

Mitchell, K., Marston, S.A. and Katz, C. (eds) (2004) *Life's Work: Geographies of Social Reproduction*. London: Blackwell.

Mooney, G. (1988) *Living on the Periphery: Housing, Industrial Change and the State*. Thesis (PhD), University of Glasgow.

Mooney, G. (2000) 'Class and social policy', in G. Lewis, S. Gerwitz and J. Clark (eds) *Rethinking Social Policy*. London: Sage.

Mooney, G. (2004) 'Cultural policy as urban transformation? Critical reflections on Glasgow, European City of Culture 1990', *Local Economy* 19(4): 327–40.

Mooney, G. and Danson, M. (1997) 'Beyond "culture city": Glasgow as a "dual city"', in N. Jewson and S. MacGregor (eds) *Transforming Cities*. London: Routledge.

Mooney, G. and Danson, M. (1998) 'Glasgow: A tale of two cities? Disadvantage and exclusion on the European periphery', in S. Hardy, P. Lawless and R. Martin (eds) *Unemployment and Social Exclusion: Landscapes of Labour Inequality and Social Exclusion*. London: Routledge.

Morton, A.D. (2006) 'The grimly comic riddle of hegemony in IPE: Where is class struggle?' *Politics* 26(1): 62–72.

Nayak, A. (2006) 'Displaced masculinities: Chavs, youth and class in the post-industrial city', *Sociology* 40(5): 813–31.

Newman, K. (1999) *No Shame in My Game: The Working Poor in the Inner City*. New York: Russell Sage Foundation and Knopf.

Pacione, M. (1979) 'Housing policies in Glasgow since 1880', *Geographical Review* 69: 395–412.

Pacione, M. (1995) *Glasgow: The Socio-Spatial Development of the City*. Chichester: John Wiley and Sons.

Pahl, R.E. (1989) 'Is the Emperor naked?' *International Journal of Urban and Regional Research* 13(4): 711–20.

Pakulski, J. and Waters, M. (1996) *The Death of Class*. London: Sage.

Pateman, C. (1970) *Participation and Democratic Theory*. Cambridge: Cambridge University Press.

Peck, J. and Tickell, A. (1995) 'The social regulation of uneven development: "Regulatory deficit", England's South East, and the collapse of Thatcherism', *Environment and Planning A* 27: 15–40.

Peck, J. and Tickell, A. (2002) 'Neoliberalising space', in N. Brenner and N. Theodore (eds) *Spaces of Neoliberalism: Urban Restructuring in North America and Western Europe*. Oxford: Blackwell Publishing.

Planning Resource (2009) www.planningresource.co.uk, accessed 13 January 2009.

Poulantzas, N. (1967) 'Marxist political theory in Britain', *New Left Review* 58: 67–78.

Putnam, R. (2000) *Bowling Alone: The Collapse and Revival of American Community*. New York: Simon and Schuster.

Raco, M. (2000) 'Assessing community participation in local economic development – lessons for the new urban policy', *Political Geography* 19(5): 573–99.

Rainer (2008) *Why do the Young Pay More? Young People, Debt and Financial Exclusion*, www.raineronline.org, accessed 17 June 2009.

Randolph, B. (1993) 'The re-privatization of housing associations', in P. Malpass and R. Means (eds) *Implementing Housing Policy*. Milton Keynes: Open University Press.

Reay, D. (1998) 'Rethinking social class: Qualitative perspectives on class and gender', *Sociology* 32(2): 259–75.

Reay, D. (2005) 'Beyond consciousness? The psychic landscape of social class', *Sociology* 39(5): 911–28.

Reay, D. (2011) 'A new social class paradigm: Bridging individual and collective, cultural and economic in class theory', *Key Articles in British Sociology*, from http://www.sagebsa.co.uk/code/viewPDF.aspx?&filename=Diane_Reay_Culture_and_Class.pdf, accessed 18 December 2011.

Rifkin, J. (1996) *The End of Work: The Decline of the Global Labor Force and the Dawn of the Post-Market Era*. New York: Putnam.

Roberts, I. (2007) 'Working-class studies: Ongoing and new directions', *Sociological Compass* 1(1): 191–207.

Roberts, P. and Sykes, H. (2000) *Urban Regeneration: A Handbook*. London: Sage.

Rofe, M. (2003) '"I want to be global": Theorising the gentrifying class as an emergent elite global community', *Urban Studies* 40: 2511–26.

Rose, N. (1996) 'The death of the social? Re-figuring the territory of government', *Economy and Society* 25: 327–56.

Rose, N. (1999) *Powers of Freedom: Reframing Political Thought*. Cambridge: Cambridge University Press.

Russo, J. and Linkon, S. (eds) (2005) *New Working-Class Studies*. Ithaca: Cornell University Press.

Saunders, P. (1984) 'Beyond housing classes: The sociological significance of private property rights in means of consumption', *International Journal of Urban and Regional Research* 8: 202–27.

Savage, M. (2000) *Class Analysis and Social Transformation*. Buckingham: Open University Press.

Savage, M., Bagnall, G. and Longhurst, B. (2001) 'Ordinary, ambivalent and defensive: Class identities in the Northwest of England', *Sociology* 35(4): 875–92.

Savage, M., Bagnall, G. and Longhurst, B. (2005) *Globalization and Belonging*. London: Sage.
Savage, M., Bagnall, G. and Longhurst, B. (2005) 'Local habitus and working class culture', in F. Devine, M. Savage, J. Scott and R. Crompton (eds) *Rethinking Class: Cultures, Identities and Lifestyles*. London: Palgrave.
Savage, M., Devine, F., Cunningham, N., et al. (2013) 'A new model of social class: findings from the BBC's Great British Class Survey experiment', *Sociology* 47(2): 219–50.
Savage, M., Warde, A. and Ward, K. (2003) *Urban Sociology, Capitalism and Modernity*. Basingstoke: Palgrave Macmillan.
Sayer, A. (2005) *The Moral Significance of Class*. Cambridge: Cambridge University Press.
Scottish Executive (2002) *Better Community in Scotland: Closing the Gap – the Scottish Executive's Community Regeneration Statement*. Edinburgh: Scottish Executive.
Scottish Executive (2006) *People and Place: Regeneration Policy Statement*. Edinburgh: Scottish Executive.
Scottish Housing Regulator (2009) *Annual Performances and Statistical Return on Registered Social Landlords*. Scottish Housing Regulator.
Scottish Neighbourhood Statistics (2009) www.sns.gov.uk, accessed 13 January 2009.
SEU (Social Exclusion Unit) (1998) *Bringing Britain Together – A National Strategy for Neighbourhood Renewal*. Cmnd 4045. London: Stationary Office.
Sharp, C. (2004) *On the Cards: The Debt Crisis Facing Scottish CAB Clients*. Citizens Advice Scotland, Scottish Association of Citizens Advice Bureau.
Shelter (2009) *Building Pressure: Access to Housing in Scotland in 2009*, from www.scotland.shelter.org.uk, accessed 23 June 2009.
Skeggs, B. (1997) *Formations of Class and Gender*. London: Sage.
Skeggs, B. (2004) *Class, Culture, Self*. London: Routledge.
Skeggs, B. (2005) 'The making of class and gender through visualizing moral subject formation', *Sociology* 39(5): 965–82.
Skeggs, B. (2005a) 'The re-branding of class: Propertising culture', in F. Devine, M. Savage, J. Scott and R. Crompton (eds) *Rethinking Class: Cultures, Identities and Lifestyles*. London: Palgrave.
Slater, T. (2006) 'The eviction of critical perspectives from gentrification research', *International Journal of Urban and Regional Research* 30(4): 737–57.
Slater, T. (2009) *What is Gentrification?* from www.members.lycos.co.uk/gentrification/whatisgent.html, accessed 17 August 2009.
Smith, N. (1979) 'Toward a theory of gentrification: A back to the city movement by capital, not people', *Journal of the American Planning Association* 45(4): 538–48.
Smith, N. (1996) *The New Urban Frontier: Gentrification and the Revanchist City*. London: Routledge.

Smith, N. (2002) 'New globalism, new urbanism: Gentrification as a global urban strategy', *Antipode* 34(3): 434–57.
Sprigings, N. (2002) 'Delivering public services under the new public management: The case of public housing', *Public Money and Management* 22: 11–17.
Strangleman, T. (2008) 'Sociology, social class and new working class studies', *Antipode* 40(1): 15–19.
Strangleman, T. (2007) 'The nostalgia for permanence at work? The end of work and its commentators' *Sociological Review* 55(1): 81–103.
Strinati, D. (1995) *An Introduction to Theories of Popular Culture*. London: Routledge.
Scotsman, The (2008) 'Scottish home-ownership rates soar', *The Scotsman*, 16 May 2008.
Taylor, Y. (2007) *Working-Class Lesbian Life: Classed Outsiders*. Basingstoke: Palgrave Macmillan.
Taylor, Y. (ed.) (2010) *Classed Intersections: Spaces, Selves, Knowledges*. Farnham: Ashgate.
Turok, I. (2004) 'Cities, regions and competitiveness', *Regional Studies* 38(9): 1069–83.
Uitermark, J., Duyvendak, J.W. and Kleinhans, R. (2007) 'Gentrification as a governmental strategy: Social control and social cohesion in Hoogvliet, Rotterdam', *Environment and Planning A* 39(1): 125–41.
Urban Task Force Report (1999) *Towards and Urban Renaissance: Final Report of the Task Force, Chaired by Lord Rodgers of Riverside*. London: Spon.
van Wessep, J. (1994) 'Gentrification as a research frontier', *Progress in Human Geography* 18: 74–83.
Virdee, S. (2006) 'Race, employment and social change: A critique of current orthodoxies', *Ethnic and Racial Studies* 29(4): 605–28.
Virdee, S., Kyriakides, C. and Modood, T. (2006) 'Cultural codes of belonging: Racialised national identities in a multi-ethnic Scottish neighbourhood', *Sociological Research Online* 11(4).
Waites, M. (2005) *The Age of Consent: Young People, Sexuality and Citizenship*. Basingstoke: Palgrave Macmillan.
Wacquant, L. (2002) 'Scrutinizing the street: Poverty, morality, and the pitfalls of urban ethnography', *American Journal of Sociology* 107(6): 1468–532.
Walkerdine, V., Lucey, H. and Melody, J. (2001) *Growing up Girls: Psychosocial Explorations of Gender and Class*. Basingstoke: Palgrave Macmillan.
Walls, P. and Williams, R. (2004) 'Accounting for Irish Catholic ill health in Scotland: A qualitative exploration of some links between "religion", class, and health', *Sociology of Health and Illness* 26(5): 527–56.
Watt, P. (2006) 'Respectability, roughness and "race": Neighbourhood place images and the making of working-class social distinctions in London', *International Journal of Urban and Regional Research* 30(4): 776–97.

Watt, P. (2008) 'The only class in town? Gentrification and the middle-class colonization of the city and the urban imagination', *International Journal of Urban and Regional Research* 32(1): 206–11.
Werbner, P. (1999) 'Global pathways: Working class cosmopolitans and the creation of transnational ethnic worlds', *Social Anthropology* 7(1): 17–35.
Williams, D. (2004) *The Glasgow Guide*, from www.glasgow-guide.co.uk, accessed 18 August 2008.
Williams, R. (1977) *Marxism and Literature*. Oxford: Oxford University Press.
Williams, R. (1986) *Keywords* (new edition). New York: Oxford University Press.
Williams R. (1993) 'Can data on Scottish Catholics tell us about descendants of the Irish in Scotland?' *New Community* 19: 296–310.
Williams, R. and Walls, P. (2000) 'Going but not gone: Catholic disadvantage in Scotland', in T. Devine (ed.) *Scotland's Shame? Bigotry and Sectarianism in Modern Scotland*. Edinburgh: Mainstream.
Willis, P. (1977) *Learning to Labour*. London: Saxon House.
Willis, P. (N. Dolby, G. Dimitriadis (eds) with P. Willis) (2004) *Learning to Labor in New Times*. London: Routledge.
Wilson, W.J. (1987) *The Truly Disadvantaged: The Inner City, the Underclass and Public Policy*. Chicago: University of Chicago Press.
Weis, L. (2004) *Class Reunion: The Remaking of the American White Working Class*. New York: Routledge.
Wright, E.O. (1985) *Classes*. London: Verso.
Wright, E.O. (1997) *Class Counts*. Cambridge: Cambridge University Press.
Young, J. (2007) *The Vertigo of Late Modernity*. London: Sage.
Young, M. and Wilmott, P. (1957) *Family and Kinship in East London*. London: Penguin Books Ltd.
Zukin, S. (1988) *Loft Living: Culture and Capital in Urban Change*. London: Radius.
Zukin, S. (1995) *The Cultures of Cities*. Oxford: Blackwell Publishers.

Index

accumulation, flexible 6, 9, 14, 24, 25, 26, 27, 41, 152
Alison (Partick resident) **71**, 74, 99, **99**, 110–111, **127**, 143, 145, 151
Anderson, P. 22
Angie (Partick resident) **72**, **100**, 103, **127**, 128, 143, 162
Angus (Partick resident) **72**, 99, **100**, 105, 118–19, **127**, 158
   STOP campaign 129, 130–31, 153

base-superstructure model 20–21, 35, 43, 46, 56
Bauman, Z. 45, 122
Bea (Partick resident) **71**, 74, **98**, **104**, 106, 117–18, **127**, 149–50, 151, 173, 176–7
   Golden Friends 74–5, 91, 101, 136, 138
Beck, U. 45
'Bedroom Tax' 30, 39, 184, 189, 194
benign gentrification 62–3, 150, 151
Betty (Partick resident) 70, **71**, 87, **98**, **104**, **104**, **127**
Bilal (Partick resident) **72**, 91, 92, 94, **99**, 104, **104**, 105, 106, 107, 120–21, **127**
Bourdieu, P. 15, 16, 47, 48, 49, 55, 187
Brian (Partick resident) **71**, 77–8, 79–80, 83, 95, **99**, 102–3, 120, **127**, 151–2
Britain 19–20, 25, 36, 37, 39, 189
bulimic society 5, 10, 52–3, 155, 161, 183, 188

Caulfield, J. 34
choice 5, 34, 50, 52, 125, 135, 153–4, 161, 194–5
class 2, 8, 15, 18, 42, 43–4, 45, 47–8, 54, 55, 191, 197

class analysis 2, 9, 14–15, 41, 42–4, 45–50, 52, 54, 56, 57–8, 122, 183–4
class culture 40, 47, 48–9
   emergent 10, 21, 23, 44, 57, 188
   middle-class 44, 48, 95
   working-class 10, 44, 48, 49, 52, 53–4, 67, 95, 121, 174, 188
class identity 8, 9, 15, 42, 45–6, 47, 53–4, 57, 67, **126–8**
   dis-identification 10, 47–8, 49, 70–71, 73, 76, 78, 79, 83, 95
   see also working-class identities
class position 2, 15, 42, 43–4, 45, 47, 55, 67, 97, 122
   disassociation 2, 8, 9, 15, 42, 47, 48–9, 67, 70–71, 78, 94–5
   mobility 113, 116, 120, 121
community 49–50, 52, 190, 191
community campaigns, *see* Glasgow Harbour development; Mansfield Park development; Tesco development; Thornwood Park development
community studies 2, 14–15, 42, 43–4, 50–51, 190
consumer citizenship 10, 31, 125–6, 131, 141–2, 143, 152–3, 154, 185, 194, 195
   regeneration strategies 14, 24, 56
control 10–11, 95, 156, 186, 192–3, 194–5
cosmopolitanism 51, 61, 92–3, 104, 156, 192
Craig (Wider Action Officer) 136
culturalist class theorists 2, 15, 42, 43, 46–7, 48–9, 153, 183, 190

Darren (Partick resident) **72**, 84–6, 90, **98**, 102, 104, **104**, 107, **127**, 166, 177
David (Partick resident) **71**, 93, **99**, 103, 115, **128**, 149

debt 77, 80–81, 154, 155, 162–5, 166, 180, 183
deindustrialisation 1, 7, 8, 13, 14–15, 24, 27, 41, 42, 44, 45, 73–4
dis-identification 10, 47–8, 49, 70–71, 73, 76, 78, 79, 83, 95
disassociation 2, 8, 9, 15, 42, 47, 48–9, 67, 70–71, 78, 94–5
displacement 1, 10, 36, 37, *38*, 39, 125, 155–6, 171–2, 183, 184, 188–9
   latent generational 156, 175–7, 189, 196
   perverse 156, 174–5, 189
   spiralling 156, 182, 189
   strategic 156, 177–81, 189

elective belonging 9, 50–51, 52, 96–7, 98, 102, 105, 106, 107, 122, 193
elective fixity 9, 10, 98, 118–21, 122, 193, 194
emergent culture 10, 21, 23, 44, 57, 188
end of work 67–8, 69, 73

Fi (Partick resident) **72**, 77, **99**, 113–14, **127**, 141, 143, 151, 154, 162, 169–70, 178
fixity to place 97–8, 112, 119, 122, 155, 156, 184, 193
flexible accumulation 6, 9, 14, 24, 25, 26, 27, 41, 152
FoMP (Friends of Mansfield Park) 136, 137–8
Fordism 13–14, 19–20, 24, 25, 44, 190
funding regimes 64, 135–6, 137, 167, 201–2

Gary (Partick resident) 68–9, **71**, 81–2, 90–91, **98**, 103, 104, **104**, 107, 112, **127**, 177
gentrification 1, 3, 9–10, 32–5, **33**, 40–41, 122–3, 183, 186–7, 195, 197
   displacement 37, *38*, 188
   hegemony 6–7, 9, 15–16, 41, 57, 186, 188
   regeneration strategies 9, 14, 31, 35–40, **38**, 125–6
   restructuring 5–6, 7, 56, 185–6

state-led 1, 3, 36, 39, 40, 49, 64, 125, 155, 193, 194
Giddens, A. 16, 30, 45
Glasgow 5, 7, 29, 40, 53, 57, 58–61, 68, 77, 93–4, **150**
Glasgow Harbour development 3–5, 61, *62*, 126, *142*, 143–9, 153, 160–61, 186, *196*, 199–200
   house prices **150**, **173**
Golden Friends 74–5, 91, 100–101, 107–8, 136, 138
Gordon (Partick resident) **71**, 89–90, **98**, 102, **104**, 106, 107, 128, **128**, 176, 182, 193
   debt 162, 165
   mobility 115–16, 120, 121
governmentality 16, 30, 55
Gramsci, A. 6, 17–18, 19, 56, 190, 195

habitus 16, 48, 49, 55, 187, 190
hegemonic bloc 7, 18, 20, 25, 49, 185
hegemony 6–8, 10, 13–14, 15, 16–19, 20–23, 24, 27, 55–7, 188, 190, 195
   gentrification 6–7, 9, 15–16, 41, 57, 186, 188
Helen (PHA) 134–5
   Mansfield Park development 132–3, 134
high school students, USA 53, 89
homeownership 15, 29, 39, 40–41, 122, 134–6, 149–51, 152, 154, 173–4, 175–7, 201
   PHA 134–5, 176, 177–81, 195
house prices 91, **150**, 150–51, 173, **173**, 174
housing associations 59, 134–5, 137, 172, 174–5, 184, 201–2
   rent arrears 180–181, **181**
   see also PHA

'incomers' 97, 98, 99, **99–100**, 100, 103, 105–6, 109–11, 121, 131, 178
   middle-class 121, 156–7, 158–9
individualisation 9, 44, 45, 46, 47, 49, 56, 189–90
industrial working-class 2, 7, 8, 10, 19–20, 26, 31, 42–3, 44, 45, 46, 49, 97

Janey (Dumbarton resident) **72**, 76, 92, **100**, 109–10, 111, 120, **127**, 147–8, 157, 174–5, 194
Jimmy (Partick resident) **71**, **99**, 113, 114–15, **127**, 143, 147, 157–8, 160
debt 81, 162
John (Partick resident) 69, **71**, 99, **99**, 105, 118, 119, **126**, 129, 144–5
Joseph, J. 22–3

Kathleen (Clydebank resident) **72**, 75–6, **98**, 102, **104**, 119–20, **127**

landlordism 5, 59, 189, 196
latent generational displacement 156, 175–7, 189, 196
Leona (Partick resident) **71**, **98**, **100**, 104, **104**, 106, 111, 112, 120, 121, **127**, 149
Lisa (Partick resident) 68, **72**, 74, 104–5, 108, 112–13, **127**, 139–40, 143, 161
local attachment 98, 100, 102, 109, 111
'locals' 51–2, 97, 98, **98–9**, 100–105, **104**, 106–9, 111–12, 121–2
locational narratives 4, 15, 55, 197
Loretta (Partick resident) 69, **71**, 74, **98**, **104**, 106, 107, **126**, 129, 148, 152
Lou (Partick resident) **72**, **100**, **128**, 140, 149, 162
    Glasgow Harbour development 149, 188
Louise (Partick resident) **72**, 74, 76, **99**, **126**, 137–8, 168–9, 178, 179–80

Mansfield Park development 126, 132–4, 136, 137–8, *139*, 139–41, *141*, 152, 154, 202–3
Mary (Partick resident) **71**, 74, **98**, 100–101, **104**, 107, **127**
Mhairi (Partick resident) 68, **72**, 74, **100**, 118, **127**, 161
middle-class 1, 34, 37, 41, 61, 109, 118, 125–6, 161, 191, 192–3
    elective belonging 9, 97, 106, 193
    'incomers' 121, 156–7, 158–9
    place attachment 52, 53, 56, 96, 97, 121

STOP campaign 129, 130, 131, 152, 153
middle-class culture 44, 48, 95
mobility 52, 69, 90, 112, 113, 115–16, 120, 121, 122

Natasha (Partick resident) **71**, 76, 89, 92, 93, **99**, 113, **127**, 143, 147, 157–8, 159–60
debt 81, 162, 163–4
National Statistics Socio-economic Classification, *see* NS-SeC
Nayak, A. 53–4, 57
neighbourhoods 14, 15, 44, 46, 49–50, 52, 55, 97, 122, 190–91
    working-class 2–3, 7, 8, 10, 62–4, 97, 185, 190–191
neoliberalism 2, 6–7, 14, 24, 25–6, 27, 28, 30, 194, 195
New Working Class Studies, *see* NWCS
Newcastle 53–4, 57
Nick (Partick resident) **72**, 92, **99**, 111–12, 114, 118, **126**, 136–7
    Glasgow Harbour development 144, 145–6
Norma (Partick resident) **72**, 74, 76, **100**, **127**, 168, 169, 178–9
NS-SeC (National Statistics Socio-economic Classification) framework 55, 68, **71–2**, **73**
NWCS (New Working Class Studies) 8, 53–4

ontological insecurity 1, 45, 51, 57, 71, 96, 97, 106, 121
Other 51, 52, 58, 91–2, 93–4, 104, 118, 183, 184, 192
Othered 4, 10, 94, 107, 136, 156, 161, 166, 192, 195

participation 9, 10, 24, 29–30, 125, **126–8**, 153, 155, 183, 185, 195; *see also* consumer citizenship
Partick 61–6, *63*, *65*, 68–73, **71–2**, *117*, 121–3, 152–4, 156–61, 162–9
    Glasgow Harbour development 3–5, 61, *62*, 126, *142*, 143–9, 153, 160–61, 186, *196*, 199–200

house prices 91, **150**, 150–51, 173, **173**, 174
'incomers' 98, 99, **99–100**, 100, 103, 105–6, 109–11, 121
'locals' 98, **98–9**, 100–105, **104**, 106–9, 111–12, 121–2
Mansfield Park development 126, 132–4, 136, 137–8, *139*, 139–41, *141*, 152, 154, 202–3
Tesco development 126, 128–31, 152, 153, 154, 200–201
Thornwood Park development 142–3, 152–3, 154
perverse displacement 156, 174–5, 189
PHA (Partick Housing Association) 63, 138–40, 174, **181**, 196
homeownership 134–5, 176, 177–81, 195
Mansfield Park development 132–4, 137, 139–40, 203
social housing 153, 172, 173–4, 177–8, 181, 184, 201–2
place attachment 50–51, 52, 96, 97, 98, 121, 122, 191, 196–7
middle-class 52, 53, 56, 96, 97, 121
working-class 9, 51, 97, 109, 121, 191, 194
post-Fordism 24
Poulantzas, N. 22
private landlords 5, 59, 155, 172, 189, 195, 196

Red Clydeside 7, 58, 70, 129
regeneration 1, 2–3, 5, 24, 28, 29, 31, 37, 41, 56, 61
regeneration strategies 9, 14, 24, 28–30, 31, 35–40, **38**, 125–6, 155–6, 187, 191
regulation school 14, 24, 25, 26–7, 56
rehabilitation strategy 62–3, 150
rent arrears 180–81, **181**
'rent-gap' 1, 34, 35, 41, 187
Rent Strikes 5, 58, 59, 196
restructuring 3, 5–6, 7–8, 9, 24–31, 34, 42–3, 46, 54–5, 56–7, 185–6

S-C-A (structure, consciousness, agency) model 42, 43–4, 46, 47

Savage, M., Bagnall, G., and Longhurst, B. 48, 50–51, 52, 97, 98, 102, 106, 190
Savage, M., Devine, F., Cunningham, N., et al. 48
Savage, M., Warde, A. and Ward, K. 1
Sean (Partick resident) **72**, 86–7, 90, **99**, **127**, 168
debt 162, 163, 166
sectarianism 20, 58, 90–92
Skeggs, B. 75, 76, 77, 119
Slater, T. 32, 37, 57
Smith, N. 3, 34, 37, 41
social capital 76, 155, 156, 167, 183, 187, 195
social housing 37, 39, 40, 137, **172**, 172–4, 176, 184, 188–9, 195–6
PHA 153, 172, 173–4, 177–8, 181, 184, 201–2
rent arrears 180–81, **181**
spiralling displacement 156, 182, 189
Sprigings, N. 180–81
state-led gentrification 1, 3, 36, 39, 40, 49, 64, 125, 155, 193, 194
Steve (Partick resident) 69, 70–71, **72**, 82–3, 90, **100**, 106–7, **127**, 140–41, 167, 171, 180, 189
STOP campaign 128–31, 152, 153, 154, 200
strategic displacement 156, 177–81, 189
Stuart (Partick case) 69, **71**, 99, **99**, 105, 118, 119, **126**, 144
STOP campaign 129, 130
Sylvie (Partick resident) 4, **72**, 74, 87–9, 90, **100**, 113, **127**, 128, 143, 189
debt 162, 165
Glasgow Harbour development 4, 5, 148–9, 165, 166

Tesco development 126, 128–31, 152, 153, 154, 200–201
Thornwood Park development 142–3, 152–3, 154
traditional working-class, *see* industrial working-class
traditional working-class culture, *see* working-class culture

traditional working-class identity, *see* working-class identities

urban entrepreneurialism 4–5, 14, 24, 28–9, 30, 31, 153
urban policy 1, 14, 24, 27–8, 31, 32, 35–7, 40, 41, 61, 91–2, 190
urban restructuring 2–3, 5–6, 8, 10, 13, 52, 55, 56, 57–8, 185, 189–90, 197
   hegemony 6, 13, 15, 16, 17, 23

Weis, L. 53, 89
Williams, R. 20–21, 22, 44, 49
working-class 1, 19, 41, 55, 163, 183–4, 187–8, 192, 193, 194–5
   industrial 2, 7, 8, 10, 19–20, 26, 31, 42–3, 44, 45, 46, 49, 97
   place attachment 9, 51, 97, 109, 121, 191, 194

working-class communities 2–3, 5–6, 7, 14, 31, 36–7, 43–4, 46, 52, 58–60, 185, 191
working-class culture 10, 44, 48, 49, 52, 53–4, 67, 95, 121, 174, 188
working-class identities 7, 9–10, 35, 42–3, 44, 52, 56–7, 67, 91, 94, 96–7, 188, 189–91
   dis-identification 70, 71, 76
working-class neighbourhoods 2–3, 7, 8, 10, 62–4, 97, 185, 190–191
working-class subject 9–10, 125–6, 152, 154, 155, 156, 183, 184, 195

Young, J. 5, 10, 52–3, 188
young people 63, 84, 89–90, 95, 116, 151, 160, 164–7, 175–7, 196

Zukin, S. 35